AUGSBURG COLLEGE & SEMINARY
George Sverdrup Library
MINNEAPOLIS 4, MINNESOTA

WITHDRAWN

Nations in Alliance

NATIONS IN ALLIANCE

The Limits of Interdependence

by George Liska

The Johns Hopkins Press, Baltimore

© 1962 by The Johns Hopkins Press, Baltimore 18, Maryland
Distributed in Great Britain by Oxford University Press, London
Printed in the United States of America
by The Haddon Craftsmen, Inc., Scranton, Pa.

Library of Congress Catalog Card Number: 62-14359

This book has been brought
to publication with the assistance
of a grant from The Ford Foundation.

In Memory of Edvard Beneš

who placed in trust with his Western allies
a nation's rightful claim and his own honor,

so that they might arm, conquer, and win through
to freedom's finest hour

Preface and Acknowledgments

Following upon *International Equilibrium,* a general statement with institutional emphases, and the discussion of social and economic conditions in *The New Statecraft,* this volume focuses on the military-political features of international order and security. In each of the complementary treatises, I have started from the patterns of the past trying to assess their relevance for the present and the future. The result is not a system but merely a somewhat systematized discussion; not a theory but mere theorizing about what was, is, and might be.

Research for *Nations in Alliance* began under the auspices of the Center for the Study of American Foreign and Military Policy at the University of Chicago, directed by Hans J. Morgenthau. I saw it through the press while on a grant from the Rockefeller Foundation. I actually wrote the book as a Research Associate of the Washington Center of Foreign Policy Research, affiliated with the School of Advanced International Studies of the Johns Hopkins University. In that capacity, I was privileged to participate in weekly roundtable discussions of major foreign-policy problems, marked by a stimulating confluence of informed experience, generalizing spirit, and speculative fancy.

This work, like the writer himself, owes much to Arnold Wolfers, the Washington Center's director. He is responsible for the book's existence, while only I am responsible for not writing a better one under well-nigh ideal conditions. Next to him and Robert W. Tucker, who inspired substantial additions, Robert E. Osgood and William Burden, were the other associates in the Center who wisely and critically commented on the manuscript as a whole or on some of its more technical and obscure parts. Mrs. Emmy Clubb and Mrs. Ruth Frank shared the editorial labors. I am deeply grateful to all of them.

Finally, I wish to record here my appreciation to The Johns Hopkins Press for authorizing Chapter V to do double duty as my contribution to a symposium of the Washington Center on neutralism, edited by Laurence Martin.

Contents

Preface and Acknowledgments . . . vii

PART I: PATTERNS AND PRINCIPLES

INTRODUCTION: CONTINUITY IN ALLIANCE POLITICS . . . 3

1 ALIGNMENTS AND REALIGNMENTS . . . 12
  Conflicts and Powers . . . 12
  Reasons for Alignments . . . 26
  The Rationale of Dealignment . . . 42
  The Rationale of Realignment . . . 55

2 THE COHESION OF ALLIANCES . . . 61
  Ideologies and Styles . . . 61
  Consultations and Compromise . . . 69
  Capabilities and Pressures . . . 86
  Pretensions and Coercion . . . 103

3 THE EFFICACY OF ALLIANCES . . . 116
  Integration and Independence . . . 116
  Deterrence and Auxiliaries . . . 124
  Restraints among Allies . . . 138
  Negotiations between Alliances . . . 147

PART II: TRENDS AND POLICIES

INTRODUCTION: THE CONTEMPORARY
INTERNATIONAL SYSTEM　　　　　　　　161

4 THE DISSOLUTION OF ALLIANCES　　　168
　Parallels and Differences in East-West Alliances　169
　Strains and Symmetries　　　　　　　　175
　National Unification and Diplomatic Revolutions　185
　Alignment Alternatives and Transnational Union　195

5 NON-ALIGNMENT AND NEUTRALISM　　202
　The Rationale of Non-Alignment　　　　203
　The "Blocs" and Stabilization　　　　　　219
　Subversion *versus* Containment　　　　　231

6 THE FUTURE OF ALLIANCES　　　　　255
　Material Build-Up and Multipolarity　　　255
　Nuclear Diffusion and Multilateral Deterrence　269
　The Rise and Decline of Nations　　　　284

Index　　　　　　　　　　　　　　　　293

Nations in Alliance

PART I:
Patterns and Principles

Introduction: Continuity in Alliance Politics

ALLIANCE IS as original an event in politics as is conflict; it associates like-minded actors in the hope of overcoming their rivals. It is impossible to speak of international relations without referring to alliances; the two often merge in all but name. For the same reason, it has always been difficult to say much that is peculiar to alliances on the plane of general analysis. The intimations of great historians, a Thucydides or Ranke, are the final product of long study; more recent formulations constitute a beginning of quest for greater precision of statement. The present study sets out to follow a winding middle path between the landmarks of history and the wider panorama of generalization.

IN CONTEMPORARY international politics, alliances have played as great a role as ever; and the United States has been unquestionably the power with the greatest stake in alliances. Alliances merely formalize alignments based on interests or coercion, but such formalizations have been more important for the "free world" and its leader than for the adversary. American alliance policies have not been original creations of unprecedented circumstances. They have parallels in both recent and remote past; and they have adapted to contemporary conditions many patterns and techniques of older and closely related nations, particularly Great Britain and France.

In the formation of the American approach to foreign policy, the first major diplomatic experience of the nascent United States does not loom large. The "permanent" alliance of the American revolutionaries with dynastic France was too short lived; so was the remembrance of the fact that *raison d'Etat* can bring together very unlike partners. Thereafter, the American strategic concept was closer to the British one. The new country's security, too, rested on divisions within the European continent: it was implemented in informal and unavowed alliance with the British, punctuated by spells of rivalry.

Both the "alliance" and the antagonism were intensified by underlying affinities. Fluctuations between excessive idealism and realism, empiricist preference for dealing with situations after they had arisen rather than before they arose, discrepancy between professed purpose and action, and a certain imperviousness to a feel for foreign conditions and mentalities—these are all criticisms made both of British and, more recently, American foreign policies.[1] Such weaknesses may afflict the diplomacy and the alliance policy of most or all other countries; but the similarities of attitude of the two English-speaking nations have been more solidly rooted in common philosophic, religious, and common-law traditions as well as in their insular station. They have been nurtured by long and intimate relations between the United States and Britain and by the long predominant role of

---

[1] See H. Nicolson, *Diplomacy* (2d edn., 1950), pp. 135–42, on the British mentality.

"Anglo-Saxon" elites in the making of American foreign policy.

Contrariwise, the strategies and the style of the French for a long time after the War of Independence recommended themselves less. Not only were American relations with France less continuous and intimate but the two nations were not diplomatically close except in the trying conditions of wartime coalitions and French weakness. For America to move toward the French model after World War II, she had first to witness the collapse of the wartime utopia of a great-power concert perpetuating the informal diplomacy of the Big Three, and she had to face a strategic problem fundamentally like that of France after World War I. Once circumstances were favorable, however, the French exemplar found support in congenial elements of the pluralistic American political culture—such as the formalism implicit in a written constitution and the rationalistic penchant of the new class of military and civilian technicians contending with complex problems beyond the reach of experience.

Action for peace and security had to be organized, not improvised as a reluctant departure from "splendid isolation." While the French had sought to convert the League of Nations into a grand alliance against Germany, the United States came to see in a similar light the role of the United Nations with respect to the Soviet Union and its satellites. The security organization of the day was to be an instrument for coercing the aggressor rather than an updated forum for conciliating powers with legitimately conflicting limited interests.[2] And while, to that end, the French had adapted to their uses the largely Anglo-American idea of collective security, the United States adopted in the main

[2] On French and British attitudes toward the League of Nations, see A. Wolfers, *Britain and France Between Two Wars* (1940); W. M. Jordan, *Great Britain and the German Problem 1918–1939* (1943).

the French implementation of the idea. Wilson's strictures against "international militarism" and military pacts met with the fate of Clemenceau's derision of Wilsonism.

When a deadlocked institution threatened to bar collective resistance to expansionist power, responsible Americans were ready with the arts of instrumental legalism to make the organization serve free-world security. The Uniting for Peace Resolution following upon the police action in Korea marked the climax of that period. The more enduring part of the revised concept of the United Nations was, however, an active policy of alliances under the aegis of regionalism.

Like France thirty years earlier, the United States set about to gather around itself a clientèle of lesser allies in order to contain the adversary, and safeguard the alliance leaders against the cumulative effect on their national security of unchecked subversions elsewhere. Germany was potentially stronger than France from the beginning; the Soviets were apparently readier than had been the Germans to move into the vacuum created by America's postwar withdrawal. Charged at home with overextending national resources in far-flung commitments, the two internationally conservative alliance leaders were beset abroad by their lesser allies' conflicts among themselves and with local opponents. The territorial disputes of the successor states to the Habsburg Empire had been no less a strain on the French alliance system than were postcolonial conflicts on the American; and while in the earlier period a Tardieu (and many another) Plan had looked forward to a Central-Eastern European "federation," the Marshall Plan came to be implemented to promote a Western European one. Being endowed with relatively self-contained economies, the two principal allies found the economics of containment even more intractable than its politics and logistics. In this respect, too, France's position was both weaker and stricter than that of the United

States; with few politically motivated exceptions, only allies were eligible for French financial support.

The turning point came in the mid-1930's for France and in the mid-1950's for the United States. Soviet ICBM's did to this country what the remilitarization of the Rhineland did to France: they apparently blocked the conservative powers' military access to the assailants of their wards in the hour of need. The strategic transformation, and the concurrently rising influence of "neutrals" in the global security organization of the day, favored on the whole the British conception of the organization as a forum for informal contacts and conciliation. Assuming that lesser states would acquire more independent military capability and the principal guarantor's military forces become increasingly mobile, the trends seemed likewise to rehabilitate somewhat the dominant British view of alliances. In this view, *ad hoc* arrangements for particular crises are the norm, since they leave the defensive great power free to adjust to existing conditions the ways of applying a tacit general guarantee of lesser states. "Permanent" peacetime alliances and guarantees are reserved for special cases; they help implement either political control jointly with friendly postcolonial elites or postwar accommodation jointly with wartime allies and enemies.

In the late 1930's, France became a vassal of Britain in all but name; in the late 1950's, the United States found renewed comfort in having in Britain a nominal equal. Both kinds of relationship served to rationalize a less forward policy by the need to secure the support of a reliably cautious power. As the United States faltered in evolving a long-term strategy of its own, the British have tended to forget the fiasco of their interwar diplomacy when claiming preferred status in allied councils, while the French, when resisting Anglo-Saxon supremacy, have been prone to ignore the fact that it was their own practice which was being turned against them. Like her lesser allies before, France was now expected to supply manpower and real estate without proportionate control over the *casus belli* or the policy preceding it. Even America's resented policies in the colonial realm were not intrinsically different from France's security strategy in the days of the League. Both powers sought to conciliate the more aggressive force in the colonial sphere in order to gain vacillating states as allies against the principal enemy. The only difference has been in the identity of the "more aggressive" forces—not the Italys now but the Ethiopias.

A study of alliance with contemporary relevance can adopt one of two courses. It can emphasize the revolutionary character of modern weapons and dwell on the resulting problems of strategy. In such a case it will have little use for the insights and incidents to be drawn from the history of the European state system. Or, one may stress continuities between the past and present, in the belief that traditional patterns become again relevant when unsettling innovation has found an equilibrium within its own compass and has been absorbed in its larger environment.

An equilibrium of the suggested kind has been coming into existence under the label of "stability" in mutual deterrence. Both parties to the contemporary conflict seem to possess the strategic capability to deny a decisively favorable change, in the form of meaningful victory, to the side initiating a nuclear war. The stalemate has released non-nuclear instrumentalities of conflict for aggressive and defensive use in traditional association with diplomacy. A parallel trend has been restoring alliances between greater and lesser states to a condition more like the traditional one. In the late 1950's an intermediate generation of nuclear weapons and delivery systems made it apparently necessary—notably for the United States—to locate the major ally's strategic deterrent and retaliatory facilities on the territory of lesser allies; this tended to distort the guarantees of a smaller state by a stronger power into a direct safeguard of the guarantor himself. The distortion disappears when the guarantor more or less willingly foregoes the facility and falls back again upon the only indirect and ultimate advantage to be gained for his security from supporting the lesser ally by forces adapted to local conditions and needs.

The new technological equilibrium has by no means been definitely or reliably "stabilized"; the absorption of the new weapons into their sociopolitical environment has been even more precarious. There has been little positive response to the new military technology in the area of political controls and organization; absorption has assumed instead the form of a perverse psychological adaptation. Every progression in the new weapons system has been met with a parallel regression in the belief that the weapons could and would be used for specific political ends; a major nuclear war has tended to become "unthinkable" as an occurrence and "unimaginable" in its course and dénouement, should it occur by accident or miscalculation. The tendency has been only accentuated by the difficulty of defining the conditions of stability and agreeing on the value of surprise, first strike, and passive or active defense. As a result, the so-called stability has often been acted upon in the politics of both nuclear and non-nuclear states while it was technologically at best in the process of becoming. The new weapons frequently lapsed gradually from nature's threat to man into one more means of bluff and blackmail among nations; and "politics as usual" has not been least pronounced in interallied relations, governed by fairly conventional, short-term and domestic, considerations.

It is too soon to tell whether the rise of an expanding major power with a revolutionary social ideology will prove to have disrupted continuity in international politics more, or less, than has revolutionary weaponry. The political intelligence of man and the politics of a state system have a way of revolving around relatively few recurrent patterns and problems, drawing on a limited range of basic techniques of statecraft. Within these limits, the range of possible relations among friendly states or unequally powerful states is comparatively great; but equal adversaries without a basis for genuine communication depend for direct contact on the smallest fund of formalized procedures of diplomacy, not in order to reach lasting agreements but to avoid the admission of complete alienation. Ideological conflicts impede the working of the traditional methods, while making them more than ever indispensable; and the zealots of social ideology are likely to follow for some time further those of religion and nationality in equating conquest with conversion and in using converts to facilitate conquest. But a case can be made that the struggle among proponents of rival social ideologies has already been largely "territorialized," as were its predecessors in the past.

Finally, the growing number of actors with highly varied cultural backgrounds is no more likely to reshape international politics fundamentally. It is probably true that differences in cultural norms, like those in ideological beliefs, aggravate relations by facilitating misinterpretation of the different parties' motives, objectives, and actions. But, in the past, culturally diverse communities did not find it impossible to relate themselves to each other within the conventions of essentially European diplomacy; this was true both after an expansionist civilization like Islam's subsided into one of conservative political communities, and before a political society representing a highly individual culture launched upon a career of expansion, as in the case of

Japan. More recently, some cultural norms may have inclined newly independent actors—in, say, South Asia—toward withdrawing from power-political conflicts and from uncompromising confrontations of interests and rights. And Middle Eastern actors may be inclined to see the political process as nothing more than a continual playing off of one power or party against another. Such individual outlooks may be more or less in keeping with this or that Western model of international politics in a period of crisis; but the practically more significant, if partly derivative, differences lie elsewhere. They bear on the individual countries' varied phases of political and economic development toward the largely accepted Western model of the state, functioning for order and welfare at home and for security and stability internationally.

There may thus be at work two contrary trends: continuity in the forms and techniques of international politics will be strengthened as the new states cease to be *new* and become *states;* and radical discontinuity in the forms and methods of international politics will probably appear only in retrospect, marking the culminating point in an evolution of the state *system* toward a different kind of order. The danger of upheaval due to revolutionary creeds and weapons will in the meantime promote continuity directly by encouraging outside assistance to the developing countries; and the same threat may promote indirectly a revolution in the methods of international politics—in the direction of quasi-parliamentary, welfare-statist, civil-warlike, or still another kind of essentially "domestic" politics. Some of these activities may become less the functional substitutes for nuclear conflict than they largely are today. In the meantime, however, their utility in conflict or in co-operation will go on depending on the distribution of especially the greater powers' presumed *capacity* to wage war with all available means, if necessary.

I
Alignments and Realignments

ALLIANCES PERFORM their several functions through movement as much as through being. The main movements are alignment and realignment. The actor making decisions about alignment seeks to maintain or improve his position in the global, regional, or domestic arena. Alignments are always instrumental in structuring the state system, sometimes in transforming it. While "system" denotes interaction of several independent actors, "structure" refers here to the number and configuration of greater and lesser powers and conflicts.

Conflicts and Powers

When they are sufficiently intense, and security is the chief concern, conflicts are the primary determinants of alignments. Alliances are against, and only derivatively for, someone or something. The sense of community may consolidate alliances; it rarely brings them about. When community feeling is sufficiently strong, it commonly seeks other institutional forms of expression. Cooperation in alliances is in large part the consequence of conflicts with adversaries and may submerge only temporarily the conflicts among allies.

The dynamics of alignment is most apparent when two major core-powers are surrounded by lesser allies. On the face of it, the core-powers have attracted the lesser countries into alliance; in fact, superior power does not attract. The weaker state naturally fears that its identity will be abridged by aligning with a more powerful one; and the strong state, too, will often shun association with the weak for fear of overextending its commitments and resources. Movement toward alignment sets in only when another state intervenes as a threat. The weaker state rallies then to one stronger power as a reaction against the threat from another strong power. The stronger state assumes the role of a protective ally, interested mainly in keeping the resources of the potential victim out of the adversary's control.

Apparent attraction of greater power is thus a consequence of revulsion; and the addition of a lesser ally's power is often incidental to denying this power to the adversary. For such tendencies and objectives to result in alignment, the lesser state must be accessible to the potential ally directly or at least indirectly. "Indirect" access may mean no more than the stronger power's capacity to exert political or military pressure on the threatening state so as to relieve the latter's pressure against the smaller state.

Geographically conditioned responses to superior power are apt to be modified by cultural, ideological, and economic pulls. Their relative weight in determining alignments varies from case to case. A weaker power will be commonly anxious to seek alignment with geographically remoter powers; the tendency will be only intensified if it has cultural differences with the more powerful neighbor. Among such differences are those dividing Catholic, Westernized Poland from Orthodox, and now Communist, Russia in Europe; and the kind of cultural differences that exist between Latin

American states and the United States in the Western Hemisphere. The natural ally of Poland was historically France, while Britain, Germany, and most recently the Soviet Union "attracted" Latin American countries, such as Argentina and Cuba, whenever they revolted against American predominance. Where they exist, ideological affinities among regimes are merely the immediate impetus to such alignments or their consequence. Conversely, cultural affinity can dampen the flight away from superior power, as shown in different attitudes of Canada and Mexico toward the United States and of Bulgaria and Poland toward Russia.

The most direct attraction that stronger states hold for the weaker is probably in response to trade and economic needs. The attraction is only provisional, however, until the resentment of economic dependence and an opportunity to draw on alternative sources and outlets set off a political reaction. At different times, Japan has responded differently to the economic attraction of the West and of China. And even good-neighborly Canada, which has had little reason to shy away from the United States on grounds of national security for some time, has been looking across the Atlantic in reaction against American cultural and economic penetration. Much stronger was the instinct of some of the weaker Central-Eastern European countries pulling away from Germany, and more recently from Soviet Russia, whenever the main Western powers of the moment were able and willing to supply economic outlets, to keep open politico-military access, and to hinder the local power from employing coercion for the purpose of forestalling permanently the lesser countries' flight into a countervailing alignment.

As a result of various kinds of conflicts which occur on the global, regional, and domestic planes, the interacting system of states tends to be polarized by alliances. The conflicts which primarily determine alignment are not always the dominant ones. A "dominant" conflict is one which would raise the winner or winners to preponderance and might even transform the relevant system's prevailing political culture and structure.

The East-West struggle is not the only globally dominant conflict which polarized the modern state system around two core-powers. Another was the conflict between the Bourbons and the Habsburgs over preponderance in the then "global" European system.

At the peak of the conflict, the rivalry pitting France against Spain and Austria was the dominant one, rather than the religious-ideological contest between Protestantism and Catholicism. The conflict produced religiously mixed alliances, notably in the case of the Franco-Swedish alliance in the Thirty Years' War; and the religiously mixed character of the alliances in turn made it virtually impossible for either of the competing churches to emerge victorious and supervise the reorganization of the state system. A Catholic triumph could have come about only in the unlikely case of France's parting with ascendant Sweden and joining the Habsburg powers in an all-Catholic coalition; and a Protestant victory would have required Sweden to defeat the Catholic powers with the aid of Protestants in the North of Europe—chiefly Denmark, Saxony, and Brandenburg. When free to choose, however, the lesser Protestant powers shunned a Swedish alliance out of a sense of regional rivalry and fear of domination, much as Catholic Bavaria reacted against neighboring, though also Catholic, France.[1]

Communist Yugoslavia's split with the Soviet Union is

[1] A good discussion of the Thirty Years' War may be found in G. Pagès, *La guerre de trente ans* (1939); see also C. V. Wedgwood, *The Thirty Years' War* (1938). On the "diplomatic revolution" I have consulted chiefly R. Waddington, *Louis XIV et le renversement des alliances: préliminaires de la Guerre de Sept Ans 1754–1756* (1896); D. B. Horn, *Sir Charles Hanbury Williams and European Diplomacy 1747–1758* (1930), Part II; Sir R. Lodge, *Great Britain and Prussia in the Eighteenth Century* (1923)), Chaps. 3, 4; W. L. Dorn, *Competition for Empire 1740–1763* (1940). On "international system," see M. A. Kaplan, *System and Process in International Politics* (1957), Part I; also L. Binder, "The Middle East as a Subordinate International System," *World Politics* (April, 1958), pp. 408–29.

only a recent instance of the pattern. The dominant conflict tends to determine the alignment policy of the major protagonists; within the resulting conditions other states consult their particular regional and domestic interests and tend to downgrade the major powers' ideological concerns as well as their programs for a future order.

When one dominant conflict divides two powers or groups of powers, alliances merely formalize a built-in polarity; they have a more creative role when two major conflicts divide three or more powers. Two such conflicts were gradually supplanting the Bourbon-Habsburg rivalry in European diplomacy of the mid-eighteenth century (whereas a second, North-South, issue was merely being added to the unresolved East-West conflict in the second half of the twentieth century). One was between France and Britain over the balance of trade and empire overseas; another occurred between Austria and Prussia over the balance of power in the Germanic middle of Europe. The two sets of adversaries gravitated spontaneously into opposing alliances of two major powers in both possible combinations. The so-called old system, still rooted in the waning Austro-French enmity, associated France with Prussia and Austria with Britain; following the diplomatic revolution of 1756, Britain aligned with Prussia and France with Austria.

Alliance policy matters most when none of several conflicts is manifestly dominant in a multipolar system of several powers. This was the case in Europe during the period 1815-1870 and, to a diminishing extent, after 1870. The Franco-German conflict was then emerging as a potentially dominant one, owing to the assumption that another German triumph over France would have seriously affected the European balance. Different alliance policies may then forestall a polarization of the state system, retard it, or virtually bring it about.

In an ideal multipolar system, each power should be able to align with any other power, depending on the particular issue. In fact, each state has some alliance handicap in the sense of being unwilling or unable to align with one or more states with which its relations are relatively most hostile. In that respect a multipolar system is but a set of partial, alternately activated bipolarities. If all states have alliance handicaps, alliance making will be impeded for fear that an initial move toward alignment might start polarizing the system into an unpredictable and dangerous configuration. A power may nonetheless set off the chain reaction of alliance making in order to forestall the most dreaded pattern of division of the system. It will do so when it believes its alliance handicap to be greater than that of other states.

The Austro-German alliance of 1879, which initiated the polarization of the state system preceding World War I, can be interpreted in these terms. As a German alliance with France was practically impossible, and French participation in any anti-German coalition certain, Germany apparently had to make sure of Austria-Hungary.[2] The thesis of a necessary alliance with Vienna made the feared Franco-Russian alliance inevitable, when later statesmen in Berlin spurned Bismarck's finesse with Russia, lacked his firmness with Austria, and departed from his non-committal friendship with Britain. Once Germany severed her tie with Russia and challenged Britain (unattainable as ally) to a naval race, hitherto impossible alignments appeared necessary and, therefore, feasible. France's isolation vanished as Russia began to fear hers and as the splendor went out of Britain's. The progression toward polarization was complete when the necessary alliances became dogmatic ones, their conservation being placed over and above other concerns.

If one takes a different view of the map of conflicts in

[2] The interpretation is essentially Bismarck's. An alternative and possibly supplementary interpretation would stress Germany's interest in stabilizing Austria-Hungary internally. For Bismarck's exchanges on the subject with the Emperor, see *Die Grosse Politik der europäischen Kabinette 1871–1914*, Vol. III, Nos. 455 ff., pp. 26 ff. A recent discussion of the historical background is to be found in W. E. Mosse, *The European Powers and the German Question 1848–1871* (1958).

post-1871 Europe, the first—Austro-German—alliance appears somewhat less necessary. The alliance handicap of Germany was not at all unique or altogether novel. Before 1870, a Franco-Prussian alliance was already highly unlikely; it could occur only on a non-German issue, mainly in Italy, somewhat as a Franco-Austrian alliance could be brought about only on a Near Eastern issue. Moreover, the impossibility of a Franco-German alliance after 1871 constituted a handicap for France, too. The handicap was a lesser one since France was now a defensive power and could hope for assistance against Germany in the interest of the European equilibrium even without prior commitments; but the overall handicap was also a greater one because, unlike Germany, France had other rivalries to worry about. She had a colonial conflict with Great Britain, in particular over Egypt, and an ideological one with Russia over "revolution" and Russian revolutionaries in Paris. France may have been willing to pay a high price for an anti-German coalition; but no one was ready to exact that price before Germany applied pressure to other powers, as it were on France's behalf.

These other powers were not free of handicaps either. Britain had two conflicts, one with France and another with Russia over Asia; and Russia, too, had a second conflict—with Austria-Hungary over the Balkans. Only Germany had a single one. The issue of Alsace-Lorraine was without question the most serious; but conflicts over Egypt, Constantinople, the Balkan principalities, India, and China made other combinations as impractical as a Franco-German alliance was "impossible."

A dominant conflict affects the global system of a given time in its entirety; but lesser conflicts are often more immediately significant in filling out the complete pattern of alignments. We have noted the way lesser states seek protection against great regional powers. Conflicts among the lesser states themselves may contravene the resulting alignment tendencies, for some of them at least, as local adversar-

ords of the Fronde, rebelling against the French monarchy, oncluded formal treaties of alliance with autocratic Spain n the name of constitutional liberties. Similarly, just before he French Revolution, the democratic party in the United rovinces was allied to the *ancien régime* against the Dutch onarchical party's alliance with oligarchical England; only e victory of the Orangists restored the United Provinces om a geopolitically unnatural alliance with France to the ditional, protective alliance with Britain.³

There is least opportunism in such trans-national alignnts when they involve ethnic groups, such as the ethnic up alignments across state boundaries in Central-Eastern rope before and after World War I. In contemporary rnational politics, an opportunistic alignment occurs n parties to the internal economic and political conflict themselves with one of the superpowers without adoptits view of the East-West conflict. The typical alignment s the proponents of stable development by conservative ods with the United States, while the proponents of d-draft development by social-revolutionary methods are d with the Soviet Union or Communist China. The on recalls somewhat the alignment of "popular" parties Athens and later Macedon and of "oligarchical" parties Sparta and later Rome in the Hellenic city-state system. n opposite alignment can take place when a conservaegime would pre-empt the Soviet-bloc alliance from adicals, as in Afghanistan and Morocco at the time of riting, or when a social-revolutionary military group pts some kind of alignment with the United States cal "reactionaries," as happened in South Korea.

interplay of domestic, regional, and global conflicts gnments extends to one more level the interplay of l and global conflicts and alignments. While the egional interplay is part of the balance-of-power de-

ban, *Ambassadors and Secret Agents: The Diplomacy of the First lmesbury at the Hague* (1954), *passim*.

ies seek great-power support by aligning on different sides of the larger, dominant conflict.

One great power can rarely have as allies both parties to a local conflict. To be sure, both Greece and Turkey have remained in the Atlantic Alliance despite the conflict over Cyprus, while both Poland and Czechoslovakia are aligned in the Warsaw Pact, despite similar disputes. In the late 1930's, Yugoslavia moved toward Germany for a safeguard against Germany's ally, Italy, when France had failed to serve as a check on both. But such exceptions from the rule merely mean that the free play of alignments has been in abeyance due to the overwhelming challenge or sheer coercion from one power.

Otherwise, the more natural distribution of local rivals will assert itself. Prussia's quest for immunity from Russia by moving toward Russia's ally, Britain, in 1756, only drove Russia to Prussia's enemy, Austria, as part of the so-called diplomatic revolution. And Denmark and Sweden could no more be expected to appear on the same side of a larger conflict in the seventeenth century than Serbia and Bulgaria could before World War I or Czechoslovakia and Hungary before World War II. Following the latter war, non-alignment with an antagonistic bias rather than outright counteralignment has been an Egypt's or an India's response to the alignment of a local rival in the East-West struggle.

When two or more states in a particular region join different sides of a global conflict, the region itself becomes an integral part of the global system, and the global system itself becomes somewhat more of a unified system by way of local divisions. In the late fifteenth century, competitive alliances of the Italian city-states with barely consolidated France and Spain integrated the previously self-contained Italian system into a larger Western European system; and the system became fully European when a like process subsequently brought in the so-called Northern powers. A genuine world system took shape as local sovereignties and conflicting alignments spread into the Southeast of Europe and on to the Far East, Afro-Asian Middle East, and the Asian and African South. The southern part of the Western Hemisphere may actually be the last region to become more than fitfully a part of world politics in this sense and manner.

A regional system as such can be said to consist of states which are parties to local conflicts that determine alignments within and beyond the region. In addition to local states, a regional system can then comprise outside powers that are "present" as allies on a local issue. Thus the Middle East, notoriously difficult to define in geographic terms, as a regional system consists of local and outside parties to the Arab-Israeli and the inter-Arab conflicts; the United States and the Soviet Union have been more intimately involved in it than Turkey, Pakistan, or, so far, Morocco. And the Middle East as a regional system was most integrally a part of the global system when Iraq pre-empted membership in the West-sponsored Baghdad Pact and a hostile Egypt responded with a tactical alignment with the Soviet Union. Matters were roughly similar in South Asia in regard to the Indian-Pakistani conflict prior to the emergence of the Sino-Indian conflict over frontier regions. This latter conflict between two major powers may develop into a regionally dominant conflict, reshaping the region's structure and alignment politics, in a way that the Kashmir issue never could.

When analyzed in these terms, domestic systems have much in common with regional ones. As political development progresses, however, a unifying national authority tends to make the domestic system separate and distinct from the international one. Factions cease to act directly as "allies" of outside powers; the state alone has a foreign policy. Domestic interest groups can only try to influence the government's foreign policy and act internationally as agents of the sovereign authority, if at all. Only insofar as the central authority does not realize the ideal of foreign policy monopoly, is the domestic system an integral part of the inter-

terminant of alignment, the relationship of domestic and international conflicts is distinct from and may be contrary to balance-of-power pressures. The question whether interstate or intergroup conflicts prevail in aligning a country depends, of course, on their relative intensity; and the intensity depends in turn on whether the authority of the ruling group is more immediately threatened by an external or an internal adversary. When domestic factors determine alignment, the groups committed to an alliance are likely to be more homogeneous and the commitment of individuals more personal, as long as it lasts. Iraqi oligarchy's commitment to the Baghdad Pact was as personal as was that of the Dutch "Patriots" to their earlier alliance with France. When international factors determine alignment, the commitment may rest on a broader, but also more heterogeneous, foundation. West Germany's adhesion to the Atlantic Alliance, for instance, was backed for different reasons by neo-Nazis alongside constitutional democrats.[4]

Lesser actors often seek their advantage in the rivalries among greater powers. When the configuration of power and geography permits choices, the major powers themselves often have to manage regional or domestic conflicts if they are to draw out of them a favorable pattern of global alignment. Like other alliance makers and breakers, the Soviets mediated or sought otherwise to moderate territorial disputes between actual or potential lesser allies—thus between Czechoslovakia and Poland and, more recently, Communist China and nonaligned India—while abetting other territorial conflicts—thus India's with an ally of the West, Pakistan. The eagerness of a major power to pacify will be least when lines of the regional conflict and the global one coincide. Neither of the superpowers was particularly anxious to mitigate the latent dispute between West Germany and Poland over the latter's

[4] K. W. Deutsch and L. J. Edinger, *Germany Rejoins the Powers: Mass Opinion, Interest Groups, and Elites in Contemporary German Foreign Policy* (1959), pp. 31–32.

western frontier; the attitudes would change if and when a settlement could be used to detach the local adversary of one or the other power's lesser ally from the opposing combination without at the same time reducing the ally's interest in *his* alliance with the pacifier. And only when great-power contestants can expect to do no better than divide local rivals between themselves without a net advantage for either—or when local rivals themselves know how to manage their differences without great-power involvement—is there a basis for neutralizing a region or a country as an arena of alignment politics.

The policies of play-off, mediation, and neutralizing can be employed toward group conflicts within countries as well as toward regional conflicts. There are some differences, though.

One difference is in degree only. It is still more difficult to secure internally competing groups as allies than it is to win regionally competitive states. A strong power may risk strains with two mutually hostile smaller states and possible loss of one of them; to attempt to secure too many supporters within a country, however, may alienate the stronger groups (against which the others may be seeking protection) and forfeit the country at stake. The dilemma is greatest when an ideological bond unites the outside power and a minority group within a lesser country, the ruling group of which aligns itself with the outside power on opportunistic grounds. Both superpowers have been beset by this problem with regard to Communist and liberal-democratic minority groups respectively. Principle as well as expediency require keeping the minority group in reserve until it becomes strong enough to supplant the ruling group without disrupting the alliance. The sleight of hand is not easy to master.

Another difference between domestic and regional systems concerns the effect of external powers on the structure of the less inclusive system. In the dynastic state system, a multipolar international structure tended to be reproduced domestically in the form of "parties," identified with different outside powers—a French party, a Spanish party, an Imperial party, and the like. An extreme instance was pre-partition Poland. Notably in ambiguous balance-of-power situations, a party was expected to sway policies and alignments at least temporarily in the patron's favor. In return, the outside power embraced the domestic quarrels of its party, especially if the tie was not only a mercenary one. In bipolar global and regional structures, the number of influential parties was, of course, smaller. There was no Russian party in the aforementioned domestic contest in the United Provinces, although there was definitely a French party and a British party. The conditions are not substantially different today. Both superpowers attempt to have a party in contested countries, so that their domestic structures at least mirror the "bipolar" international system as is; in addition, the superpowers use their influence to reproduce within disputed countries the pattern which each side desires for the state system and practices at home—pluralistic for the West, uniform in the East.

While global structures tend to coincide with domestic ones, they tend to differ from regional ones. A bipolar global structure may very well go with multiplicity of relatively independent lesser countries within regions. The two major powers may even contribute to the disparity as they seek to break out of a deadlocked struggle: they tend to activate new participants, perhaps simultaneously with developing new elements of strength in new areas of power. The contest of the Habsburgs and the Bourbons in the sixteenth and seventeenth centuries brought new states into the system—notably the United Provinces, Sweden, Brandenburg-Prussia, and, indirectly, Russia and Turkey; and it accelerated the opening up of the Western Hemisphere as other states became aware of the material advantages which Spain drew from overseas.

Multipolar contests revolve typically around a new balance of existing power, possibly polarized by means of alignments.

Out of a bipolar contest tends to develop a balance of new power, covering a range from the gold of mercantilism to presumably man-centered economic growth, from mobile infantry to intercontinental missile, and from Northern and Eastern Europe to the extra-European East and South—indeed, all the way into outer space. As former dependents outgrow the control of older powers and major allies, the new power is likely to be diffused in a multipolar structure globally as well as regionally. The last phase is repolarization around new core-powers which had grown up in the protective shadow and partly as a result of preceding conflicts. Illustrations must wait until the theme is taken up again with regard to the present and the future.

Reasons for Alignments

Alignments have long been associated with the balancing of power in both theory and practice. In economic terminology, alliances aim at maximizing gains and sharing liabilities. The decision to align, in what form, and with whom—or not to align, as part of a deliberate policy—is made with reference to national interests. But no abstract criterion can supply reliable guidance in either making or analyzing alignments without reference to concrete conditions and conflicts, and to particular objectives in matters of security, stability, and status.

In theory, the relation of alliances to the balance of power is simple enough. Put affirmatively, states enter into alliances with one another in order to supplement each other's capability. Put negatively, an alliance is a means of reducing the impact of antagonistic power, perceived as pressure, which threatens one's independence. The object is to check or divert pressure with counterpressure, applied at the point of the adversary's initiative or at his weakest point; the art is to achieve best possible results within the limits of economy. In order to act "economically," alliance builders must not collect haphazardly all available allies and seek the most demanding commitments; they must consider the marginal utility of the last unit of commitment to a particular ally and the last unit of cost in implementing commitments. Like strictly national efforts to increase one's capability, and probably more so, alliances entail purely political costs in addition to material ones. These costs consist of counterattack, counteralignment, or other adverse responses by the target state and other states.

Apart from "why" and "how much" alliance, there is the question "with whom." In practice, states tend to be either too free or not free enough to follow the guidance, however uncertain and ambiguous, of the balance of power.

There is commonly too wide a range of choice in minor conflicts among roughly equivalent actors. It is then not easy to know with whom and against whom to align on the basis of a general precept. On the other hand, actors may be unable to follow the precept of the balance of power when it is clearest—in the event of a bid for hegemony. Some lesser actors are then likely to be more accessible to one great-power side; and access will lead to constraint unless the other side is able and willing to translate capability into effective counterpressure. Even when free, of course, states may be unable or unwilling to align "rationally" for reasons of domestic or regional conflicts, ideological or historic biases, or because of special inducements to opportunistic behavior.

The ambiguity of the balance of power, and the innermost character of alliances as transactions which are distinct from accidental ties of culture and feeling, conspire to inject the notions of "interest" and of "gains" and "liabilities" into both analysis and policy determination.

All association depends on the existence of identical interests. The interests may be identical from the outset; or they may be capable of becoming identical in and through the association, or capable of merging in a higher, more inclusive, common interest. Pending the evolution, provisionally disparate interests of members must be at least compatible with each other and with the maintenance of the initially identical interests, if the association is to succeed. Originally disparate interests and the motives for acting as if interests were identical can converge into joint action and association. Such convergence can, however, be confidently asserted only after the event; in advance, one can only guess or hope that disparate interests will converge. There are no intrinsically "convergent" interests.

The chances of convergence are best when there are complexes of interests, encompassing identical, disparate, and even conflicting ones. Such complexes of interests are more likely to converge when actors rate disparate interests differently, preferably in an inverted hierarchy of importance. A certain amount of identical interests must, moreover, complement the conflicting ones and serve as a basis for adjusting them. But, again, it is not so much particular interests that are "complementary," as complexes of interests, motives for ignoring conflict in interests, and resources for implementing both identical and disparate interests.[5]

We can try to illustrate with the United States-Pakistan alliance. There are identical interests bearing on security against the Soviet Union and Communist China. The nearest thing to complementary interests would be American concern with the Sino-Soviet alliance and Pakistan's concern with an alignment of India or Afghanistan with the Soviets and China. These interests would be, for all practical purposes, virtually identical. The actuality of India's neutrality and the Kashmir issue introduce disparate, and even conflicting, interests into the structure underlying the alliance. The conflict cannot be resolved under existing conditions

[5] On "complementary" and "convergent" interests, respectively, see H. J. Morgenthau, "Alliances in Theory and Practice," in A. Wolfers, ed., *Alliance Policy in the Cold War* (1959), p. 188; E. B. Haas, *The Uniting of Europe: Political, Social, and Economic Forces 1950–1957* (1958), p. 152.

and could affect the success of the alliance as it is implemented.

The two allies may have misunderstood each other when entering into the alliance; but the alliance may survive the conflict for two main reasons. One is that the Kashmir issue is only one of a complex of interests and concerns between the United States and Pakistan, as well as between the United States and India and, in the final analysis, between Pakistan and India. The second and related reason is that, while the Kashmir issue is a vital one for Pakistan in the longer run, Pakistan also shares the still higher priority assigned by the United States to the avoidance of an overt Pakistan-India conflict on the Sino-Soviet periphery. Pakistan has other, compelling, reasons for enduring the extent to which this priority is imposed by the United States. They include the joint American-Pakistani interest in building up Pakistan's defense and economic potential. These identical interests could converge into alliance and joint implementation only because the partly conflicting purpose of the build-up—*also* against India in Kashmir for Pakistan and *only* against the Sino-Soviet bloc for the United States— could in practice be treated as non-existent. It could be treated as such because of the common concern over Sino-Soviet aggression and subversion and the hope that events in South Asia will eventually help resolve the Kashmir issue or subordinate it to a larger security concern associating Pakistan and India with each other, with or without the United States.

The American-Pakistani alliance exists, therefore, not so much because of complementary interests as because of identical interests despite conflicting ones—as do all alliances, in different ratios of the two kinds of interest.

As for notions of gains and liabilities, they are like the balance of power in one respect at least. They, too, indicate conduct clearly only in extreme cases—of indisputable gain or liability and, especially, stark disproportion between gains and liabilities. Short of such extremes, a tangible gain may be offset by an intangible liability; a certain one by a hypothetical one, an immediate one by an ultimate one, and so on.

Moreover, the question arises: interests and gains (or liabilities) in what? We answer in terms of internal and international security, stability, and status of states and regimes. The three main grounds for alignment are variously interrelated and interdependent. Actors are directly interested in security, internal stability, and status; in international stability they tend to be interested only indirectly, as the condition of respect for their security and status, and conditionally, depending on satisfaction with their role in upholding international stability.

The gains and liabilities associated with each of the main grounds of alignment can be grouped into pairs. The pair peculiar to security is protection and provocation, the first to be derived from a particular alliance and the second producing counteraction or counteralliance. Stability is threatened by material and political burdens and strains flowing from alliance, while gains consist in economies from pooling of resources and in material and moral supports by allies. And if alliance can enhance a member's status in the form of superior recognition and wider influence, these gains must be scored against possible losses in independence and equality due to co-ordination and subordination—to allied consensus or to a major ally. In order to assess a particular alignment all these factors must be compared with hypothetical gains and liabilities of other alignments; with non-alignment; or at least with a different implementation of an unavoidable alliance.

What are the salient features of the several grounds for alignment? Take security first: to promote it an alliance must enable members to deter or coerce. While deterrent alliances are implicitly defensive, alliances for coercion can aim either at offense or defense. The trend has been away from an unabashed equivalence of defensive and of offensive alliances toward a virtual monopoly of defensive alliances. The monopoly was at first one of ideology; more recently it has become also one of fact, due to the difficulty of translating increased strength into decisive political or military advantage.

The most common type of commitment is to mutual military assistance, as an alternative to being isolated and overpowered by the adversary or patronized by a guarantor.

The addition of strength is not mechanical, and deficiency of power is not always a liability. In the grand alliances for security against hegemonic powers, the key state must commit itself first; the lesser states may have to advertise weakness in order to secure such a commitment and avoid the choice between vain resistance or acquiescence. The "involvement" of the United States in NATO and SEATO as the necessary preliminary to a comparable effort by lesser states has many precedents, such as England's often reluctant leadership in the grand coalitions against Louis XIV, Napoleon, and the two German bids for hegemony. The lesser powers may, however, lack the readiness as well as the means to develop their strength for and through the combination, or they may simply fail to acknowledge the threat. The major power will then try to involve them despite themselves—as the Western powers vainly sought to do in the Middle East in the 1950's. A merely nominal alliance may then have to suffice, increasing somewhat the possibility of local defense and the suspected expansionist's uncertainty.

Nazi Germany's and the Soviet Union's formula for involving a country short of—or prior to—absorbing it as a dependency has been a treaty of non-aggression or neutrality.[6] The commitment to mutual assistance implies a common

[6] W. W. Kulski, *Peaceful Co-Existence: An Analysis of Soviet Foreign Policy* (1959), pp. 301 ff.; W. Welch, "Soviet Commitments to Collective Action," in *Alliance Policy in the Cold War*, p. 279; R. Torngren, "The Neutrality of Finland," *Foreign Affairs* (July, 1961), p. 604. The Soviet Union has neutrality treaties with Iran and Afghanistan. The treaty with Finland is a hybrid; a mutual-assistance pact guarantees Finland's neutrality.

danger; the non-aggression or neutrality formula implies reciprocal threat. Both formulas provide a basis for "friendly" intervention by the bigger state and make it technically difficult or impossible for the lesser state to join an adversary coalition or enforcement action against the treaty partner, even though the partner himself may constitute the real outside threat. By itself, pledges of non-aggression or neutrality add only indirectly to the deterrence of encroachments against the lesser state by others; they may, however, be less provocative in the eyes of unaligned states.

There is an intermediate formula. In 1870, Russia observed benevolent neutrality in favor of Prussia, but was believed ready to join Prussia if Austria-Hungary joined France—while, perhaps, Britain was somewhat more likely to intervene if Russia gratuitously abandoned watchful neutrality for outright assistance to Prussia. The upshot was a "guarantee against a coalition," or, put positively, commitment to assistance against "two or more" powers. The purpose was to neutralize the power of the target state, Austria, by vetoing its addition to the adversary of one's "ally." The arrangement may be only tacit and informal, as it was in the above case; formalization by treaty may cover both aspects—benevolent neutrality and outright assistance—or leave the question of assistance vague or only implicit. The so-called Bismarckian system of alliances comprised all variants.[7]

[7] The simplest formulation is in the tentative draft of a Russo-German pact (never actually concluded). "In the event of a war between England and Russia [or, alternately, between France and Germany], Germany [Russia] will remain neutral, and undertakes to prevent, by force if need be, any other Power from joining with England [France]." Cf. J. Y. Simpson, *The Saburov Memoirs, or Bismarck and Russia* (1929), p. 83. Articles III and IV of the Triple Alliance of Germany, Austria-Hungary, and Italy add up to a similar commitment and specify "benevolent" neutrality. Cf. W. L. Langer, *European Alliances and Alignments 1871–1890* (1950), p. 245. The commitment to outright assistance is implicit only in Article I of the Alliance of the Three Emperors (German, Austro-Hungarian, and Russian), which refers explicitly, however, to the localization objective. *Ibid.*, p. 418.

There is significant difference between a commitment seeking to prevent other states from joining an ally's adversary and a commitment which obligates the contracting party to join its ally in any circumstance. One aims at equalizing the belligerent sides and confining the conflict at the same time; the other entails expansion of conflict.

The conflict is most likely to remain confined to the original contestants when they and the interested guarantor powers are about equally strong relative to each other, thus minimizing the temptation for either to seek gains that would jeopardize international stability. In 1870, the relative strength of France and Prussia was apparently equal; so was that of Austria-Hungary and Russia. When the test of arms proved French and Prussian power to be unequal, and the stature of unified Germany was further increased relative to other powers at the expense of France, it was too late for an immediate countervailing adjustment in Austro-Hungarian and Russian policies, and the reversal of alliances had to wait. Still, conditions for confining the conflict to original belligerents were infinitely more favorable in 1870 than in 1940. On the later occasion, Japan's commitment to the European Axis powers had the avowed object of deterring the United States from entering into a belligerent alliance with Britain; America was to be confronted with the certainty of a two-ocean war and the uncertainty of being able to contribute a net increment to British power. But Germany was unable to conquer Britain before revealing fully her far-reaching ambitions, and Japan herself sought too many gains for herself for the "deterrent" alliance not actually to stiffen the American posture.[8]

The typical objective of a mutual-assistance alliance is to contain an adversary, with incidental effect on international stability. The guarantee against adverse coalitions

---

[8] F. W. Iklé, *German-Japanese Relations: 1936–1940* (1956), p. 176; P. W. Schroeder, *The Axis Alliance and Japanese-American Relations* (1958), pp. 124, 138.

would also confine the conflict. The alliance policy that would most deliberately add the objective of stability to that of security is one designed or implemented so as to contain an exuberant ally.

One way of controlling a revolutionary force is to crush it at its inception. That is the rationale of preventive or punitive action against an anti-status quo power by conservative coalitions and against social revolutionary threats by "holy alliances." The best or only hopeful way of influencing a revolutionary force that cannot be crushed is to associate oneself with it. The maxim fits alliances most accurately when the internationally conservative ally serves as a kind of mooring for a government embarking upon a "revolutionary," anti-status quo foreign policy in order to gain prestige and undercut potentially revolutionary domestic opposition; the conditions of domestic and international stability are then at their most interdependent. Here belong, in some respects and phases, alliances of the internally unstable Orleanist monarchy and of the Second Empire in France with Britain, and that of Austria-Hungary with Germany. In exchange for its services, the conservative power cannot but exact a decisive part in defining the ally's methods and objectives; for that reason alone internally unstable and externally adventurous regimes will skun this kind of alliance as long as they can afford to.

To be sure, restraining function is not necessarily related to domestic pressures. The avowed purpose of France's alliance with Austria in 1756 was to stabilize Europe once the two conservative great powers had defeated expansionist Prussia and England. When Austria subsequently sought to reshape the alliance into a revolutionary and unequal one—by seeking aggrandizement only for herself in order to make up for the definitive loss of Silesia to Prussia—the French responded by bringing the alliance's conservative bias to bear against their ally as well as Prussia. The French foreign minister went so far as to deny Austria the benefit of *casus foederis* in her war with Prussia (over the Bavarian succession in 1788), on the grounds that a defensive alliance was inconsistent with support for territorial acquisitions. Vergennes held two vital assets: Austria needed France, who had an equivalent alternative to Austria in a Prussia anxious to rejoin her; and the Frenchman was able to offer Austria compensations in Italy to make up for vetoing acquisitions in Central Europe and in the Balkans (against the Turks).[9]

Roughly a century later it was enlarged Prussia under Bismarck that became the restraining ally of Austria.[10] Bismarck retained *his* alternative option in the target-state (Russia) to check the ally; and to make up for a strict interpretation of the defense commitment, Bismarck kept offering compensations to Austria in the Ottoman Balkans, to be divided in a new balance of power between Russia and Austria. Bismarck's Russia was Vergennes' Prussia, and what Vergennes would have allowed the Austrians to do in Italy Bismarck would have them do in the Balkans. The prerequisites of effective restraint collapsed when post-Bismarckian Germany threw up the Russian option and when nationalism and economic imperialism conjointly disposed of a negotiated Balkan partition forever. Before this happened, however, Russia had been only too glad to accept Bismarck's control over allied Austria as the best alternative to a Russo-

[9] G. Grosjean, *La politique rhénane de Vergennes* (1925), pp. 56–59, 75–76, 94–95.

[10] For this to happen, Prussia had to disrupt the German balance of power (previously invoked by Vergennes partly in the interest of Prussia) and, in the act, also the European balance. Two alliance developments, due largely to the new force of nationality, were chiefly responsible. First, the erosion of the liberal Anglo-Franch entente, intended by the British to contain and control the foreign policy of Napoleon III—a revolutionary one not least because of Napoleon's desire to serve the principle of nationality as well as to utilize it for much needed success abroad. And second, the difficulty, if not impossibility, for the Emperor of the French to replace the "liberal" alliance with England by the "conservative" alliance with Austria— not least because of nationalist German opposition to fighting Prussia on the Rhine on the side of the "hereditary" enemy.

German alliance. Russia would have Germany vouch to her for the conduct of Imperial Austria somewhat in the way the United States would have Soviet Russia vouch for Communist China in the nuclear age.[11]

The task of restraining is made easier when the commitment is not automatic. And there is automatic restraint in a commitment which does not pledge assistance to any one state against another particular state. This is accomplished by two kinds of commitments, both of which were applied to the Franco-German conflict. The first is the above-mentioned commitment to assist "against two" or more powers; another is the commitment associated with Locarno in the post-World War I period, to assist "both of two" potential adversaries against each other, depending on who is the aggressor. Both formulas aim at combining security for allies with restraints on them and stability for the system as a whole. The Locarno formula has become British property as much as the other formula was Bismarck's; it is a means of *détente* as much as of deterrence. The one may help limit conflict, the other aims at liquidating the aftermath of great wars and guaranteeing postwar settlements—traditionally in Europe and more recently in Asia.[12]

Regardless of the nature of the commitment, to exert restraint over an ally is one of the most delicate political tasks, even among ideologically congenial partners. Restraint contravenes the principle of interallied solidarity and raises in an acute form the question of the restraining partner's motives and purposes. The margin for ambiguity is especially great when a major ally asserts influence through groups closely identified with him. The Germans

[11] See Simpson, *Saburov Memoirs*, pp. 76–77, on the Russo-German-Austrian triangle.

[12] See B. Williams, *Stanhope: A Study in Eighteenth Century War and Diplomacy* (1932), p. 310, on the Locarno-type Quadruple Alliance following the wars of Louis XIV. Sir Anthony Eden defines the "thought" behind the Locarno Pact as "that of a reciprocal defensive arrangement in which each member gives guarantees." *Full Circle: The Memoirs of Anthony Eden* (1960), p. 150.

and the Hungarians in the Habsburg monarchy were the guarantors and beneficiaries of the Dual Alliance with Germany and, after the reversal of fortunes, the Slavic groups in the successor states enjoyed the same role and status with respect to alliance with France. The minority groups of the moment became the natural allies of the rival power. More recently, local Communists, white colons, emerging capitalist middle classes, or religious groups, have supplemented and largely replaced ethnically defined groupings. The utility of such groups, however defined, continues to rise and fall with the related outside power's weight in the regional or global balance of power. Their role can be most decisive in cases of uncertain or unstable alignment when, on the model of the Germans and Hungarians in the Empire, a group helps "dig a ditch" between the regime and other groups and *their* preferred international friends.

To promote a group within an allied country politically may be part of a material build-up of the country itself; the objective can be described as one of stability. On the economic plane, alliance promotes internal stability most commonly when pooling of resources and division of roles among members enables a regime to stop short of mobilizing disaffected groups and interests; beyond that, alliances may entail outright subsidy or other form of material support. The vital counterpart to any such support is political and has to do with prestige. Domestic stability is inseparable from the status of the regime and, through the regime, the country. A change has occurred in this respect, however.

In the past, alliance with a respected power was especially valuable for unstable regimes. It enhanced significantly their status and fastened their hold on domestic authority. The alliance helped subdue domestic oppositions by certifying the regime as internationally acceptable and stable. Alliance went thus one step beyond recognition of existence as a matter of fact or law; it marked the adoption of a country and its regime as a desirable close relation within the larger family of nations. Both the regime and the opposition had reason to assume that the alliance created a new vested interest in the regime's permanence. Were the government to disappear, it would jeopardize the alliance tie, presumably useful for the other power as well. The original function of the Triple Alliance, for instance, was not so much for Germany and Austria to guarantee Italy against France as it was to confer on Italy the status of a great power and enhance her regime's stability against domestic enemies.

The relationship was not always one-sided, and the status-giving function of alliance was not always confined to lesser and recently-created states. Following upon the last grand coalition against Louis XIV, the Regent in France and the new Hanoverian monarch in Britain bartered recognition and support against each other's legitimist rivals in dynastic succession. The allies lost their common purpose when the succession issue failed to arise in France and the Jacobite challenge wore off in England; exchange of legitimacy between regimes gave way to a contest over the two powers' status within the alliance, and soon led to the dissolution of the tie.[13] Louis XV's First Minister, Cardinal Fleury, was not the last French statesman to bid for equality with allied Britain; not all were equally fortunate, however, in disposing of not too costly alternatives in the eastern part of the Continent in conditions of less than total military and diplomatic conflict.

In a democratic age, following World War I, the successor governments in Central and Eastern Europe were still ready to act like the Regent beset by the "old court." They

[13] Williams, *Stanhope;* A. M. Wilson *French Foreign Policy during the Administration of Cardinal Fleury* (1936); P. Vaucher, *Robert Walpole et la politique de Fleury 1731–1742* (1925). Other than status concerns were, of course, present from the start. Among them were Britain's political and commercial interest in keeping Spain from joining France under one monarch; and Britain's need for an ally who would help consolidate the postwar status quo by means of judicious "peaceful change" in the teeth of a disgruntled ex-ally, the Holy Roman Emperor, and an ex-enemy, Spain.

did so on the assumption that their status, as well as their stability and security, would be enhanced by alliance with one of the great-power victors of the preceding great war, especially with respect to disaffected minorities at home. Since then, in an anti-colonial age, alliance with a major power has come to cost status rather than confer it. It seems to curtail *full* independence rather than preventing *mere* independence from turning into isolation.

Whenever the needs of security are compelling and clearly indicate a particular alignment, concerns with domestic stability and status will be subordinated. Neither would survive a failure in security, and a successful security response will tend to enhance both. But such clear priorities are rare. Requirements of external security are often hypothetical; requirements of stability for the country and of status for the regime seem to be immediate and manageable. Individual power-holders may of course interpret "stability" in static and repressive terms. But in this they are not altogether free agents, especially when external allies back domestic demands for stable transformations rather than sheer stability.

To note such dynamics may seem to invalidate the preceding analysis as unduly static. It emphasizes security and stability, in contrast with the role of alliances in national expansion and in the transformations of international systems. There doubtless have been alliances for aggrandizement of parties, designed to isolate the victim or also to combine forces in war, regardless of prior agression or provocation. Whatever their form, however, offensive alliances tended to be uncommonly fragile. The best of allies do not easily maintain the singleness of positive purpose that is necessary if offensive action is to be effective. And the very success of an expansionist alliance tends to transform prior disparity of interests into conflict, most flagrantly when partners covet the same territory and seek equal gains. States neither should, therefore—nor do they any more as a rule—embark on an aggressive career unless they can do without allies or can fully control them.

The only overtly offensive alliance since the Axis has been the Arab League. The League campaigned against Israel in a regional system exhibiting the characteristics of traditional diplomacy and conventional warfare; its record of failure was no less conventional. Most recently, revolutionary and expansionist regimes such as Nasser's and Castro's have preferred only informal alignments with a greater power. Their not altogether successful strategy has been to secure protective great-power backing without subordination to a major ally's control and restraints, while thrusting forward in virtual alliance with like-minded groups within target countries.

In the Sino-Soviet bloc, to the extent that alliances have any autonomous effect, the Warsaw Pact has probably had on the whole a restraining impact on the Soviet Union, if only because of the domestic preoccupations of most of the member regimes; the dampening impact of the Sino-Soviet alliance on the more aggressive Chinese partner has been commonly assumed abroad. In the Western system, individual members have been alternately anxious to receive the backing of allies for offensive, or counter-offensive, actions; few of them would, however, accept a sweeping reformulation of common purposes into offensive ones. In both alliance systems, the partitioned countries are most ambivalent, and they constitute at least a partial exception to the rule. Their immediate concern is defensive security; their ultimate reason for alliance is the "offensive" one of unification. The attitude resembles that of France before World War I, seeking in the alliance with Russia a safeguard against a "pre-emptive" German attack as well as a basis for eventual reunification with Alsace-Lorraine. The two allies restrained each other for quite some time from pushing forward in areas attractive for one but merely distracting from the main purpose of the alliance from the viewpoint of the other.

The weapons of mass destruction have only confirmed the presumption against offensive alliances. Both the risks of a "pre-emptive" attack and the possible advantages of a surprise attack favor national action rather than inter-allied coordination. The character of weapons or anything else cannot, of course, rule out the possibility that originally defensive alliances are propelled in offensive directions as allies embrace each other's grievances to forestall the threat of a major transformation to their disadvantage. Here belong the so-called tightening of the adversary alliances prior to World War I and the gradual stepping up of war aims on the part of both the defeated and the ultimately victorious coalitions in both world wars.

As a result of such developments the basic structure of the international system may be transformed. When alliances and alignments become primarily defensive, what can be their relationship to positive transformations of the system? The fundamental dynamics consist of the growth and decline of individual nations in their capacity to innovate, apply, and bring to bear on other states the momentarily decisive components of power. Within these limits, the role of alliances in linking existing to potential structures can be of two kinds. More commonly, alliances are made to prevent undesired transformations, and incidentally they promote an unintended transformation of the main actors or of the basic structure of the system. Or alliances can reshape the structure, at least temporarily, in the desired direction. A fully successful offensive alliance might do so; but the more likely method at present is material assistance toward internal growth of states, extended as part of alliance policy. Assistance to non-aligned states too may be part of alignment policy. It may be intended to reconcile "neutrals" with the assisting power's alliance with another state in the region; or assistance to the non-aligned country may aim at developing it into a power which could help promote security and stability in changed conditions of the future.

The Rationale of Dealignment

Once an alliance is made, it is expected to endure until the purposes of the allies are fulfilled. In fact, however, alliances are highly vulnerable to failure and break-up. One kind of break-up is separate peace concluded by an ally in war. I shall describe as "dealignment" any movement out of an alliance either in war or in peace, regardless of whether such a movement is completed or not. Among the aspects to examine are the who's, how's, and why's of separate peace: the partners; the strategy and tactics; as well as the economics, politics, and ethics of the separate-peace variety of dealignment.

Choice of a partner is the first step in a separate peace. A losing member of a losing alliance, or a member abandoned by less unfortunate allies, will automatically address himself to the adversary who can give him peace; so will a winning state that would formalize its gains while the going is good. The choice is less obvious when a power seeks to detach other states from an adversary alliance by offering them separate peace. Much will depend on the power's objectives and on what price it is willing to pay and what gain forego in the present in order to win more or lose less in the future.

Only limiting cases can be suggested. To break up an alliance and secure immediate general peace, a power must make separate peace with a key member of the opposing combination; this member is likely to be a leading ally. Merely to curtail an alliance, lesser opponents will be more suitable as separate-peace partners; the weakened leading adversary is then likely to be amenable to a general peace later. As a rule, a power would address itself to a major opponent when it was moderately winning or desperately losing; to lesser opponents when it was moderately losing or strikingly winning. In limited conflicts the choice of the partner is least predictable because most opportunistic.

ALIGNMENTS AND REALIGNMENTS 43

The choice will be determined by experimentally discovered propensity of individual powers for an immediate arrangement and possible postwar alignment. In the intermittent and protracted peacemaking of the War of the Austrian Succession, for instance, the favored partner of Britain was Prussia and, later, Spain, while France flirted with the Dutch and the Austrians. But the two major allies remained throughout potential separate-peace partners for each other as a means to speedy termination of the whole affair.

In contests over hegemony, however, the weapon of separate peace will always be used to isolate the principal opponent. In the peace negotiations associated with the name of Westphalia, Spain sought separate peace successfully with the United Provinces and unsuccessfully with Sweden; France wooed Bavaria as a lever to a peace arrangement with Austria, leaving out and isolating Spain. A peace settlement between the leading powers, France and Spain, had to wait for decisive military defeat of one side. In the total wars of the twentieth century, the lesser states too had increasingly to be coerced by defeat or subversion before they were ready for a separate arrangement.

How to induce another power to make separate peace, or else how to detach it from a counter-coalition, is the first question of strategy. The basic techniques are coercion, enticement, or combinations of the two, unless force alone suffices to compel a separate peace which is tantamount to unconditional surrender. To force defection by means short of the enemy's destruction, pressure has to be applied at the militarily or psychologically weakest point of the adversary alliance. A composite is only as strong as its weakest member. The precept was followed when Louis XIV sought to detach Savoy from one of the many hostile coalitions; when, by economic means, France sought to press Italy out of the Triple Alliance before World War I; and when, prior to clashing with Japan in World War II, the United States tried to edge her out of the Tripartite Pact. Following World War II, the Communist powers were applying a similar strategy to the Western alliance system, mainly in relation to Taiwan and West Germany.

The weakness of the link is a relative matter. It grows with the disparity between allied support and the goals and ambitions of the state subject to the pressure. The ambitions of the above-named targets exceeded considerably their capacities; and they failed to get adequate allied support to offset the pressure and help them realize their objectives. Consequently, Savoy concluded a secret treaty with France pledging the neutralization of Italy, while in the later instances Italy and Japan successively diluted their commitments to Germany to the point where they differed little from conditional neutrality. On the other hand, the failure of an alliance to snap the weakest link of the adversary combination will seriously strain its own cohesion.

Weakness in an alliance may lie in the internal domestic order of an ally, too. A major shift in European diplomacy occurred when Louis XIV failed to sustain his ally, James II, against Protestant opposition headed by his arch-enemy and James' successful rival, William of Orange. England was thus pried out of the French orbit for good and became the core-power of anti-French alliances.[14] When issues are only international, positive inducements tend to accompany pressure; when the causes are domestic, inducements should follow upon pressure and favor a successor regime. The United States did not heed this precept when it failed to make concessions to the Konoye government in Japan after American pressure had helped force out the pro-Axis predecessors.

Mere enticements are rarely if ever sufficient. The Habsburg powers were unable to make Sweden part with France

[14] See J. J. Jusserand, ed., Vols. XXIV–XXV (*Angleterre*), in *Recueil des instructions données aux ambassadeurs et ministres de France depuis les traités de Westphalie jusqu'à la Révolution française* (1929). On the transactions between France and Savoy in 1696, see P. Sagnac and A. de Saint-Léger, *Louis XIV, 1661–1715* (1949), pp. 402–403.

and conclude a separate peace in the 1640's; they tried skillfully to magnify and exploit differences between the allies, but were unable to generate the required military pressure at crucial periods.[15] Napoleon's mastery in dissolving alliances through peace overtures failed him with the decline of belief in his military power and skill; the impact of "peace offensives" of the Soviets had been no less contingent on the military might in the background. There is good reason for this, having to do with the most common strategy of the party wishing to act separately.

What is the strategy, in addition to the generally useful complaint of inadequate consultation? It is to propose a joint course of conduct to one's allies necessitating some sacrifice on their part. One variant is to ask allies to make general peace on terms which are satisfactory to the would-be defector. Another, possibly complementary, variant is to apply to allies for military relief in the expectation that they cannot or will not comply. At the very least, the party contemplating separate peace finds out whether the step is necessary; when the allies actually do fail to cooperate, the would-be defector is released from loyalty to the alliance. The aforementioned Duke of Savoy went through the motions of asking for large-scale military assistance and obtained his allies' sanction for separate peace with France when they proved unable to divert troops to Italy. In the earlier Thirty Years' War, the French themselves employed in a similar manner the ambiguous terms of the Swedish commitment against the "House of Austria," asking and being refused assistance against its Spanish branch.[16] As long as a joint course of action by allies is sufficiently plausible to be feared by the adversary, the strategy may have the additional advantage of securing the best possible terms from him.

[15] G. H. Bougeant, *Histoire des guerres et des négociations qui précédèrent le traité de Westphalie* (1751), Vol. II, pp. 40–43, 127 ff.
[16] The commitment under the Franco-Swedish treaty was to "make war on the Emperor, on the House of Austria and its Adherents . . ." and to "constrain them to make peace." *Ibid.*, Vol. I, p. 404.

The basic strategy of dealignment indicates a counterstrategy of the ally who is intent on preventing separate peace. On the positive side, he must retain the capacity to satisfy reasonable demands for joint action. On the negative side, he must retain the capacity to prevent separate peace by controlling an asset which can be used to make the transaction impossible for the ally or unattractive to the adversary.

To make the transaction impossible implies the ability to coerce; to make it unattractive, the ability to withhold and outbid. The ability to coerce must be direct, physical; the ability to punish by mere withdrawal of assistance wanes as the recipient becomes able to terminate his role in the conflict. The ability to withhold and outbid depends primarily on the possession of an asset which is indispensable for acceptable peace from the viewpoint of the enemy. For a long time, Britain's ability to outbid a would-be secessionist did not rest primarily on her ability to withhold subsidies. More important was her ability to withhold restitution of colonial conquests from the enemy, France, in exchange for French conquests in northwestern Europe. This worked against the Austrians when they bade for separate peace with France in 1748 and would have thwarted such an attempt in 1813; and it enabled the British to make virtually separate peace in 1748 and again in 1763.[17] In 1940, the control of the French fleet was a key factor in the separate truce negotiations of France with Nazi Germany. The distribution and control of nuclear capability among allies might have like implications in contemporary conditions.

The strategies of parties reflect the reasons why they seek separate peace. Both the would-be divider of an alliance and the defector may seek to compel third parties into a general peace as the necessary consequence of defection or

---

[17] Sir R. Lodge, *Studies in Eighteenth-Century Diplomacy 1740–1748* (1930), Chap. 8; Lodge, *Great Britain and Prussia in the Eighteenth Century* (1923), Chap. 4.

the only means of preventing its consummation. This was the rationale of the British whenever they decided to attend separately to the general interest. In quite different conditions, the Bolsheviks thought that they might force the Western Allies into a general peace by creating a precedent at Brest-Litovsk; the harsh terms exacted by the Germans indicated that they themselves did not share the illusion. Another reason for seeking a separate peace may stem from the desire to prevent the ascendancy of a too successful ally after the adversary's defeat. An equally unrealistic objective may be that of maintaining or enhancing one's role and status within a particular alliance or in alliance diplomacy by showing one's capacity and eligibility for separate peace. The declining Dutch were anxious to show in this way that they were still a major power in the 1740's; and both preceding motives were entertained, or advanced, by Prussia's Frederick. These questions raise the issue of the ethics of separate peace, while the underlying general reason for separate peace, to get better terms than would be available otherwise, involves its economics.

The Prussian king's self-justification rested on an indictment of the abandoned ally. According to the princely author of *Anti-Machiavel,* a sovereign must admit three main reasons for breaking an alliance commitment if he is to remain faithful to the reason of state: if the ally fails to fulfill his obligations; if he meditates deception and has to be forestalled; and if a *force majeure,* preeminently in the form of insufficient material resources, compels the breach. The French were said to be guilty of the first two offenses while Prussia suffered the "strongest and most decisive" third disability.[18] Too great a facility in separate-peace making lowers

[18] J. D. E. Preuss, ed., *Oeuvres de Frédéric le Grand* (1846), Vol. II, pp. xxvi, 94, 115–17, 127–28, 134. According to Frederick, had France succeeded in attaining her extreme objectives, a French-controlled "balance of power" of four states in Germany (the Habsburg dominions, Prussia, Saxony, and Bavaria) would have reduced Prussia to the role of a satellite. France's failure, on the other hand, would have endangered Prussia's existence and her gain of Silesia. Prussia herself was financially exhausted and could secure the benefits of arduous military efforts only by a separate peace.

one's value as an ally in the future despite a temporary rise in status. Pleading necessity is, therefore, a shrewd gesture of a party which aims at satisfying the requirements of both the ethics and the economics of separate peace. A presumed capacity for separate peace may be the greatest asset; used too often it becomes a liability. Prussia and Britain learned this several times over during the eighteenth century; since World War I, the mythical German option to make a deal with Russia has been an asset, but worth more before than after a Rapallo.

The elementary economics of separate peace is a matter of gains and losses and their durability. To make tenure legitimate, Frederick fought again and then worked hard to have the gain of Silesia ratified in the final peace of 1748. One hundred years earlier, Cardinal Mazarin stated the issue in two main points.[19] First, a party to separate peace is likely to be offered better terms than it can obtain in a general peace, possibly after more effort. And second, while it is an extraordinary bargain to get terms into a guaranteed general-peace treaty that are offered as an inducement to betray loyalty to an ally, it is still a good bargain to get somewhat less. The extra gains in a separate peace are commonly deducted from the lot of allies and must, in return, be discounted by the greater uncertainty of the acquisition and by the liability of dependence on the former adversary for good will and support.

The Swedes did not find it to their advantage to make a separate peace in the late 1640's; and the Soviets had even stronger reasons for resisting the separate-peace initiatives of the Japanese on behalf of Germany in late 1943 and early 1944. They could expect to receive substantial concessions from Nazi Germany, but they could realistically expect to gain more from their allies by prosecuting the war to the finish. Moreover they could increase their gains still further at the expense of the would-be mediator, Japan. The calcu-

---

[19] Bougeant, *Histoire des guerres*, Vol. II, pp. 333 ff.

lation would have been different had the Soviets really suspected their Western allies of propensity to a separate peace with the Axis. By contrast, in the negotiations between the United States and Japan, which were intended to remove the necessity for war, the Japanese could hardly be expected to renounce all gains. To do that, a war must first be waged and go badly.[20]

Only in extreme circumstances are "economic" calculations of this kind seemingly irrelevant. The defector may yield to the desire for release from useless struggle in defeat; or he may seek revenge on an ally regardless of the cost to himself—another possibility which is most potent as a threat only. More commonly, calculations are impeded by the dilemmas which beset parties to separate peace. They concern the utility, the implementation, and the dynamic implications of dealignment.

What is the utility of separate peace as an alternative when there is an effective choice for or against? Proven loyalty to allies and known low propensity to dealignment may be the best way to hold allies and increase one's value as party to alignments. Cohesion and efficacy of the alliance as a whole increases as a result. But to renounce one's capacity for separate peace too conspicuously as part of a crusading commitment may reduce one's ability to secure satisfaction and to limit the gains of others—to the possible detriment of the alliance in the longer run. It can be debated whether Tsar Alexander made a mistake in 1812–1813 when he rejected Napoleon's half-hearted moves toward a separate peace with his chief continental enemy, Russia. A threat of separate peace before Napoleon's final defeats might have induced Russia's allies to satisfy all her territorial demands, provided they were unable to anticipate Russia in desertion. Short of an open threat, a less total commitment—leaving open all options— would have increased the Tsar's leverage

---

[20] On the two Japanese involvements, see F. C. Jones, *Japan's New Order in East Asia: Its Rise and Fall 1937–1945* (1954), pp. 414 ff.; Schroeder, *The Axis Alliance*, p. 108.

in pressing his war-aims in the course of the campaign; it would have correspondingly reduced the bargaining power of other allies, notably Austria.

Roughly the same argument can be applied to the relations of Western democracies with the Soviet Union during World War II. When its task is to limit the acquisitive ally's territorial ambitions, diplomacy must steer the separate-peace expedient along a narrow path between duplicity and single-mindedness. The behavior of the United States toward Japan, who was anxious to secure some accommodation before belligerency, and toward the Soviet Union, who was suspect of retaining the capacity to make separate peace during belligerency, suggests one thing. A democracy at war is more ready to make grave compromises in order to avert separate peace by an ally, than it is to arrange something like a separate peace with an actual or potential opponent. This double standard is applied despite the fact that the required compromises may be qualitatively identical and involve surrender of the same principle of self-determination for which the war had been waged.

Popular involvement aggravates the dilemmas that stem from the fact that the making of a separate peace is somehow an act of disloyalty. Governments must communicate simultaneously with diversified publics interested in the transaction: the ally; one's domestic public; and the adversary. Talleyrand's dictum about the role of language in diplomacy (to conceal thought) is now indisputably true, and the actors must depend on the ability of the counterparts to read correctly suggestive facts and permissible symbolic actions.

Take the two World War II cases, for instance. The separate peace proponents in Japan (the Konoye group) and in Italy (the Badoglio group) had to speak and act so as to conceal their intentions from the ally (notably in the case of Italy, still partly occupied by the Germans) or the ally's domestic friends (notably in the case of Japan, with her pro-Axis extremists). The same words and acts, however, aroused suspicion of bellicosity or at least duplicity on the part of the adversary. In order to master the contradiction, one must dare presume certain things about the potential defector, pressure him into clarifications, and protect him against the consequences. The presumption of propensity to separate peace can rest on highly secret and symbolic communication. A change in the directors of foreign policy alone may indicate instability in the system and its external orientation; and the identity and prior foreign-policy views of the new elite are more important than immediate statements which may have to be overcompensatory. Both the Prime Minister and the Foreign Minister of the Konoye government were known to be moderates, and Marshal Badoglio was known not to be the Duce. Similar conclusions could be drawn, in earlier mentioned instances, from the ascendancy of the Tories in England just prior to Utrecht and of the King's Friends just prior to the peace of Paris.

There are, of course, doubtful cases. The identity of a Badoglio and of a Pétain might have misled those who identify military rank with bellicose politics. The less clear the propensity of the elite, the more important it is to press the elite into some revelatory act; and the clearer the propensity to separate peace, the more essential it is to protect the elite so that it can reveal itself. The two requirements may coincide when the elite requires not so much a physical protection against the ally's sanctions, as the Italians did, but rather a political protection against charges of wanton betrayal of the ally. The adversary's coercive pressure must then supply the exonerating proof of necessity. The embargo against Japan produced, pressed, and protected the Konoye government. The results could not last forever, however, unless rewards demonstrated the success of a moderate course. In the Japanese case, inducements would have had to be material; when the adversary has been weakened and needs an honorable way out, they may be merely symbolic and face-saving.

The pitfalls of dealignment may recommend the expedient of a tacit, partial separate peace in a particular sector of operations. A tacit truce seems to avoid decisive commitments either way and to reduce one's risk as a result. It may be profitable, too. The mercantile English and Dutch, when aligned against France and Spain, often differed over the limits of hostilities and of concurrent trade with the enemy.[21] In any limited war, including a cold one, each ally's use of available capabilities is a matter for *ad hoc* determination. The sphere of undeployed resources is one of "peace," which may be evolved in tacit collusion with the adversary. The ally who exposes himself more can try to compromise the partial defector into equivalent involvement—thus the British insisted with success on "total" war in commerce for the Dutch, too. The ally who tacitly limits or suspends his part in a conflict will be least receptive to such pressures when he tries to impede a hegemonic ally's success, as the Austrians did in 1813. And the more deeply involved ally will be hesitant to force the issue when to do so would reveal conflicts of interest and his inability to penalize defection. This was Nazi Germany's difficulty when Spain's Caudillo consented not to act against the Anglo-American invasion of North Africa, an area whose division he had been unable to agree upon with his Axis partners.

In peacetime, a partial dealignment may take the form of a restrictive interpretation of one's commitment or of restrictions placed on the use of facilities made available to an ally. Restrictions on use have become crucial in modern, integrated alliances. In an earlier period, Italy vouchsafed to France interpretations weakening her commitments to Germany prior to World War I, and Japan was apparently ready to do likewise for the United States, had she received

---

[21] On the conflicting concepts, see G. N. Clark, *The Dutch Alliance and the War against French Trade 1688–1697* (1923), pp. 5-6 and *passim*.

parallel assurances in return. Parties to adversary alliances may exchange reassuring interpretations and thus reduce the danger of both provocation and miscalculation, without detriment to deterrence and alliance loyalty. Things are different when such assurances are granted unilaterally, without concert with allies, and when an ally concedes an interpretation which in effect nullifies the commitment. He then virtually renounces "free hand" to act under the guise of recovering freedom *not* to act.

Tacit separate accommodation has obvious drawbacks for the longer run, which put a premium on formalizing and completing the dealignment. Unless the transaction is formalized, both sides can reverse themselves in changed conditions with great ease. The risk is greatest for the party which concedes more in immediate advantages while the other party is not formally committed to perpetuate the reward in time of victory. One can then find himself with both strings snapped in his bow. Frederick in a way had to move from an informal convention toward separate peace; and Metternich would have had to make separate peace with Napoleon, and possibly join him against the Russians, or else abandon Austria's temporary suspension of hostilities had it not wrought the desired effect on the forward allies. As for Franco, he had to be reassured by formal commitments by the Anglo-Americans regarding the postwar period, as the price for a partial dealignment which made lasting sense to him only as a token of ultimate realignment.

Such pledges can be cautious. Unlike the American President, the British confined their assurances to the integrity of Spain as a country independently of its regime. But any pledge limits the legitimate freedom of the benefitting party with regard to the defector.[22] On the other hand, the failure to formalize a wartime understanding with postwar consequences in any form might make it mandatory for both

[22] For the facts and a different interpretation, see Sir S. Hoare (Viscount Templewood), *Complacent Dictator* (1947), pp. 168–70.

parties to retain indefinitely an active capacity to enforce the tacit agreement. Theoretically at least, the party linked to the losing side would have to increase its capability as that of its belligerent allies declined or else find itself at the mercy of the victors later.

In any event, the balance of power is the source of the most fundamental dilemma of separate peace. A party follows its dictates when deserting a too successful ally; a defector violates these dictates when he initiates a stampede away from the losing side. The separate peace maneuver defeats itself from the standpoint of the defector also in the first case, however, when he is unable to tip the scales against the winning ex-ally. He then confronts a strong former ally without much comfort from the ex-enemy.

A critical issue is that of timing. When can defection still help a losing side, and when is it worth a concession to the winning side; or when, in a stalemate, are separate-peace arrangements desirable for both sides? The ambiguity built into the balance of power will alone make it difficult for potential partners to evaluate identically the "objective" situation, let alone agree on terms which would conform with the state of the balance. In the changing strategic picture of World War II, there was hardly a moment when the Western Allies, the Soviet Union, and Nazi Germany could have done so. To be satisfactory, the terms must weaken the ex-enemy decisively, while keeping him strong enough to act as a weight or buffer against the ex-ally. Another disparity bears not so much on timing as on space. An American-Japanese agreement would have made sense, and might have been feasible, in terms of the Far East alone. But it would have released Japan's resources—otherwise pinned down in China—against, say, the Soviet Union, while immobilizing the American government at home politically. Such a turn of events might have had a disastrous effect on the European and ultimately the global balance.

Balance-of-power dilemmas propel dealignment into complete realignment. In order to avoid confrontation with a victorious ex-ally or to identify his cause with that of winning ex-enemies, the defector will be tempted to throw his full weight into another scale. In some circumstances, complete realignment may be the only alternative to retro-alignment, that is, reverting to original partners so as to correct a previous miscalculation.

Mere dealignment will be the terminal point when it is sufficient or when full realignment is impossible. It will be impossible when the realignment of A's ally B to C is vetoed by C's ally D, and might force retaliatory realignment of D to A. Such a reversal of alliances would nullify the advantages for C of B's realignment and be less advantageous for C than a mere dealignment by B. The veto is likely to be inspired by D's particular conflict with B. When alliances coalesce around several conflicts, this will increase strains within them toward defection, but will also impede the movement's completion. The mere fact that Austria would not have tolerated Prussia's realignment during the War of the Austrian Succession was in itself enough to stop Prussia at the point of dealignment and to push her into temporary retro-alignment with France. On the other hand, in the same war, Britain prevailed upon Vienna not only to admit a regional rival into the alliance against France but even to pay the territorial price for Sardinia's belligerency. Austria's reluctance to repeat the feat in favor of Sardinia's great-power successor in 1915 led Italy into belligerency against her ex-allies after a brief spell of neutrality.[23]

The Rationale of Realignment

There is no fundamental difference between dealignment and outright realignment. Realignment, too, is due to such

[23] On Italy, see L. Albertini, *The Origins of the War of 1914* (1957), esp. Vol. III, Chaps. 6, 7.

things as coercion, conflict of interests and strategies, and changes in domestic authority and in power relationships.

Coercion is strong and effective pressure. Inability to resist it compels a power to re-evaluate the gains and liabilities of existing policies. Both Austria and Prussia swung to Napoleon's France and back again in function of military defeats and victories. When external coercion releases a nation from an alien regime, it may actually enlarge the area of freedom. Realignment will then be particularly violent, as reprisals and retribution attend change. Unlike many other regimes, the Franco regime in Spain escaped coercion by the victorious allies of the last war. Its gradual, controlled realignment was facilitated by the regime's ability to adjust somewhat the domestic power structure and ideology to the new alignment of forces in the world at large.[24]

There are various degrees and forms of coercion. Italy's shift in the First World War was less due to forcible pressure than was her shift in the Second; in both instances external influence merely confirmed widespread popular inclination and geopolitical factors favoring realignment. The result was the appearance of opportunism. No state is immune to coercion of some kind, however. Britain's shift from an understanding with Russia to alliance with France against Russia in the crisis which led up to the Crimean War, in the 1850's, was due partly to French coercion. France confronted the reluctant British with the choice of alliance in the Near East or hostility in Belgium, where France would seek compensation for being excluded from the Ottoman affair.[25] The blackmail, accompanied by military demonstrations in both geographic areas, proved to be a decisive supplement to the growing divergence of interests and interpretations between Britain and Russia concerning the partition of the Ottoman Empire.

[24] See E. J. Hughes, *Report from Spain* (1947), p. 96 and *passim*, in contrast with H. L. Mathews, *The Yoke and the Arrows: A Report on Spain* (1957), p. 125.
[25] V. J. Puryear, *England, Russia and the Straits Question 1844–1856* (1931), pp. 220 ff., 246 ff.

Conflicts of interest between allies may be sufficiently great, however, to prompt realignment without external pressure. For an existing tendency to become action, the other side must be receptive, and, of course, conflicts with alternative allies must not outweigh grievances against present ones. In one way or another, intra-alliance conflicts bear on the gain-loss equation concerning policy aims and alliance strategy. In the Thirty Years' War, divergences between France and Sweden failed to culminate in realignment only because of the main conflict's gravity. Moreover, the two allies were able to conduct the strategy of converging on the German land mass from two different sides. And the main cause for a rupture disappeared with the danger of upsetting territorial and political gains for the Protestant power. Conversely, the divergence of strategic concept on the Habsburg side was largely responsible for the failure of the alliance, despite substantial unity of policy aims. A like divergence precipitated Austria's realignment from Britain to the traditional French enemy in the mid-eighteenth century. While Austria's main concerns were in Central Europe, the main strategic interests of her Spanish and subsequently British ally were in the Low Countries.[26] In neither case was material subsidy by the major ally sufficient to overcome divergence in strategic priorities.

Austria's propensity to realignment bore fruit when the director of her foreign policy, Kaunitz, succeeded in three concurrent operations. First of all, the Austrians reassessed the idea of traditional conflict with France; this review revealed identical interests between the two conservative powers confronted with upstart powers in Europe and overseas. Second, the Austrians pressured Prussia, the incompatible ally of the desired French partner, into acts creating at least a semblance of conflicting interests between Prussia and France. (One such act was Prussia's treaty with Britain, France's new chief enemy; another was Prussia's "preventive" invasion of Saxony, a friendly and related court.) And

[26] Waddington, *Louis XIV et le renversement des alliances*, pp. 129 ff.

third, the Austrians muted existing conflicts of interests between the desired alliance partner and an older ally, Russia. Russia was induced to respect the liberties of France's Eastern-European allies, Poland and Turkey, and to moderate her territorial claims in the region. The adaptations removed Prussia's main safeguard against a Franco-Russian alliance, while Prussia's attack on Saxony gave the hitherto antagonistic powers a common grievance. On the other hand, the survival of partly repressed conflicts (between France and Russia as well as between France and Austria) weakened the new alliance system during and after the ensuing seven years' hostilities.

Sagacious diplomacy was required because the reversal of alliances was not necessary. On one side, Austria had a solid base for realignment; on the other side there were only minor irritations between France and Prussia. The break was precipitated by Prussia's attempt (matching Britain's) to satisfy too many interests and guard against too many contingencies without giving up the basic alliance with France. The Prussian king's obsession with status, as an independent and equal ally, may have prompted his restlessness beyond the needs of mere security.

When he has any freedom, the defecting ally will often use mediation between the contesting parties as the chief strategy of realignment. The strategy goes beyond offering co-operation in expanded efforts with one's ally, to the threat to act in unison with the side willing to limit its pretensions. The strategy of dealignment plays upon the doubted resolution of the ally and is meant to justify the strategist's passing to inaction; the strategy of realignment plays upon the doubted reasonableness of the ally and is meant to determine or justify the strategist's subsequent involvement. Since dealignment may be but a half-way station to realignment, the two strategies will merge in practice. In 1756, Prussia first offered to act jointly with France against Britain; when her half-hearted offer was spurned, she at first tried to stay neutral and offered to mediate between France and Britain.

A critical issue is the good faith of the mediator. Ideally, he should align with the side which meets his terms. Strictly speaking mediation is incompatible with alliance with one party to the conflict, since mediation presupposes impartiality. In practice the ally becomes a neutral for the purposes of mediation; technical incompatibility is brought up only when a power wishes to prevent mediation by an associate or, conversely, wishes to be disengaged from the alliance commitment as a prerequisite to mediation.

Metternich sought a release from alliance with Napoleon before he employed mediation to move Austria toward the anti-French alliance. Like the England of Charles II in the Dutch wars of the 1670's, Metternich could embark on the tricky maneuver on behalf of Austria for two main reasons: both countries lay outside the main path of military operations; and in both instances the French ally tolerated mediation in the potentially conflicting beliefs that it was better to have peace terms mediated by an ally and that it was better for the ally to mediate than join the adversary. In the actual event both mediators went beyond mediation to realignment, partly under the pressure of public opinion. It is a moot point whether the "preliminary" peace terms presented to Napoleon by Metternich were moderate and, if so, why? What is less controversial is that the Austrian did not act as a bona fide armed mediator. He was not prepared to guarantee the offered terms as final and to reaffirm the French alliance if Napoleon accepted the terms on this basis and the Allies did not.[27]

Metternich's biased mediation was but a pretext for re-

---

[27] A. Sorel, *L'Europe et la Révolution française*, Vol. VIII (1904), p. 172 and *passim*. More favorable to Metternich is H. A. Kissinger, *A World Restored: Metternich, Castlereagh, and the Problems of Peace 1812–1822* (1957), Chaps. 5–8. Metternich's role appears less important in Sir C. Webster, *The Foreign Policy of Castlereagh 1812–1815* (1950), pp. 103 ff.

alignment. The ostensibly similar diplomacy of a successor of Metternich's in the Crimean War some forty years later, Buol, was not. Buol's main concern was in limiting the gains of all belligerent parties: expansionist Russia, as well as Britain and France, bent on containing her. Buol's mediation could be more impartial than Metternich's, because Russia's objectives shrank as Britain's expanded and because Austria's truly vital interests were soon satisfied in the Balkans. Austria actually made a treaty with the Western powers, directed against her ally and savior of 1848; but she refused to implement the realignment militarily once Russia accepted the essence of Buol's peace program.[28]

Most recently, the "neutrals" in the cold war have sought to limit and terminate the great power conflict. It remains to be seen whether their policy can be effective without the sanction of alignment with one of the great powers and, if so, whether they will mediate in good faith. The nonaligned countries meet some of the prerequisites. They are located outside the main path of the East-West conflict, and both sides to the conflict prefer to conciliate the noncommitted rather than alienate them with subsequent advantage to the adversary.

---

[28] G. B. Henderson, *Crimean War Diplomacy and Other Historical Essays* (1947), esp. pp. 153–89; Puryear, *England, Russia and the Straits Question*, pp. 340 ff.; H. Temperley, *England and the Near East: The Crimea* (1936), Book IV, Chaps. 10–14.

2
The Cohesion of Alliances

THE REASONS for making and breaking alliances define indirectly the main conditions of their cohesion and efficacy. I shall now discuss the conditions of cohesion explicitly, proceeding from the intangible and procedural elements to the material ones.

Ideologies and Styles

If allies are to stay together despite setbacks, the grounds for alliance must be rationalized. To do so is the function of ideology, which more than anything else makes alliances into social institutions. As a handmaid of action, ideology feeds on selective memory of the past and outlines a program for the future. A typical alliance ideology will define the basis and, by implication, the limits of alliance solidarity; it will be formulated so as to add incentive to joint action and to screen intra-alliance strains and splits. Beyond that, alliance ideology merges with the rationalization of the struggle which has brought it about, if only because it cannot avoid characterizing the identity, intentions, and capabilities of the target state. While this characterization will be rather definite, the statement of the allies' ulterior objectives is liable to be more tentative and general.

Defensive coalitions designed to contain a hegemonic bid are rich in ideological lore; alliances of democratic states, particularly in time of war, are richest of all. This is readily explained by the heterogeneity of interest in a defensive coalition and by the need to transform alliances of democratic states under stress into communities of friendship among peoples. By contrast, offensive alliances of autocratic states will be held together by the prospect of gain; if they have an ideology, it will be the ideology of the leading have an ideology, it will be the ideology of the leading member. The alliances led by Louis XIV and Napoleon, the Central Powers and the Axis Powers, were weaker on ideology than their opponents; if at all, they moved to imitate their rivals only when their fortunes had declined beyond repair. Baron Lisola, Frederick von Gentz, Wilson, and Churchill, all spoke on behalf of the defense. Even today, the West is a match for the otherwise more ideology-conscious Communist East in this respect.

The construction of alliances, their implementation, and their perpetuation have specific ideological requirements. When an alliance is being put together, the ideology will emphasize the joint interest of potential allies in combining their resources. It must carefully balance assertion of great power and threatening intentions on the part of the challenger with the affirmation that allied power is adequate to deal with the threat if properly developed and combined. To facilitate coalescence, the ideology will emphasize pressing common interests, while ignoring or minimizing divergent interests among allies. "Let bygones be bygones" is the slogan whatever may be the allies' private reservations. In the period of implementation, the ideology of an alliance at war will differ from one at peace. If there is war, the power of the opponent is a visible fact; the ideology will stress the opposing power's hidden vulnerability which alone makes interallied effort into a rational undertaking. In time of peace, the ideology will continue to stress the gravity of the opponent's capability and intent, modulating the motif of his vulnerability in order to offset excessive optimism or pessimism. In both war and peace there are then two sides to the ideology: one is turned outward and is part of psychological warfare to demoralize the opponent; the other is turned inward, and idealizes relations among allies in order to build psychological hindrances to individual selfishness, separate peace, or realignment. The keynote is solidarity and equality in the dark present, as a token of things to come in a faintly suggested, brighter future.

To assure the future, one may have to exorcise the past. The ideology of the period of construction and implementation tends to obliterate the past history of allies, unless the past is one of traditional friendship. By contrast, the period following the peak of a threat requires that the common immediate past be glorified as creating both a moral obligation and an irrefutable political argument for perpetuating the alliance. At this point, the ideology stresses the immutability as well as the immorality of the adversary, attributing to him magical powers of resurgence and incurable addiction to evil. The merely preventive objective of the alliance with regard to the enemy must, however, at this stage be legitimized by means of a positive program for the state system as a whole. The intellectual task is to make the two objectives appear complementary, and to define the positive program so as to contain the tendency of the alliance to disintegrate, as conflicts among allies again come to the fore. This is a difficult task, especially when alliance ideology comes to be differentiated more and more along national lines. As signs of an imminent break-up of the alliance multiply, nationalized alliance ideologies will be chiefly concerned with exonerating a particular member-nation from blame for the dissolution and with reasserting the nation's ability to do without the departing allies, to find other allies, or to stand alone.

We have noted earlier the beliefs of Frederick the Great,

justifying separation from allies by reason of state. The views are not unique, and the ideology *about* alliances of a sovereign seeking territorial aggrandizement need not be substantially different from that of a contemporary nationalist leader seeking to restore his country's grandeur. Ideologies about alliances reflect the holder's beliefs concerning international behavior, in general, and behavior of states in alliance, in particular. Frederick justified Prussia's secession by the behavior imputed to his wartime ally, France; the ideology of de Gaulle reflects dogmatic skepticism regarding the behavior and motives of France's allies in a more recent and greater war.

The nationalist position, as exemplified by de Gaulle, is built on two major premises. One holds that ideology of allied co-operation is a thin disguise for the hegemonic striving of the major ally or allies. The other holds that subordination to allies is equivalent to servitude imposed by the enemy. The premises dictate the major conclusion: the struggle with the adversary must not be allowed to obscure the duty of self-assertion within the alliance.

Both premises and conclusion reflect beliefs bearing upon the states' entry into the alliance, their policy within the alliance, and their likely exit from the alliance. States join a struggle as allies only when they are directly assaulted in their territory or interests. This is especially true of powers which are shielded by nature, as the sea powers Britain and America have been until recently. The United States entered both World Wars late and only when compelled to do so by the adversary. Alliances among land powers who do not have a margin of security, such as France and Russia, are somewhat more dependable. Once in the alliance, however, the hitherto sluggish power strives for supremacy, under the cover of solidarity, and practices expediency under the color of principle. Thus the United States strove for hegemony in and by way of the wartime alliance. Among other things, it played on divisions among political groups in allied France while proclaiming the primacy of the military effort over political considerations. In the concluding phase of an alliance, the same ally which joined in the fray last, when his hand was forced, must be expected to leave first, as soon as he can. His sacred egoism will then prompt him to make a separate arrangement with the adversary or, if such is ruled out, with another major ally, in either case ignoring and excluding the lesser powers.

One's beliefs about the behavior of others will breed convictions about the right conduct for oneself. In a view like de Gaulle's, a state can count only on itself, even within an alliance. Since the major allies were compelled to enter the alliance by acts of the enemy, it is up to the lesser allies to compel respect for their rights within the alliance. The fundamental posture must be one of firmness, principle, and self-dependence. The requirement of firmness is so paramount that a lesser state must fulfill it even at great peril. The behavior of the leading allies themselves proves that "logic and sentiment do not weigh heavily in comparison with the realities of power . . . what matters is what one takes and knows how to keep." [1] For a leader of character to act so as to stake out a principle strengthens his nation's moral position in the present; and, even if he fails to receive immediate satisfaction, he has reserved the rights for the future when the power position has improved. Agreement for its own sake has no value. The answer to expediency is to force issues and reveal ambiguities. To do all this, and more, a state must remain self-dependent. This does not exclude co-operation, but it defines its terms as strict *quid pro quo* reciprocity and limits it by the requirements of equality and independence. By retaining independence a nation can be a match for other allies in hegemonic politics, in withdrawal from the alliance, in separate arrangements, and in

---

[1] The quotation is from de Gaulle's *Mémoires de guerre*, Vol. 11 (1956), p. 240 (my translation). The recommendation to firmness "at great peril" was dispensed to the Shah of Iran. *Ibid.*, Vol. III (1959), p. 58.

exclusion from settlements. Independence enhances one's value as ally for other powers and as political leader of equal or lesser states.[2]

The nationalist's dogmatic view stands in contrast with the more pragmatic, associationist policy and, if the term is appropriate, ideology. The pragmatic view favors a supple, *ad hoc* approach, which, depending on mutual convenience, may lead either to informal accommodations or to formal commitments. Its practitioners—de Gaulle's wartime counterpart, Churchill, or, in the postwar period, an Adenauer—prefer to wheedle concessions out of a stronger ally. They wait out the crystallization of an identity of interests within the alliance rather than precipitate fights over conflicting interests. Having once decided that the alliance is necessary, the associationist believes in making it work.

In stating the dichotomy in these terms, one can hardly doubt which attitude is more conducive to the cohesion of an alliance. But the nationalist position has the virtue of stating in stark, absolute terms what are subdued traits in the moderate attitude, too, so long as alliance-interest is not something superior to the interests of members. The nationalist ideology is, moreover, in the ascendant among politically less developed countries. It fits both the current phase of their historical development and their memories of past conduct by other states.

Historical phase and memory are always operative. The General's ideology was as much a response to past events as was the similar ideology of a Social Democrat, Kurt Schumacher, in West Germany.[3] The first was impressed by the suspected downgrading and abandonment of France by the United States, the exclusion of France from Allied councils, the exploitation of France's weakness in the Levant by the British, and, during the last German counter-offensive in

[2] The synthesis is based on de Gaulle's *Mémoires de guerre*, Vol. II, esp. pp. 2, 21–22, 24, 36, 73–74, 80, 187–88; Vol. III, pp. 58, 195, 200, 570.
[3] See F. R. Alleman, *Bonn ist nicht Weimar* (1956), pp. 138 ff.

the Ardennes, the danger that "integrated" French troops would have to be withdrawn from Allied command in the middle of hostilities if they were to defend positions of symbolic value for France. On his part, the Socialist opposition leader reacted to the reputation of his party as unpatriotic, while the country's responsible Chancellor sought antidotes to national chauvinism in an associationist philosophy and practice.

As for the historical phase, a developing new state may find itself in self-isolation on the way to fuller political involvement. For an "ancient" state, the phase may be one of restoration or interregnum after a titanic effort in expansion or defense; or the nation may be experiencing resurgence after the restoration period has run its course and given way to a new élan for prestige and aggrandizement. The great continental European powers have been through such patterns. So have the maritime powers, Britain and to some extent the United States, although they withdrew and re-intervened largely in response to the dynamics of the continental states themselves. A certain dovetailing of phases and moods of the members is as essential for the cohesion of an alliance as is the dovetailing of particular interests in a compromise. If all members were in an expansionist or prestige conscious mood, the alliance would be unlikely to work—unless it turned its energies outward; nor is it likely that nations in an apathetic mood could constitute any but a highly conservative, inward-oriented alliance on the model of the Locarno Pact of the 1920's.

Lastly, there is a connection between a nation's alliance ideology and behavior and its predominant diplomatic style.

A diplomatic style is the intangible product of other intangibles. It is influenced by the needs of the moment; but at a deeper level it mirrors a nation's political culture. The classic French style, for instance, reflects the values of the *politiques* and the jurists of absolute monarchy, while the British diplomatic style mirrors the mercantile and parliamentary predispositions of the nation of shopkeepers and compromisers.[4] And the style of politically developing new states is likely to be influenced by established styles. No nation practices an internally consistent and immutable national style, although older powers may incline more consistently toward one or the other side of certain style alternatives. They may also know with a surer instinct when to depart from their norm while consulting with allies, demonstrating their or their adversaries' power and intentions to allies and neutrals, and while negotiating with an opponent.

With these reservations in mind, what is the difference between a formalistic and an informal diplomatic style? The difference corresponds roughly with the difference between dogmatic-nationalist and pragmatic-associationist ideology of alliance behavior. More traditionally, the formalistic style has been associated with the doctrine of the *raison d'Etat* as a transcendant and relatively stable standard, while the informal style is more in keeping with a foreign policy keyed to particular and changing interests within a society. The formal style stresses procedure, method, and institutions; the informal style stresses substance and results. Consequently, where the first is meticulous the second is deliberately vague. Even when it actually surrenders to convenience, a diplomacy practicing the formal style will express itself in the guise of a principle, while informal diplomacy will address itself to the facts of the matter even if serving an ideal. Both styles are concerned with prestige. But formalistic diplomacy is compulsive about upholding prestige, while the practitioner of informal diplomacy acts as if assured of status. The first is, therefore, more authoritative while the second tends to be permissive, although not egalitarian; the first inclines to be forceful to the point of being coercive, whereas the other will experiment with tact and conciliation.

[4] A. Sorel, *L' Europe et la Révolution française*, Vol. I (1885), pp. 217 ff., 247, and *passim;* H. Nicolson, *Diplomacy* (2d edn., 1950), pp. 131 ff.

The formalistic style is congenial to the power whose needs, rights, and interests clash directly with those of another state. Such a power will favor a relatively active strategy designed to anticipate and take precautions; it will typically resort to long-term peacetime treaties of alliance. Conversely, the practitioner of informal diplomacy will be content to wait out developments and then improvise responses; since in his view verbal and institutional symbols merely express underlying facts, he will trust only conjunction of interests and find unwritten, implied, and tacit assurances to be enough. Informality is a luxury for the secure; as such, it was available in the past to countries like Britain and the United States, who could maintain their great margin of security by adjusting the needs, rights, and interests of third countries in a relatively casual and leisurely manner.

Consultations and Compromise

Ideology and diplomatic style condition the procedures of interallied consultation, which in turn bears upon material conditions such as capabilities and pressures. Like cohesion, consultation may become an end in itself. And like ideology, consultation may seemingly and temporarily make up for basic deficiencies. The value of consultation in and of itself can be great if consultation affirms the internal constitution of the alliance, as one of equality and solidarity among allies. In other circumstances, too great a concern with consultation may impede the military efficacy of the alliance and the political influence of individual members with outside powers.

Since alliances lack both a central authority and a basic law concerned with the observance of procedural rules, they are not fully developed constitutional structures. In their internal life, alliances move beyond the condition of anarchy; but as corporate actors, alliances approach the pole of anarchy in their external relations and depend on a more inclusive "global" order to impose procedural limits on their interactions. Hence alliances are not only intermediate forms between constitution and anarchy, but also mixed forms. Their external relations feed arbitrariness into their internal relations, and internal restraints occasionally affect their external behavior. Interallied relations are, therefore, more complex than relations between adversaries; and consultations are less determinate than negotiations.

Consultation includes negotiation and goes beyond it. The object of bona fide negotiation is to settle or suspend a particular issue, as an alternative to conflict or coercion. Parties to consultation negotiate in order to concert behavior toward an issue or a third party. Whereas, in a formal sense, parties to a negotiation are equal, parties to consultation are often in unequal positions. One consults because he is more interested in concerting conduct than is the other, consulted, party. The aim of concerting action or attitude creates between parties to consultation a sense of community; the typical "community" between parties to a negotiation is the negative one of apprehending the effects of failure. The component of negotiation in consultation shrinks or expands depending on relations between allies, which can be more or less antagonistic, and on the kind of issue and interests, which can be more or less controversial and vital for one or all parties.

As a component in consultations, negotiation introduces formal diplomacy into interallied relations.[5] The methods of diplomacy reflect its dual task. On the one hand, diplo-

[5] The virtual identification of diplomacy with negotiation (see, e.g., Nicolson, *ibid.*, p. 15) is supported by Richelieu's emphasis on *négociations continuelles*, encompassing probably both permanent contact and specific *pourparlers*. See Chap. 6, Part II, of *Maximes d'Etat ou Testament Politique d'Armand du Plessis, Cardinal duc de Richelieu* (1764), pp. 32 ff. In the Italian state system, diplomatic techniques evolved in the context of antagonistic relations between sovereigns, pathologically suspicious of a temporary, uncertain ally still more than of a declared enemy. G. Mattingly, *Renaissance Diplomacy* (1955), pp. 58 ff. and *passim*.

matic procedures and courtesies are frequently called upon to gloss over latent antagonisms and infractions of independence and equality, and to disguise coercion as concession to principle. On the other hand, diplomacy must reserve essential interests by means of the utmost formal precision. In pursuing these tasks, diplomatic negotiators share the tricks and techniques of other votaries of bargaining, designed to make interests converge at a point closer to one's initial position than to that of the adversary. Unlike what may be the case among horse-traders, however, the crudity of the undertaking imposes on diplomatic negotiators the requirement of pretense in order to safeguard the prestige of the parties. Diplomacy is concerned with the parties' reputations —for formal integrity as well as material power—because diplomatic relations are fluid and must be continuous. Continuity stems from the fact that no transaction is complete and separate in itself, and cannot be the last one between particular parties even if they come to distrust each other's probity. And the fluidity of relations has to do with the fact that today's adversary may be tomorrow's ally and vice versa.

Fluidity decreases when alliances become "permanent." However, concern for prestige and precision is thereby only modified, and it may even grow. Under any circumstances, a power has to nurse its prestige in order to hold its own in an antagonistic environment and to increase its value as an ally. But, as long as a nation can dispose of its power freely by realignment and test it in open conflict, it need not worry all the time about its commitments being precise and its reputation for power remaining intact. In a permanently operative association, individual prestige and formal precision in delineating commitments and interests become all the more important as allies become less free to employ their national power and as practical requirements of the joint function appear more compelling.

Interallied consultations cannot be governed, therefore, only by pragmatic concern with the best possible joint performance. Alliances are not the only forms of association beset by such ambivalence, for so are coalitions of political parties and functional symbioses of management and labor. They are all subject to two conflicting requirements. One is the requirement of consensus to ensure joint efficacy with regard to an external public (i.e., competitive producers and consumers of policy alternatives and alternative products). The other requirement is for the individual parties to uphold their separate interests and independent identity within the association so as to retain the ability to act separately outside the association when it has temporarily or permanently ceased to fulfill its purpose. There are doubtless differences among these and other similar co-operative-competitive composites; the crucial identity lies in their members seeking simultaneously to maximize individual advantages and both maximize and share advantages procured jointly.[6]

In the circumstances, occasional negotiations are necessary to define and redefine the basic terms and limits of co-operation, while continual consultations adjust co-operation to outside challenges. Moreover, the mere fact of consultation reassures not only against a sense of dependence on the stronger party, but also and more generally against the ambiguity which surrounds "independent" actions and their motivation. Particular acts may be undertaken to increase a

[6] The differences between the two kinds of coalition and between the coalitions and the labor-management relationship have to do with the equivalence of the competitive counterparts, the intensity of competition over the same public, product, or profit between the parties as well as with opposing counterparts, and the extent to which the competition is continuous or rises and falls with particular international crises, domestic elections, or rounds of industrial adjustments. To draw the parallel between organized groupings seems to be more accurate than, but may be complementary with, the equation of alliances of free member-states with the position of individual citizens in a free democracy, grouped in majorities and minorities, with respect to coercion as against consent. See L. B. Pearson, *Democracy In World Politics* (1955), p. 43. C. P. Kindleberger, "International Political Theory from Outside," in W. T. R. Fox, ed., *Theoretical Aspects of International Relations* (1959), pp. 76 ff., discusses "maximizing."

party's contribution to joint maximizing of gains; or they may be intended to enhance the party's position as an alternative to sharing. Who can tell whether an action is meant to be in the collective or in the individual interest and, in the latter case, whether it is also in the "real" or "ultimate" interest of the alliance? Similar questions arise when one political party in a governing coalition advocates a policy or when price and profit policies of management and wage demands of labor are referred to the common interest in raising the level of consumption at large.

The general character of consultation influences its more specific aspects. These bear on participation, scope, and intended conclusions in consultation—in other words, whom to consult, on what issues, and toward what object. In negotiations, the issues, parties, and objectives tend to be given and to determine each other. Hence the greater concern with how to negotiate. The question of how to consult is subordinate, though not an easier one to answer.

Whom to admit to a part in consultations is a fundamental option. Equality among allies would convert strains into stimuli for accommodation; a hegemonic alliance would repress strains underneath the supremacy of the leading ally. To be meaningful, participation in consultations must not stop with the right (and duty) to approve the policies of the major ally or allies. The range of participation must extend to formulation and implementation of alliance policy; moreover, individual allies must both consult and be consulted on policies which fall within the purview of the alliance. The debate over the extent of participation is never ending. The lesser allies of, say, France and Sweden in Münster and Osnabrück in mid-seventeenth century would have found little fault with the proposition that consultations in NATO should "reach into the field of policy-making as well as policy-clearing." [7]

[7] L. B. Pearson, *Diplomacy in the Nuclear Age* (1958), p. 28.

Most lesser allies take a realistic view of their proper share in consultations. Their main concern is a formal one. They wish to be consulted in a way which would give a decent semblance of reality to their standing as partners and to the representative character of the major ally's diplomacy. Only when they are directly involved do lesser allies demand the right of veto as well as that of remonstrance. On the other hand, the major ally wishes to be consulted chiefly in order to have the opportunity to authorize or veto action, or to be able to dissociate himself from the inception, implementation, and consequences of a lesser ally's conduct. The formal aspect is less important to him unless his paramount status within the alliance is in jeopardy.[8]

A party's role in consultations depends on its capability and concern. If capability, contribution to joint effort, and immediate or ultimate responsibility for allied actions are great, so will be the claim to being consulted. The major ally's right to be consulted may entail the duty to consult others, however, when his capability and the use he makes of it become potentially fatal to all. The title to decision-making based on ultimate responsibility of the major actor is then matched by that of ultimate co-liability of all, equally vulnerable, allies. The lesser partners invoke their great concern to offset their inferior capability to contribute to a joint effort. In practice, the combination of great concern and small capability is more likely to make one consult others rather than be consulted by them.

Two patterns of consultation habitually express the claims of capability and concern: a relatively stable pattern of more frequent and intimate consultation among major allies as distinct from all allies; and an *ad hoc* pattern of consultation in cases of special concern to a particular ally. We may take West Germany as an example of both patterns of consulta-

[8] See, for instance, Eden, *Full Circle*, (1960), p. 634. "The [official American] attitude was . . . that the President had been slighted because the allies had acted without permission. The allies must pay for it, and pay they did." The event was, of course, the Suez incident in 1956.

tion. Bonn was consulted on the German issue even before it became a leading ally in NATO. On the other hand, when in 1959 it explored with the Spanish government the possibility of securing bases in Spain, Bonn seems to have cleared the policy only with the major Atlantic allies separately. It did not formally consult the NATO Council which includes the lesser allies, too. More generally, participants in "summit" meetings have prepared for them by way of highly differentiated consultations with lesser allies and neutrals.

Participation in consultations determines the extent to which an alliance is one of equals; the scope of consultations bears on the degree to which members practice solidarity. To decide for and against equality in principle is easier than to define the limits of solidarity and independence. The scope of consultations depends on the immediate needs and conveniences of allies; but these in turn reflect the tendency of an alliance to be "limited" or "total" in terms of the degree of liability that allies commonly assume for each other's actions and interests.

The alliance is a total one, even if the underlying security commitment is defined more narrowly, when two conditions are met: allies practice the precept of solidarity—one for all and all for one—in their conduct; and they do so all over the global system of the day. The scope of consultations conforms to the unlimited liability that allies are presumed to assume for each other's actions and interests. In a limited alliance, by contrast, consultations are more likely to conform to the scope of the specified security commitment, which also tends to set limits to the allies' practical liability. The scope of the commitment is in turn defined by the kind of action that is pledged to follow, automatically or under specified conditions, upon a particular kind of threat in a particular geographic area. Prior consultations may be one condition of the commitment's going into effect. But some consultation will be assured by the play of needs and fears, regardless of such stipulations. When the commitment is stringent (and integration of interallied resources intimate), the obligated parties will insist on being consulted during a crisis so as to make sure that the *casus foederis* was necessary; when the commitment is limited (and integration is loose), the prospective beneficiary himself will be anxious to consult in order to make allied assistance certain.[9] In a limited partnership that allows for both collective action and interallied restraint on individual action, solidarity is not so much an instinct as an ideal standard of action at best.

The major Western allies have differed about their principal alliance's place on the spectrum of solidarity and global concern. The French have been the most consistent advocates of a total alliance, at least in principle; they would do for NATO in the second half of the twentieth century what their forbears did for the initially limited Franco-Russian alliance at the century's beginning. The British, following more pragmatic traditions and anxious to safeguard traditional ties, have favored a pattern of particular arrangements for different strategic areas. The United States has been closer to the British in favoring limited alliances, but closer to the French in viewing all or most particular issues and arrangements as being related to a dominant East-West conflict.[10] A power with less capability than concern will, as a rule, seek to expand alliance functions in both scope and depth. To make substantial contributions, such a country must invest all of its resources in the alliance; it neither will nor can do so unless the alliance covers all of its concerns. A greater power has excess capabilities; it will prefer to employ them outside a particular alliance in order to distribute its investments and segregate the liabilities.

[9] R. Hilsman, "Coalitions and Alliances," in W. W. Kaufman, ed., *Military Policy and National Security* (1956), p. 171, speaks of more solidarity and consistency resulting from the existence of a "central forum."

[10] Cf. R. Pleven, "France in the Atlantic Community," *Foreign Affairs* (October, 1959), pp. 19–30; M. Howard, "Britain's Defenses: Commitments and Capabilities," *ibid.*, (October, 1960), esp. p. 84; M. M. Ball, *Nato and the European Union Movement* (1959), pp. 133, 137.

Whatever the source of the differences in concept, however, they will constitute a prime source of interallied differences over particular strategies.

Both limited and total alliance are pure types, with flaws and shortcomings when put into practice. A limited-liability alliance either restricts consultations to issues that bear directly on the security commitment, or fails to identify issues of common concern predictably. Any attempt at limitation runs into the difficulty of distinguishing between "direct" and "indirect" causes of overt conflict and between strains which originate within and without the compass of the alliance proper. If it is difficult to draw a clear line between, say, Cyprus and Quemoy as occasions for strains within NATO, it is no easier to distinguish the "vital" interests which may exempt allies from the duty to consult less vitally concerned partners in a limited alliance from interests that do not. In principle, the vital interests of individual allies— of the British and French in the Suez issue and of the Americans in the Taiwan problem, for example—can be placed above the more general interests of the other allies, such as the concern to avoid general war or to avoid alienating non-aligned countries. This may justify reticence on consulting, when to consult is to be restrained from action; the non-consulting ally may prefer the advantages of a free hand and pay for it with a diminution of allied backing. However, such a suspension of alliance being problematic, allies will seek to associate themselves with the active party's policy-making, regardless of the limits of their actual commitment.

The allies' liability for each other's action and, consequently, their right and duty to consultation are thus unlikely to find a natural limitation in the character of particular issues and interests; the latter's location in particular geographic areas is no more likely to solve the problem for a limited alliance. Its members must identify from time to time the areas which are to be covered by consultation— only those defined in the security commitment and covered by military planning, or also other areas. If the alliance is multilateral, members must moreover identify the parties that are to be consulted on different issues in individual areas; the choice is currently between allies with past, including colonial, interests in an area and allies with present interests there, backed by capabilities. Whatever choice is made, some allies and local states are likely to be alienated; informal arrangements are therefore more convenient and likely.

The shortcomings of the limited-ability alliance strengthen the case in favor of global competence for a major alliance like NATO. Any but a total alliance—that is, one which practices solidarity in conduct and is global in concern—suffers from an imbalance between commitment, which tends to be unlimited in practice, and scope of consultation, which can be limited only artificially. To redress such an imbalance, members will try to disengage themselves partially from the alliance. The argument for a total alliance seems especially cogent when it is applied to one homogeneous alliance only; it is emotionally appealing when the particular alliance, like NATO, is the chief safeguard of a beleaguered civilization. Without a leader, an alliance system lacks a head; without an inner core of solidarity, it has no heart.

A total alliance concept is, however, no more free of flaws and shortcomings than is a limited alliance concept. If solidarity meant automatic support of allies for each other's unilateral actions on matters of vital interest, unlimited mutual liability would leave little room for reciprocal restraints, despite the ritual of consultations. If, on the other hand, consultations amounted to effective decision-making and solidarity was read to mean unanimity, it might allow only a generally agreeable action or no action; if mere majority sufficed, the will of the major allies only might determine the supposedly real interest of the alliance. And finally, were solidarity to be administered by global powers only, it might degenerate into automatic support of powerful allies by lesser ones.

What, one may ask, is a global power at a time when the smallest state is co-liable to the consequences of the most remote dispute? The stakes are no less if the domain is small; they actually increase with the ease of obliterating a country. By the criterion of capability, a global power is one which can act in any area of the world—not only by sending a long-range rocket—and whose action has a chance of being accepted as somehow representative of local attitudes and interests. In this sense, only the United States is a global power within the non-Communist world. Britain and France have claimed the status on the strength of their residual interests and dependencies; but their ability to act and have their action tolerated in outlying regions has been highly uneven.

Other questions arise. What would be the result of dissent by a nominally global power in a system of policy-making? Would France, for instance, in return for a global co-ordination of policy (demanded because American policies are judged to be at once inept, hegemonic, and intrinsically isolationist) not only surrender her independence in Europe, but also open her remaining colonial problems to authoritative consultation by allies? Or would France continue to shield these problems behind the screen of domestic jurisdiction or paramount regional responsibility? If she kept excluding them, the result would be a major ambiguity. To outside observers an Atlantic Alliance with an extended consultation regime would appear more than ever responsible for all actions of its members everywhere. By their actions, the allies of France—or of any other power—would have to dispel the unwanted and unwarranted appearance of such responsibility. One has only to remember the Anglo-American arms shipment to Tunisia in the late 1950's. The two allies failed to consult the NATO Council and on at least one occasion ignored France herself for the same reason for which France demanded a veto power—because Tunisia had been a dependency of France. Parallel problems would arise if the United States excepted the Western Hemisphere, or if Britain excepted the oil-rich sheikdoms in the Middle East, from the area of mutual liability *and* shared responsibility.

Furthermore, there are at present several alliances in the non-Communist world. The NATO powers may suffer from the Far Eastern policy of the United States, but non-European members of SEATO or of OAS can be drawn into the ramifications of NATO policies in Central Europe. While the concern of all regional alliances is potentially global, only one alliance within an overlapping alliance system can combine a global concern with interallied solidarity in conduct. The other alliances would be reduced to a secondary status; they would become agencies for implementing and dealing with the consequences of policies which had been agreed upon by a global policy-making directorate or a regional committee within the total alliance. Being already a pseudo-NATO, a SEATO would also become a sub-NATO.

There is thus a real conflict of valid concerns on each side of the issue. The globalists have a point, and so have the regional pluralists and the unilateralists. What can be done? One radical solution is to avoid multilateral regional alliances. They are a device peculiarly suited to raise, but not to solve, the dilemmas of collective consultation. Another radical possibility is to consolidate the several alliances of one side to a dominant conflict, and make the super-alliance a total one. Some advantages might be lost, such as specialized study and treatment of regionally critical target-states and issues by the several alliances; but the areas of consultation and commitment would henceforth coincide. Before it considers any radical solution, the non-Communist world will experiment with informal arrangements to co-ordinate policy among the several alliances. Overlapping membership of the greater powers in several alliances, selective informing of lesser allies or allies in less directly involved alliances, and tacit or explicit mandates for the key ally will continue to serve as tenuous connecting links in the system.

The reference to a "mandate" raises the question of the product at which consultations aim. This question is related to the remaining questions: when to consult? when to avoid consulting?

Consultations may aim solely at an exchange of information. When the parties seek decision concerning action, and their interests are not identical, there will be need for a compromise. What are the chief methods of arriving at a compromise? Parties can concede to each other and dovetail their non-identical interests; they may split the difference between them; or they may agree only on the core of overlapping identical interests, the rest being excluded. The first type has been called "inclusive" compromise in contradistinction to the split-the-difference compromise and to the third, "exclusive" compromise. The inclusive compromise is a way of implementing solidarity; the other two are more in keeping with a limited alliance.[11]

There are, accordingly, three different forms of compromise. But, it might be argued, to agree to pursue jointly only identical interests is not a genuine compromise; and to have to exclude all other elements is a failure of compromise. The compromise is at best only procedural; it consists in defining the core of identical interests and agreeing to postpone attempts at substantive compromise on the rest. The split-the-difference compromise, too, may be downgraded. As a technique among allies (as distinct from adversaries) it is apt to magnify the dissatisfaction which attends any, even partial, failure to uphold one's interests. And in a logical sense, this kind of compromise may be only a form of the inclusive or dovetailing compromise in matters of policy which do not entail divisible quantities but encompass a variety of aspects and interests. A split-the-difference

[11] On the "dovetail" pattern, see K. W. Deutsch, *et al.*, *Political Community and the North Atlantic Area* (1957), p. 90; on "inclusive" and "exclusive" compromise, D. A. Rustow, *The Politics of Compromise: A Study of Parties and Cabinet Government in Sweden* (1956), p. 231.

compromise would take place if, for instance, parties agreed to act on the 5th of October, rather than on the 1st or the 10th, with five-thousand troops instead of one or ten-thousand—an implausible situation. In actual negotiation, the difference is likely to be "split" in that one party concedes to the other party all or most on one aspect, say in regard to timing, while the other side does the same on another aspect, say the preliminaries of action. The final compromise includes, then, as many mutual satisfactions as possible, dovetailed into each other.

To sum up, identity of interests requires no compromise (except possibly on identifying these interests and adjusting their priorities); interests which are non-identical to the point of being conflicting cannot be split but must be mutually conceded, or else excluded from the product of consultations. It is easier to compromise when structures of interests are complementary—i.e., when parties rank in a different order of priority non-identical, conflicting interests on a particular matter. While disparity in hierarchical ranking facilitates compromise, it may impart to an agreement the quality of compromise if the interests of the parties are identical, but have different priorities for the respective parties.

At the extremes, compromise bears on questions of solidarity between close allies and of war between adversaries. In 1954, to illustrate the first point on Anglo-American relations within NATO, the United States wanted to institute search proceedings on the high seas against ships suspected of carrying arms to the Guatemalan government and, subsequently, to block action in the U.N. Security Council concerning the invasion of Guatemala from foreign territory. The British government complied with the request for support of its more vitally interested ally, despite doubts on grounds of legality. With an eye on the same American government's failure to reciprocate in the Suez crisis, and thus complete the dovetailing pattern, Sir Anthony Eden wrote in retrospect:

Her Majesty's Government agreed to cooperate with the United States Government, or at least not to oppose them, taking the view that first priority must be given to the solidarity of the Anglo-American alliance. If allies are to act in concert only when their views are identical, alliances have no meaning.[12]

The United States apparently ranked its interests in the Suez affair too high to "sacrifice" them to interallied solidarity; it certainly ranked these interests higher relative to Britain's than the British had ranked theirs in the Guatemalan affair relative to America's. In a vastly different context of conflict, the United States and Japan were unable to reach a compromise in the negotiations over Japan's Tripartite Pact with Germany and Italy prior to Pearl Harbor, despite divergence in the order of strategic interest of the two parties in the contested areas: Manchuria, British and Dutch parts of Southeast Asia, and Europe, respectively. Other than strategic interests were in the picture and there was not enough underlying unity of concern to facilitate a "deal" in the sense of barter of mutual concessions. Together with the analytic dubiety of the split-the-difference compromise, the requirement of some such underlying consensus makes negotiations-within-consultations among allies more promising than negotiations with adversaries. Between antagonists, an attempt to arrive at a compromise based on the exclusion of non-identical interests is liable to reveal the absence of any concrete identical interests out of which to fashion a compromise.

Among allies, a compromise or a compromise-free identity of interests may lead to a decision on joint action or to something less. The essential joint action of an alliance concerns the commitment: how to implement it before and as a result of a *casus foederis*. The Atlantic allies made decisions on collective rearmament and have had to decide how to deal individually and collectively with particular threats—Berlin for instance. Furthermore, allies may decide to act jointly

---

[12] *Full Circle*, p. 151 and, for the quotation, p. 155.

in a functional area—such as the economic exploitation of third countries or, more recently, assistance to them. For fear of antagonizing non-members and limiting their own freedom of action, the Atlantic allies have shunned binding decisions on individual or collective action outside the NATO area in particular. They have preferred non-binding resolutions and recommendations concerning action by individual members. The first resolution of the NATO Council regarding Southeast Asia and the Far East (passed in December, 1952), for instance, confined itself to pledging in general terms the support of the allies for action by the major powers which was in harmony with the aims of the Atlantic community.[13] The proviso of "harmony" implies a conditional mandate to the great powers to act on behalf of the alliance.

A mandate to act within some limits on behalf of other states implements the idea of a concert of powers. An instance is Europe's mandate to France to intervene in Spain in the 1820's. In some form, a mandate of this kind is a valuable international technique, and may be the sole alternative to a decision to act jointly or not at all. This is particularly the case when lesser states which take part in consultation cannot match concern with capability; when a state with vital interests in a regional matter is prevented from acting because it has lost local legitimacy; or when only some powers are members of all alliances within a pluralistic alliance system. A mandate delegates to the authorized power the representation of the interests of the other allies within the limits set by consultation and compromise. The authorizing parties retain some control over the agent, if only by the implied right to refuse to acknowledge the agent's action as conforming with the mandate, to be bound by the action, or to extend to the results their alliance commitments. On the other hand, the agent's action is legitimized when he has observed the terms of the delegation, even if it is not successful. There is, finally, a kind

[13] Ball, *NATO*, pp. 129 ff.

of accountability after the act, which may take the form of a report within the alliance.

Such a report may resemble mere information. Information is the least exacting form of consultation; great powers are wont to employ it to satisfy lesser members of an alliance, occasionally soliciting their views to improve appearances. The lesser NATO allies were thus consulted in 1955 and 1960 prior to impending summit meetings. A major ally, too, may be the recipient of mere information but can refuse with greater effect to treat information as tantamount to consultation.

When allies do not inform and consult each other, they may act in tacit agreement. Such agreement reflects the absence of the conditions which normally induce consultation: the belief that an exchange of views can help find a way out of a dilemma about which parties do not know what to do; impart collective sanction to acts of the party or parties who know only too well what they wish to do; and secure outright support by others in an action or in an ensuing conflict. When an issue is such that consultation patently can produce none of the beneficial results but, on the contrary, will threaten cohesion, non-consultation becomes the lesser evil. The Cyprus issue, dividing three NATO allies, was not brought before the Council for formal consultation as long as there was any prospect of solution by other means.

The situation is different when allies are not consulted because their partners act or contemplate action in secrecy. Frederick II did not consult (or inform) France before concluding his neutrality treaty with Great Britain in 1756; Hitler did not permit his ally Japan to be advised of the impending attack on the Soviet Union, with whom Japan had just concluded a non-aggression treaty at Germany's behest; and, of course, Britain and France kept their counsel before announcing military intervention in the Suez area. Such procedural omissions strain alliances; but the cohesion of an alliance grows as it develops the capacity to absorb *faits accomplis,* especially if previous consultation accomplished little or nothing. When allies concede each other the privilege of occasional unilateralism, they may have arrived at a tacit constitutional compromise—to tolerate self-help in the dovetailing of non-identical interests. In return, the non-consulted ally may be entitled to disclaim liability for the consequences.

If only the wisdom, rather than the loyalty, of the non-consulted ally is questioned, the decision not to consult is a gamble rather than a precaution. The gambling ally rates highly the ultimate identity of interests among the allies in general and on the critical issue in particular. And he rates low the resentment which will follow upon the concealed action, believing that to appease the non-consulted ally will require fewer concessions than would prior consultation. Such must have been the calculation of Frederick II and of Prime Ministers Eden and Mollet in their respective undertakings. They all had, moreover, the excuse of acting only after consultations failed to devise effective alternative courses of action. By contrast, the decision to consult while anticipating objections is a gamble on the moral effect of the show of trust implicit in advance communication. A party adopting this course of action rates low the disintegrative effect of having to disregard continuing objections of the informed ally. The German Foreign Office acted on these considerations when it favored informing the Japanese foreign minister of the impending invasion of Russia.[14]

Like separate action itself, the consequences of failure to consult indicate the degree of an alliance's cohesion. They constitute a better index than does a successful consultation, since they occur in the more revealing conditions of a crisis.

Capabilities and Pressures

The procedures of consultation do not occur in a vacuum;

[14] P. W. Schroeder, *The Axis Alliance and Japanese-American Relations* (1958), p. 112.

they are conditioned by the relative capabilities of the allies and the adversaries. Neither are the consultations an end in themselves; they have to yield to unilateral action, notably of the leading ally, whenever it is necessary to bring the requirements of cohesion into harmony with those of efficacy. No association, and certainly no alliance, can long survive unless it can fulfill the needs of its members. To promote their security before all other interests, allies must be able to resist the capabilities of the adversary, translated into pressures on the alliance.

In alliances which are built around a core-power, the capability of the major ally counts most in determining the degree of cohesion. This is true, in particular, when the alliance is exposed to the stress of divergent conflicts.

The Little Entente, for example, was designed to deal with a regional conflict between the so-called successor states and revisionist Hungary following World War I. The patron of the small-state grouping, France, shared the objective of maintaining the peace settlement intact. But only Czechoslovakia shared fully France's preoccupation with Germany; Rumania's determinant conflict was with Soviet Russia, and Yugoslavia's with Italy. The different conflicts worked toward alliance with France and toward cohesion of the alliance system as long as France had, or seemed to have, the capability to protect the lesser allies against Germany, Italy, and the Soviet Union. This meant in practice that France retained the capability to deter and, if necessary, defeat Germany while containing Italy and the Soviet Union. To contain meant to restrain the two great powers from exploiting to the detriment of her protégés an involvement of France with Germany.

When French capabilities declined relative to the other powers, the limits of what she could do for her clients in Central and Eastern Europe came into the open. The system was doomed once France tried to add regionally incompatible major allies—Italy and, in particular, the Soviet Union—to the security system against Germany, without being able to protect Yugoslavia, Rumania, and Poland against them. Only if France and Britain had been clearly preponderant in the alliance of the great powers against Germany could Rumania or Poland have allowed their territory to be used in interallied operations as *their* contribution to the alliance's cohesion and efficacy.

Shared weakness and vulnerability on the part of defensive powers is not enough, any more than is shared ambition among predatory powers. An alliance's cohesion rests most safely on different kinds of vulnerability calling for reciprocal support: immediate vulnerability for the lesser, or local, allies; and ultimate vulnerability for an isolated major, or remote, ally.

We can substitute SEATO for the Little Entente. SEATO's cohesion, too, has depended on the continued capacity of the United States to protect the lesser allies of the region (and the guaranteed neutrals) by means of deterrence and, if necessary, defense against all of their respective enemies. A United States, clearly dominant in the partnership, must be able to contain the locally feared state, even if it is an ally—be it Thailand feared by Cambodia, or Japan feared by the Philippines—while drawing on its facilities against acute regional threats, in particular Communist China. The cohesion of SEATO would fail if a locally suspect ally's contribution to the American strategic posture became negotiable for opportunities of regional, economic or politico-military, aggrandizement. Japan's possible effect on SEATO (to which it is related only indirectly through Japan's alliance with the United States) is similar to that of Germany on NATO, however commanding the distance between present service and possible future threat may appear to be.

The pattern of roles and claims within an alliance will change with the rise and decline of national capabilities. Rising capability on the part of the core-power may increase cohesion and efficacy. On the other hand, members of an association of sovereign states tend to seek some kind of equilibrium within the alliance as well as with the opponents. It is not in their interest to substitute a preponderant ally for an overwhelming enemy if they can help it. Unless allies have an ideal basis for identifying with one another, unequal increase in their present and likely future capability will not favor cohesion. This is true even of alliances which were organized to cope with only one dominant conflict, when the passing of the threat may have revived awareness of temporarily submerged rivalry. Napoleon's forced retreat from Russia disclosed the latter as a rising power, apt to increase her capabilities further if her territorial ambitions in Poland were satisfied; the resulting crisis at Vienna produced a diplomatic realignment of Great Britain and Austria with Bourbon France. The danger for an alliance is less, to be sure, as long as it is on the defensive and needs all the capability there is, however distributed. And it helps if the exceptional growth in the capability of one ally is due to the expansion of internal resources. Still, the only lasting remedy to strains from an unequal growth is a political framework going beyond alliance, a framework which would enable the other parties to identify themselves fully with the rising ally's contribution to a common pool of power.

When there is not a single unifying conflict, the concern of allies over each other's capabilities will be even greater. Unequal gains arouse fears lest the successful ally abandon the struggle over issues less vital to him, if the success is a short-term military one, or lest he impose his conflict as the dominant issue for the alliance as a whole, if the achievement is one of peaceful "growth." For good reasons, the Axis partners received news of each other's military successes during World War II with mixed feelings. And the pre-World War I Franco-Russian alliance would not have been lastingly strengthened if Russia's capabilities had continued to rise relative to those of France or if a buoyant Russia had given the alliance an anti-British twist not acceptable to Paris.

To be sure, a marked decline in the capability of a crucial

ally is even more likely to set off dissolution. Nor will too great a success for an alliance as a whole weld it together. The best thing for cohesion is an even and moderate rise in capability, just adequate to implement a strategy which promises to realize the security objective of the alliance. Strains are less likely to deepen into disintegration when there are, in addition, an ideological tie beween allies and an ideological conflict with the enemy, which limit the loosening effect of both excessive success and extreme failure. These conditions prevailed in the victorious alliances of the two World Wars, except for the disparate Russian case, which necessitated a synthetic alliance ideology.

The employment of individual and collective capability is at least as important as its extent and distribution among allies. One problem is the deployment of allied resources in different areas and theaters of operations. Alliance relationships can be seriously disrupted when different allies do not assign equal ranking to various areas, target states, and conflicts. Failure to co-ordinate results in a waste of capabilities and reduces cohesion. Albeit to differing extents, the relative priorities of the central front on the Rhine and of the North German theater troubled both alliances in the Thirty Years' War; the issue regarding the importance of Europe relative to other overseas areas beset Britain and, later, the United States in their alliances. In Britain's eighteenth-century alliance with Austria, designed to deal with the Anglo-French and Austro-Prussian conflicts, only the adversaries in the two conflicts were in tacit agreement over which theater of operations was the primary one. Both Britain and France were mainly concerned with operations in the northwest of Europe and on the battlefields outside Europe; each sought to realize a balance of territorial gain by winning more in one area than she was losing in the other. For both, and particularly for England, the operations in Germany and, to some extent, Italy were merely diversionary operations. They were meant to drain the resources of the opponent and his German ally. The interest of Austria and Prussia was roughly the opposite one. Neither alliance survived the attempt to fight two different wars simultaneously.

A divergence in strategic emphasis will be more dangerous for an alliance if the adversary combination does not suffer from a like handicap. This was the plight of the Axis during World War II. Germany and Italy were interested primarily in the European and North African theaters. Their interest in the Far East and Southeast Asia was a secondary one; the areas were useful for diverting the forces of the Anglo-American allies onto the Asiatic member of the Axis. Japan's interest in Western and Eastern Europe and in North Africa was, by the same token, secondary. As a result, the Axis powers failed to evolve joint strategy even in regard to the Middle East, the natural focal area for the two wings of the global alliance. By contrast, the wartime Allies managed to enhance the impact of their capabilities and their cohesion by concerted use of their principal resources. They proceeded first against the European Axis powers in North Africa and Europe and only thereafter against Japan. Agreement was made easier by the fact that all three major allies had interests in both arenas and in a roughly identical hierarchy.

The main methods for stretching limited capabilities are to isolate adversaries and to co-ordinate capabilities and strategies of allies. Merely to aggregate individual capabilities is rarely enough. The success of the wartime Allies and, even more, the failure of the Axis illustrate the unequal merits of the different approaches.

The first approach is to isolate adversaries from each other and save capabilities for use against one enemy at a time. To that end, Nazi Germany and Japan sought to deter the United States by way of a pact directed against American belligerency; Germany sought to mediate Japan's Chinese Incident and improve Nippon's relations with Germany's temporary ally, the Soviet Union; and Japan sought to induce Germany to avoid conflict with the Soviets and subsequently to use her neutrality in the Nazi-Soviet war to mediate it. All failed, while the Soviets' nonaggression pact with Japan saved Russia from a concentric attack. The Soviets denounced the pact when the defeat of Germany fulfilled its purpose.

The second road toward cohesion and success is that of co-ordinating belligerencies and strategies. Like their adversaries, both major Axis allies could have concentrated on one enemy first—particularly the Soviet Union, after Germany activated it by invasion. Japan would have had to choose the course of northward expansion and join Germany against the Soviets before the West was fully mobilized for action. Once this opportunity was neglected, the second best arrangement for the two Axis powers would have been to proceed against both enemy sides simultaneously in a co-ordinated strategy. The area of strategic junction would then be the Middle East rather than the Soviet land mass. Instead, they chose the third strategy, which minimized the frictions but also the fruits of alliance: they proceeded separately in the hope that a mere aggregation of their individual capabilities would have an impact on the adversaries sufficient to bring victory.

The problems of co-ordinating limited capabilities have been besetting the parties to the East-West conflict, too. Even if the logistical advantage of the Communist powers' central geographic position is discounted, their aggressive initiative has made it easier for them to shift around their capabilities. On the other hand, initiative sharpens the problem of determining priorities, much as agreement on them between jealous allies may be facilitated by the primary theater's greater susceptibility to nuclear devastation. In the Western alliance system, the foci of acute conflicts have shifted back and forth in the Atlantic area, the Middle East, and the Pacific area bounded by commitments under SEATO and American bilateral alliances with Japan, Taiwan, and South

Korea. In order for the dispersion of concern not to disrupt the alliance system, the allies have had to combine flexible national and collective military capabilities with a firm subordination of divergent local issues and conflicts to the East-West struggle as having priority for all.

Nuclear weapons have placed the role of capability in maintaining cohesion in a new perspective. The superior capability of the core-power to deter or defeat attack on any ally is more important than ever. The vital protection-provocation ratio is deranged when the core-power, which controls the use of nuclear weapons, cannot be depended upon to initiate a nuclear strike if lesser allies are attacked and no other effective means of defense are available. The situation becomes critical when the developing means of long-range delivery interposes an invisible barrier between the principal military resource of the alliance leader and his allies. There is another derangement. Cohesion normally grows with the capability of the core-power to defend the lesser allies, which capability in turn rises with the leader's immunity to direct attack. In the present nuclear environment, however, civil defense and other protective measures taken by the United States (or the Soviet Union) alone might cause serious strains. The unprotected allies might not only resent the disparity for its own sake; they might also fear lest the disparity identify them as the softer target of enemy action and make the major ally less willing to risk his seemingly self-sufficient, but still precarious, national defenses on their behalf.

The alternative to monopoly is diffusion of key weapons. It is virtually impossible to predict the effects of a spread of individual nuclear capabilities on alliance cohesion. One may fear that an ally with newly acquired nuclear capability will demand a correspondingly stronger position in the alliance with disintegrative results; but the newly "independent" ally may actually be more co-operative than before, as the old fears of dependence, which encouraged the ally to develop a nuclear capability, yield to new fears of isolation in a crisis as well as to a new feeling of confidence most of the time. Considering the alliance as a whole, the diffusion of nuclear capabilities might diminish cohesion. Allies forfeit the feeling of being responsible for each other's defense; they come instead to fear involvement in a partner's unilateral response to probing actions by the adversary. On the other hand, as an alternative to redefining commitment, allies may seek a practical remedy to the trend toward disintegration. Thus suggestions for strengthening the Atlantic alliance have focused on the co-ordination or pooling of nuclear capabilities, as well as on an increase in conventional forces designed to moderate strains on the alliance that result from dependence on nuclear response. Each remedial measure can diminish cohesion in some other way, however. The above NATO scheme, for instance, raised disturbing questions regarding control over the use of a joint nuclear capability, and regarding the effect of less destructive means of deterrence on the credibility of the alliance's most potent weapon. The cohesion of NATO might suffer if the Germans came to fear the downgrading of the Strategic Air Command in favor of conventional capabilities, while other allies might fear the upgrading of West Germany as the chief supplier of conventional forces at least as much as if Germany, too, developed nuclear capability.

Once she did develop nuclear capability, West Germany would merely follow France as France followed Britain and Britain the United States. Such duplications of resources among allies are undertaken in part to promote their equality. But, again, instead of imparting equality, nuclear diffusion might concentrate authority in the hands of the major ally by way of reaction to the anarchical implications of diffusion. Diplomatic dictatorship would supplant intra-alliance democracy as an alternative to the major ally's withdrawal from an uncontrollable association of apparently self-dependent partners. Since attempts to limit an actor in political policy are a tribute to his independence as a military agent, the duty to consult, imputed to the major ally as long as he is the only independent actor, would turn against the lesser allies, only more effectively.

Speculations about different courses of action and their effect on the cohesion of alliances follow the usual pattern. A reasoned position reflects the possible consequences of a particular course of action which the party fears most, without necessarily taking into account the probability of such an occurrence. It is easier to invent supporting arguments than to evaluate their merit. Regarding military capabilities and their distribution among allies, one must try to assign weights to military and political considerations, to immediate effects and the corrective responses to them, and finally, to likely repercussions in a supreme crisis and in all the other contingencies cluttering the life-span of a peacetime alliance.

To aggravate matters, there are discrepancies in the outlook of the planner, of the responsible political leader, and of the public. The discrepancies come out most strikingly in connection with nuclear capabilities.

The planner's approach is rational, aiming at certainties and calculable probabilities. An imperfect capability is downgraded as one whose employment is not credible to the adversary or one which is altogether useless for the possessor. When the imperfect capability—e.g., to disarm the adversary by a preclusive first nuclear strike—is the chief capability of an alliance leader, such as the United States, the result is declining confidence in the alliance; when the allegedly useless capability is the token capability of lesser allies, the argument denies the possibility of even partial national self-dependence. Where the planner seeks rational strategies and economical use of resources, the responsible political leader inclines to rationalize the imperfect. The inadequate capability—e.g., for the disarming first strike—is turned into a self-denying ordinance. The denial hardly reassures the adversary while disturbing the lesser allies' trust in the alliance leader's willingness and ability to meet aggression in any form. The consequence is weakened deterrence and cohesion; the resulting desire of lesser allies to develop a national, albeit inadequate, capability points to another aspect.

Whereas the planner tends to think chiefly of military crises, the political leader is concerned at least as much with political implications prior to crises. He worries over the impact on domestic politics of the economic cost of rationally optimal capabilities, and over the effect of different military capabilities on the nation's ability to conduct diplomacy. The nation's resources may be inadequate to realize an adequate response to a range of hypothetical challenges. The leader concerned with peacetime politics has then good reason for placing the nation in the same category with the adversary—e.g., as a "nuclear" power—even if he cannot have a comparable capability in the event of war. A greater concern with military crisis puts the public itself nearer the planner, although in a very different way. Before a crisis, the public tends to be indifferent, since a major war seems to be remote and speculations about modern weapons and strategies are esoteric. In a crisis, however, the public will be neither indifferent nor will it be as rational as the planner expects the governors to be. It will tend to be emotional and even passionate. If a challenge threatens the country's vital interests, the public will require its government to be able to return threat for threat. In the event of a failure to act effectively, disposition of control and command over the key weapons determines whether the responsibility can be shifted onto the alliance leader only or whether it must be shared by the government of the humiliated or despoiled ally as well. In the first case, the alliance may disintegrate; in the second, the failure may set off new and larger efforts. The aspect is not unimportant when the adversary adjusts its pressures so as to demoralize the allies individually rather than defeat the alliance in one massive assault.

It is through pressures that allies experience the adversary's capabilities; and different ways of applying pressures will have different effects on the alliance's cohesion. A sudden increase of pressure in the form of a political demand or military threat is likely to consolidate an alliance. There is no time to conceal evasions and retreats or to devise alternatives to firmness; the windfall of a provocative pressure may then just as well be used to tighten the alliance and test it in a showdown. The opposite occurs when sudden pressures reveal conflict of interests or stark deficiency of capabilities. However, even an overwhelming threat is likely to be more effective if its maturity is somewhat delayed; a nuclear blackmailer must then be sure of his defenses against a pre-emptive attack.

Hitler was ultimately no more successful in straining the Anglo-French alliance than had been William II; it is too early to assess the effect of Soviet pressures on the Western system. They have alternated with equally sudden decreases of pressure. The tactic of shifting back and forth between aggressive and conciliatory attitudes is designed to combine the advantages of both increased and decreased pressure; it relies on the cumulative enervating effect of the pattern of alternation itself, especially when one side's increasingly cautious responses accentuate a steadily growing capability of an ever more daring other side. An even increase in pressure due to growing capability may keep consolidating the adversary alliance. The critical point is reached when it comes to be believed by members of a defensive alliance that their collective capabilities can no longer withstand those of the adversary. Disintegration may then be as sudden as the rise of the pressure was gradual. Here would belong the collapse of the Little Entente under Nazi German pressure, following on real progress in co-ordinating divergent regional interests and increasing collective capabilities.

A simple and continuing decrease in pressures has a more definite effect. Unlike an increase of pressures, a decrease does not make all conceivable responses very costly. The most dependable decrease of pressure is one due to a structural change in the system, such as the deflection of the opponent in another direction or his decline as an offensive threat. When the need for the alliance disappears with the disappearance of the pressure, the alliance will have been self-liquidating rather than self-defeating as it is when it produces an irresistible counter-pressure. Only offensive alliances feed on the decline of the target and may survive it to ease the digestion of spoils. Defensive alliances do not survive the enemy for too long. They also tend to subside to the lowest level of effort permitted by a live enemy. The decline of post-Napoleonic France under the Bourbons weakened the cohesion of the Quadruple Alliance to such an extent that the allies failed to find a new basis in joint opposition to the rising forces of revolution outside France.

Things are different when decrease of pressure is due only to an opponent's reversible policy. What seemingly disappears in such a case is the need for an implementation entailing difficult choices between costly alternatives. The balance of the individual allies' gains and liabilities in security, stability, and status underlying the initial commitment is likely to founder if the decrease in pressure continues for any length of time. As the sense of insecurity decreases—and with it the sense of the gains flowing from the alliance—awareness of unstabilizing burdens grows and so does awareness of status-diminishing limitations on independence and equality. A period of dormancy used to be the device for adapting alliances to a temporary decline in tension; in changed conditions, the Western allies have devised no comparable stance for dealing with the rising and falling policy pressures from the Soviet bloc, against the background of a steadier growth in the bloc's capabilities and the uncommitted countries' continuing ideological hostility for military alliances in general and foreign bases in particular.

Whatever may be the effect of one side's exerting pressure on the other side, reciprocal pressures between roughly equal alliance systems tend to consolidate both. This is true especially when the internal arrangements of one or both alliances are cloaked in secrecy. Traditionally, secrecy chiefly concerned the terms of an alliance; currently, secrecy mainly surrounds the capabilities and the policy intentions of totalitarian states. Antagonistic alliances are most commonly tightened in a chain of self-fulfilling suspicions—when presumption of one party's commitment or intention prompts the other party to match the adversaries and vice versa. Or, probings by one side to discover how far and in what way secretive allies are tied together and, if possible, to disrupt a suspected alliance before it is consolidated often produce the feared conditions. Frederick II's preventive strike in 1756 brought to completion the Austro-French-Russian alliance he had assumed to be consummated on the basis of inaccurate intelligence; and the diplomatic probings of another restless German monarch did the same for the Anglo-French entente before World War I.

It is up to all allies to keep a balance between their capabilities and enemy pressures. If the alliance has a core-power of preponderant strength, the leader's responsibility exceeds that of the other parties. Leadership among states is based on material capability; but it requires an equally superior ability to affirm collective purpose and to adjust to its fulfillment the techniques of leadership, such as persuasion, compensation, and sheer coercion.

If they are to withstand the adversary or come to terms with him, allies must uphold their commitment and maintain capabilities for an effective strategy. The perception of the threat defines the commitment; commitment defines the task of strategy; and strategy determines the means necessary for upholding the commitment. The leading ally can do much to that end; but he must be willing to subordinate temporarily the demands of cohesion to those of efficacy when there is conflict between the two. In so doing, the leader spares the alliance a "displacement" peculiar to permament institutions: the conversion of means into ends. A strong leader is one who understands the peculiar psychology of weakness—a psychology which fears risks and scorns timidity at one and the same time.

Only a vigorous policy can maintain effective external pressures at an even and manageable level, pending their irreversible decline. This is a material requirement for cohesion. To say "effective" pressures is to regard them as relative to the capability which can be opposed to them; to say "maintain" is to regard with some skepticism the staying power of alliances, and especially the democratic ones, because of domestic counter-pressures. The invidious task of maintaining pressures can be relaxed only in two circumstances: first, when the alliance has developed the capacity of passing periods of lessened tensions in a state of dormancy, while yet retaining the potential for instant reactivation; second, when the opponent himself can be depended upon to reapply pressures before relaxation produces disintegration, or when substitute pressures arise to fill the void. Substitute pressures are least dependable in firming up cohesion, notably when they originate in a rival issue. Theoretically, when and if Soviet pressure on NATO is reduced, it might be supplemented by the challenge of less developed countries, giving rise to novel functions on a global basis. But even if alliances were more adaptable than they actually are, the outside world is unlikely to let them live down, or transcend, their original purpose.

To maintain an even level of effective outside pressures, the leading ally must do several interrelated things. While maintaining enough capability for the main contingencies, he must either reach dependable and irreversible agreements with the adversary or demonstrate that the threat continues undiminished. The two operations tend to be mutually exclusive. A feat by the alliance leader which is necessary to impress and reassure foreign-policy elites in allied and neutral countries, for instance, may ostensibly provoke the adversary or secretly encourage him. And although they may be actually reassured, friendly elites may register public disapproval of the action in order to protect their prestige as equal allies, especially if they have not been consulted in advance. The difference between firmness and provocation is often one of the observer's perspective, as is that between flexibility and appeasement.

What matters most on the part of the leading ally is a sense of the right opportunity for untrammeled individual action. He can then dramatically exploit a coincidence of interest with the adversary or an act of manifest truculence on his part. In the recent past, the more obtuse of the Communist powers, China, has been obliging the West by persistent truculence, chiefly in Korea and South Asia; the shrewder Soviets have alternated conciliation with truculence and have often managed to turn the tables on the leader of the free world in showing him up as either indecisive or intransigent. Barring diplomatic *faux pas,* the desired demonstration to allies and nonaligned countries is easier, or may be feasible only, when the adversary is relatively indifferent to the wider repercussions of his behavior—that is, when he aims at immediate, limited gains rather than at long-term, risk-free gains.

The more ingenious is the adversary, the more important is the leading ally's ability to adjust internal conditions and gains-liabilities equations in the alliance. Apart from persuasion, he depends on the means of compensation and, in the last resort, on coercion.

Compensation is an indispensable device in international relations; it is often the only alternative to coercion. On the other hand, compensation is rather sterile as an analytical device since anything can in principle compensate for everything, or can be treated as valid compensation to save face.

Relatively simple and straightforward are compensations by territory for territory, by material subsidy for material effort, or by consultation for policy support. A matching of commensurate values is probably more common in an unequal alliance. The predominant partner in an alliance of widely unequal powers may have to stabilize imbalances in each particular sector of the partnership. Not to do so might materially disable the lesser allies or undermine their morale. In alliances of equally mature powers, cohesion will grow as allies spontaneously compensate unequal expenditures by unequal risks, or other kinds of effort, without matching or proportioning each and every activity and value. An alliance of this kind may even thrive on the feeling of uncompensated sacrifice for the common good, as an act demonstrating solidarity or the responsibility of power.

Only when an issue develops into one of prestige before domestic or foreign witnesses may compensation have to occur in the same commodity, as a mechanical *quid pro quo*. The case is clearest in negotiations between antagonistic powers, when the appearance of reciprocal concession is more important than the intrinsic value of apparently unrelated concessions. Literal reciprocity, based on bargaining and barter, supplants solidarity, based on mutual accommodation and compromise. Insistence on strictly equivalent compensation merges with coercion, which may be nonetheless real for being reciprocal.

Coercion has its place in the most egalitarian alliance, provided that the acts of coercing and being coerced alternate among members. It helps if the stronger partner's pressure is exerted indirectly on structures of interests, constituting an inducement, rather than directly on the actor's will by means of threats and warnings. In the last resort, the leading ally may coerce lesser partners into greater exertions by restricting his commitment to fit a less ambitious strategic concept. Conversely, lesser allies can rarely muster enough unified pressure to influence the major ally through his particular interests. They can "coerce" the leading ally only directly, by means of representations concerning the major ally's behavior toward adversaries and neutrals. An occasional concession to direct pressure will not debase the major ally as it does a lesser one; it may even increase the cohesion of a "free" alliance as direct pressure on lesser allies does not. This is not to say that good will can take the place of prestige even in relations among allies. But up to a point the two intangibles may be exchangeable and cumulative, inasmuch as due regard for the interests of lesser allies may increase both.

Pretensions and Coercion

Apart from the security aspect of alliances, there is the question of the internal stability of allies and their status. If the requirements of cohesion are to be reconciled with those of efficacy and change, individual allies' gains and liabilities within the alliance have to be periodically redistributed, the functions and objectives of the alliance adjusted, and the subalignments of members formed and reformed.

The most straightforward cause of the disintegration of an alliance is domestic instability producing radical change in the governing elite. A new governing group may confirm membership in an alliance in order to win the respectability which goes with continuity. It may be more important for a new group, however, to distinguish itself from the predecessor. The advantages of a new course will greatly commend themselves when the regime's predecessor was closely identified with the alliance and perhaps even manipulated it so as to consolidate his domestic position.

The successors of Bismarck, like those of Nuri-as-Said, chose a new course; Germany moved away from Russia toward Britain, Iraq moved in the opposite direction. The suspicion that Western alliances, including NATO, have served as superstructures for upholding the signatory regimes —in France, West Germany, Japan, and elsewhere—has increased the possibility of an adverse reaction, away from the alliance, under successor regimes. An opposition is probably least inclined to disrupt an alliance, after it has become the government, if it has been associated with the alliance's inception and implementation. This may have to mean that both the government and its allies give the opposition a virtual veto over major new departures. The prerequisite is, of course, that the opposition is not too far apart in basic foreign policy views from the government in power. Moreover the opposition itself must be a coherent force, able and willing to undertake the responsibilities of both internal government and international alliance. When this is not the case, the opposition may have to be kept out of alliance politics. The alliance is then, however, a bond with a government and not with a state; this may make the alliance more cohesive while it lasts but less stable over a length of time.

Pressures within member countries rarely increase the over-all cohesion of the alliance. In this respect, internal pressures differ from external pressures on allies and resemble unilateral, unco-ordinated pressures directed outward against third states by a venturesome ally. When the hard-pressed government is weak, it will seek concessions from fellow-allies in order to dampen the drive behind the opposition and avoid being replaced by it; an example was the Kishi government in Japan, fighting for its life and the American alliance. When the government is strong, it will play up domestic resistance to an alliance so as to drive a hard bargain; in its best days, the Adenauer government in West Germany had its already strong hand strengthened by the Social Democrats' ambivalence about NATO. Neither posture need lastingly strengthen the alliance's cohesion any more than does the oppositional pressure to which the government reacts, or which it exploits.

The relationship between government and opposition influences cohesion most decisively and often most harmfully when the alliance combines states at diverse stages of political and economic maturity. Political maturity is vital for alliance relationships, since it grows with the ability to accept reciprocal limitations on independence as a necessary condition of existence. By contrast, it is immature to regard such limitations as a debasement of national dignity and prestige. In both economic and political development, the progression is from some kind of primitive self-sufficiency and isolation to co-operative division of functions and resources.

Even between equally developed states, it is no easy task to assess the level of military contribution which would strain the economies of allies and impose comparable deprivations on their publics. It is no easier to compare the political gains and losses which accrue to allies from supporting, or failing to support, each other. What have been, for instance, the comparative strains on the American economy of maintaining a division in the field and on the Belgian economy of maintaining a batallion? And what would be the political cost to Belgium of supporting American actions in the Caribbean as compared with the hypothetical cost to the United States of backing Belgian interests in the Congo? The equations become unworkable when allies, attempting to span divergent stages of development, have to reduce to a common denominator disparate forms of contribution—such as the grant of material assistance and of military bases.

The main obstacle to a sense of "fair sharing" lies in intangibles. When lesser partners lack an inner sense of equal worth, it is hard to compute and impossible to prove specific instances of equality. And particular exchanges break down when a fundamental barter of legitimacies has failed. Alliances with an established power no longer serve to legitimize a new and unstable regime; such a regime cannot, therefore, use a legitimacy which it failed to receive to cover the major ally's "presence" in the country. Nationalism, added to factional struggles, has made it more likely that alliance with a major power will discredit the government of the less developed ally rather than legitimize it, and help topple the government rather than build it up. Assistance has come to be perceived as interference, support as domination, and political backing against an adversary as an incitement to a break with him. The tragic part is that in order to implement an alliance between unevenly developed allies, the major ally often has to act in ways which apparently validate the *a priori* hostility of some groups and confirm others in the cynical grounds for their co-operation.

Divergences in development can be harmful to cohesion among allies in still another way. They exacerbate relationships among the objectives of security, stability, and status.

For one thing, heterogeneous allies are most likely to enter an alliance for different reasons. The interests of parties in an alliance are identical if both parties intend to deter or defeat the same opponent. Interests are disparate when both allies are concerned with security against different opponents. The major ally's concern to equip, train, and otherwise reinforce the partner is then still matched by the concern of the other side to be equipped, trained, and otherwise reinforced; and the superficial symmetry of concerns will facilitate the implementation of the alliance. But the need for action in a crisis is apt to bring into the open the disparity regarding the main target-state. Another kind of difference besets allies when one is concerned primarily with military security, while the other is chiefly preoccupied with securing assistance for internal stability and growth. In contrast with the preceding case, strains are then likely to appear at an early stage of implementing the alliance, but the alliance is less vulnerable to sudden disruption.

Some motives for desiring alliance are better suited to symmetrical balance than others. For example, the desire to build up an ally economically and the desire to be built up constitute an easy pair; the desire to restrain is unlikely to be matched by the desire to be restrained. An exception may be that of a "conservative" government anxious to associate an ally in its internal contest with aggressive (or revolutionary) groups. Such was the case with the Restoration Bourbons in France after Napoleon, and with the not dissimilar Adenauer regime in Germany after Hitler. By and large, symmetries are enhanced by governments using allies to press for desired but unpopular measures.

Another likely effect of heterogeneity among allies, inimical to cohesion, is a derangement of relationships underlying status. The ideal relationship is one of correspondence. The more security and stability a country has, and the more it does for itself and others, the higher would be its status. The relationship is deranged when actors claim higher status to make up for poor performance in the area of security, for instability, and for dependence on others. A leading ally may countenance such overcompensations; he may single out less advanced states, aligned or nonaligned, for special forbearance while reserving the harder line for politically more experienced partners. The risk is that politically less developed governments will construe a concession from strength as a sign of weakness.

There is no hard and fast rule for conceding and denying status-building advantages to less favored governments; and status-seeking is not confined to less developed members of heterogeneous alliances. The fall of the Orleanist regime in France in 1848 can be blamed in part on the unwillingness of the British to allow foreign policy success to their unstable liberal ally. On the other hand, the directors of German diplomacy in 1914 have been blamed for deferring to the prestige needs of unstable Austria-Hungary. And different critics may use the relation of Weimar Germany with the Western European parties to the Locarno Pact to emphasize one or the other aspect of the matter. They may accuse the Germans of having tried to blackmail France and Britain into concessions for domestic reasons, or they may criticize Britain for having given priority to unity with the French over the need to bolster a domestically weak democratic regime in Germany.

In contemporary multilateral alliances, the intangibles of

prestige and influence can be very tangibly expressed in indices like membership in policy-making committees, frequency with which an ally is consulted on major decisions, and the allocation of military commands. The visibility of such preferments intensifies the contest over status, especially when there is competition over which ally, if any, is to be nearest to the leading power. Within the Atlantic alliance, Britain has sought to retain the status of the first ally of the United States. Two centuries back, the Dutch had a similar ambition with respect to Britain as the leader against France. Like the British today, the Dutch constituted a vital strategic bridgehead for the less vulnerable, and institutionally related, overseas power. Other allies can be counted upon to resist even an informal division of leadership, however, especially when the first ally is not as clearly superior in resources and contributions to the other allies as is the preponderant power to the rest.

All alliances are subject to erosion. To halt and survive the drift, allies must do something about it as they implement their commitments. A way of defining their task in the abstract is to say that allies must maintain the initial balance between the gains and liabilities which can be attributed to the alliance. To speak of "balance" is to imply that cohesion of the alliance and its efficacy can be served by either reducing or expanding functions and objectives—or only functions, if the defensive objective is given. Restriction and expansion of functions can occur simultaneously, when allies expand economic and political functions to offset reduction or stagnation in military functions. This has been the standard formula for NATO from time to time, as even those suspect of militaristic predispositions affirmed the need to give the alliance "the totality of its meaning." [15] Or, inter-allied co-operation may be expanded in a key sector of the

---

[15] See former Secretary of State Dulles' speech to the Associated Press Editors, April, 1956, cited in J. R. Beal, *John Foster Dulles, 1888–1959* (1959), p. 219.

military establishment only, for instance by way of a pooled deterrent for the Atlantic alliance. Although each crisis produces pledges of increased effort, the economy of an alliance may actually require an agreed upon deflation of early ambitions.

It is useful to look again at classical alliances and alliances at war. They relate to territory, whereas contemporary peacetime alliances revolve around functions. The distribution of territorial gains in return for the expenditure of blood and treasure raises the issue of gains and liabilities in the most concrete form. It also raises a vital question for allies—to wit, whether to define their common goals and individual prospective gains concurrently with the undertaking of burdens. There are two main possibilities: allies can agree on how to divide anticipated gains at the outset; or they can postpone the definition of war aims to the day of victory. Negotiators of alliance treaties between France and Austria, and Austria and Russia, which provoked the Seven Years' War, divided anticipated gains in advance; so did members of the Triple Entente in the early stages of World War I. By contrast, the issue was postponed by members of the winning coalitions against Napoleonic France and Nazi Germany.

Is one of the methods clearly more advantageous? A satisfactory agreement on individual gains makes it easier to allocate tasks which seem to be objectively necessary to realize the hypothetical gains. As reverses make gains more doubtful, or as originally planned efforts prove to be inadequate, a revision is necessary. Allies must scale down and reapportion expected gains or expand their effort. In either case, however, the alliance ought to be able to prosecute the best possible strategy; there is less reason to fear that the physical occupation of enemy (or other) territory by individual allies will give them undue advantage in the final settlement.

Postponement is fraught with corresponding disadvantages and risks, which only the political naïveté of the less acquisitive allies can minimize. On the other hand, postponement of agreements has the advantage of delaying an overt showdown over conflicting interests to a time when the alliance can afford it, that is, when the hypothetical gains have been realized. If all allies are predatory, an alliance can work only if the configuration of territory excludes competition over the same real estate. In the latter stages of the Thirty Years' War, France and Sweden managed to hold the alliance together as long as Sweden confined her ambitions to northern Germany, and France to the Rhine. More recently, Nazi Germany had fewer frictions over the division of territorial spoils with remote Japan than with the Soviet Union over the Balkans and with Spain and Italy over North Africa. If only one party in an alliance is predatory, the conservative status quo powers have no foolproof policy. They must try to drive the best possible bargain when the predatory power needs them most and retain the psychological and military capacity for instantaneous transition from coalition to some form of coercion when the expansionist ally does not adhere to the bargain.

In peacetime, defensive allies are less preoccupied with territory and more with savings which can be realized by "producing" security in an alliance rather than by other, unilateral or universalist, strategies. And they are concerned with possible increments in domestic stability and in status as a result of the alliance. There is a qualitative disparity between possible, hypothetical gains and the more tangible and immediate liabilities to be apportioned among allies. Unless allies deliberately attempt some such distribution, rational strategy for the alliance is again hampered by concern lest individual members unilaterally appropriate greater gains in security, domestic stability, and status than are due them on the basis of performance.

What are some of the possible distortions? They can bear upon the kind of threat against which a party is guaranteed and on the degree of assurance which it receives. The degree depends on the military and political liabilities that other allies are ready to undertake on behalf of an endangered partner. In return, the guaranteed government may be both obligated and ready to adopt domestic measures, for instance, which may temporarily increase threats to its authority. Failure to clarify the scope and conditions of commitment will impede the cohesion of the alliance and its chances for evolving an effective strategy. The guaranteed ally may resort to unilateral acquisitions of the desired gain by evading alliance burdens which play into the hands of internal opponents, or by self-protective repressions. And the other allies will have to worry lest the unstable government utilize interallied co-operation for the defense and development of its country to represent the allies as unconditionally committed to the regime's survival. Still more common are "slowdowns" by individual allies who reduce national efforts to increase relative gains in the security produced by others and to lessen strains on their economic and political stability.

Roughly the same applies to the prestige and influence of allies. In a permanently organized peacetime alliance their relative status is expressed in determinate roles and institutions, such as hierarchical military command and political consultations. Relative status can be determined by the allies themselves with little outside interference; and unlike security and stability, intra-alliance status is a finite quantity which will divide itself unless it is apportioned. It cannot, like security, be increased for all simultaneously or, like domestic stability, be increased or decreased for one without immediate effect on the stability of others. The alternative to some form of consensus is that allies will unilaterally appropriate assets which either impart status directly or may be exchanged for tokens of status which have to be conferred by others. A unilateral appropriation of territory may contribute to the allies' common objective by defeating the enemy, while at the same time threatening the abstract goal of a balance of power and small-state independence. Conversely, a unilateral seizure of status may frustrate the concrete requirements of effective deterrence and defense, while implementing the abstract ideology of equality among allies. Acts which might otherwise contribute to the total capability of the alliance or bring it up to date can be disruptive because of the status-arrogating intent behind them.

Aware of the finite character of status, fellow allies oppose such unilateral acts no less than wartime allies resist the occupation of controversial territory by an acquisitive cobelligerent. And their resistance may take similar forms, too. They may bare the ally to thrusts by the adversary in an area of his strategic weakness, or they may create assets to be bartered against the ally's withdrawal from the unilaterally seized advantage. At the close of the Napoleonic wars, the more conservative allies of Russia and Prussia first exposed the forward powers to the counterthrusts of the retreating French. Subsequently, they brought France into a secret convention for resistance to the Russo-Prussian demands. And finally, they bartered the convention against a partial reduction of the demands. In 1960, the Atlantic allies, too, had an option in the face of France's undertaking to reshape the policy-making and military physiognomy of the alliance. They could threaten to reduce their effective commitment and expose France strategically in Europe, or politico-militarily in Algeria and in the U.N., if she persisted in her unilateral policies; they could create a new asset, such as a joint nuclear capability under genuinely shared control, and bargain over the terms of France's admission to it; or they could concede to France the desired status of one of the three alliance leaders in exchange for her resuming full co-operation in the military field.

A firm stand may be necessary to compel the lagging (or too forward) partner to fall into line. The way of coercion is through a subalignment which threatens to isolate the unco-operative member. The latter can respond by leaving the alliance; or he can set up a counteralignment within the alliance as a basis for negotiating from strength. Failing that, the temporarily isolated ally may have to rally to the temporarily dominant grouping after securing whatever face-saving concessions he can. France might have to do so on the issue of military integration if the de Gaulle government fails to organize a Continental-European or Western Mediterranean grouping around an "independent" French nuclear deterrent, somewhat as Britain was moved to rally to the Franco-German center of economic and political integration once the rival grouping of the so-called Outer Seven failed as a counterpoise. The precedent had been set in an earlier dilemma of Anglo-American making, when France was compelled to accept Germany's rearmament and NATO membership as an alternative to being replaced as the leading continental ally of the United States. Before bowing to the inevitable, one can gesture in the direction of past traditions. The British Prime Minister is alleged to have invoked at one point the memory of the British-led peripheral coalitions against continental European combinations; and the French can always hark back to France's Eastern European option.[16]

In a flexible state system a trend toward disintegration will be cumulative, as each ally hurries to sell his realignment before the price goes down. In a viable permanent alliance, the appearance of such a trend can be reintegrative, as the lack of alternatives compels an adjustment. The adjustment is likely to be reasonable, owing to the flexibility of diplomatic alignments *within* the alliance. For a member of the temporary inner grouping to make unreasonable demands on the repenting rebel is to run the risk of being the next one to be isolated. This being so, it is fortunate (rather than the opposite) when intra-alliance flexibility grows with the decline of freedom to realign. The risks of coercion among allies are greater when direct pressures from the adversary are less and when the ally's unilateral measures

[16] On the subsequently denied statements by Prime Minister Macmillan, see *New York Times*, April 1, 1960, p. 3.

render him more independent militarily and politically. When the conflict with the adversary is uniquely grave, it is less risky to antagonize a fellow ally on a particular issue; and the fact that many issues are active at one time within a permanently operative alliance facilitates a mutually compensatory pattern of interallied checks and balances. The practical alternative to diplomatic alignment-politics within an alliance is stagnation or dictatorship of the major ally—or both.

When the alliance as a system of interdependent partners cannot force the deviant ally to its level, it may have to follow him to his, if it is to come to terms with two major sources of disintegration. One is a protracted imbalance in gains and liabilities of different allies; another is the domination over the alliance's objectives or functions by particular allies willing to run greater risks than others. In the aforementioned case of the Quadruple Alliance, the allies of Prussia and Russia could have demanded equivalent territorial gains for themselves. By re-establishing a balance of power through compensations, they would indicate that they, too, could do without legitimacy or national homogeneity. They did not adopt this course because their ability to curtail somewhat the gains of the two predatory powers increased their standing more than any conceivable piece of territory could have done. Similarly, the Atlantic allies of France might have set out to show that they, too, could do without integrated defense and accept the risks and liabilities of a differently implemented alliance. They preferred to adhere to the principle of integrated defense in preference to the principle of strict reciprocity at all points all the time.

Reciprocity among allies is important for cohesion, especially when anticipated gains are difficult to realize. For France's controversial eighteenth-century alliance with Austria to be accepted at home, it was more important that Austria render "efficacious assistance" to France against Great Britain in exchange for parallel French assistance against

Prussia than that France actually secure the anticipated territorial gain.[17]

It used to be relatively easy for autocratic allies to restrict initial ambitions when such a course appeared to be desirable or necessary. Matters are different with defensive allies, with democratic governments. A regime depending on popular support is loath to admit original misassessment and intervening setbacks. To expand the functions and commitments of an alliance is to respond creatively. When this is done, the challenge can be admitted without producing panic. To reduce functions and commitments in a key alliance and redefine gains and liabilities downward is to take a gamble. At worst, it may prove impossible to stop the reduction of goals short of complete disintegration of the alliance; even short of that, the government courts a possible future charge of having done less than was required and possible. Insofar as such considerations do sway policies, popular involvement diminishes not only flexibility of alignment; it also hampers adjustments in implementation of alliances which seemingly point in the direction of dissolution.

---

[17] R. Waddington, *Louis XIV et le renversement des alliances: préliminaires de la Guerre de Sept Ans 1754–1756* (1896), p. 473.

3
The Efficacy of Alliances

THE REQUIREMENTS of cohesion may coincide with those of efficacy; but cohesion due to the oppressive rule of a single power or of a single principle—such as the principle of consultation or integration—may inhibit the capacity of allies to reconcile their various needs with an efficacious strategy for all. This chapter discusses the politico-military conditions under which defensive allies can perform three main functions: always to restrain the adversary and, if and when desirable, also each other and the scope of a conflict.

Integration and Independence

One may ask, "how much cohesion?" referring to the degree that allies stay together and act together. And one may ask, "how much integration?" implying how intimately allies must be tied together so that they cannot act separately. Modern technology notwithstanding, there is no simple answer in favor of "more" of each.

An integrated capability to underpin an all-purpose strategy can be recommended for an alliance as a means to increasing its cohesion. But the same set of measures may be presumed to diminish cohesion, if one stresses the frictions attending implementation rather than the ideal consequences of achievement. Similarly, it is hazardous to predict that a particular measure of integration will lastingly increase cohesion, because it will debar members from alternative and possibly separate, if obsolete and ineffective, ways of serving the national-security interest. Quite to the contrary, the prospects of a premature disappearance of alternatives may disturb cohesion, unless all major interests are somehow safeguarded in a community arrangement. Cohesion itself cannot be the supreme value for individual allies, as long as an alliance is a limited one and is served by a permanent organization rather than serving as a short passageway to a higher form of community. And it cannot always be such for the alliance as a whole, when too much unity would decrease the political efficacy of an association, notably with regard to countries other than the adversary in peacetime. It is not self-evident that NATO, for instance, should act as a unit in the field of aid and trade, bloc-voting in the U.N., or global political strategy.

Individual countries as sovereign members of an alliance apply no single criterion in determining their preferred mix of unity, integration, and separateness. Technical possibilities may permit a measure of nonintegration, and domestic political necessities may require it, while economic necessities on the whole favor integration as the cheaper way to implement the commitment. What about the strategic necessities? Their impact is uncertain, quite apart from the fact that, in a world of nations, the demands of security must compete with those of independent status and domestic stability. These assert themselves most whenever the decline or diversion of external pressures intensifies the feeling of discomfort from too close, but not total, integration.

The conflict between military integration and independence has been a major issue in the Western alliance. The conflict is least acute when integration itself is flexible. This is the case when it ties allies together in such a way that they can act either separately or jointly, depending on whether individual or common interests predominate in a particular challenge. In such a case, integration is compatible with improvisation.

There are three relatively distinct areas of activity which can be integrated so that parties cannot act separately without crippling dislocation. The first encompasses command over forces in the field, backed by governmental consultations in the sphere of political, economic, and military policy planning and strategy. The second area encompasses facilities for communication, transport, and supply of all sorts. In both planning and combat, the movement of ideas, instructions, and forces, as well as information and warning about enemy activities in peace and war, are indispensable for effective consultation and command. And finally, the third area is one of specialization among allies in research, production of matériel, and kinds of forces to be contributed to the over-all capability of the alliance. Integration in command and consultations underpins the strategy of operations in the field; specialization concerns the strategy of material means; while integrated communications would seem to facilitate both kinds of strategy.[1]

Distinctions of this kind make it possible to assess actual and preferred policies and strategies. A measure of integration in NATO's military command and communications may appear to be excessive when compared with deficient consultation on political and economic policies. Or, too much preoccupation with the strategy of operations can be contrasted with inadequate attention to the strategy of means, bearing on research, development, and production. On the other hand, one may pick and choose within the various areas of integration, depending on one's idea of desirable alliance

[1] P. M. Gallois defines the strategy of operations as "the art of drawing up a plan of campaign and leading an army in its decisive engagements." See his "New Teeth for NATO," in *Foreign Affairs* (October, 1960), p. 78.

policy. If one favors tying allies together so as virtually to exclude separate action, the critically significant integration concerns command over battlefield forces, as well as communications and supplies. The insurance is complete, when individual (or lesser) allies specialize in particular kinds of forces and strategic tasks as part of alliance capability rather than national capability. If, however, one does not wish to preclude separate action, other kinds of integration remain possible and useful. One kind may be treated as merely a superficial form of co-ordination—for instance, standardized training, joint military exercises, and hypothetical planning. Another kind of integration, in depth, would make allies specialize in production of different kinds of matériel, while adequate peacetime stocks might still permit unilateral wartime employment of all kinds of matériel by any one ally.

In each of the multilateral Western alliances, a permanent organization of councils, committees, and staffs has served as a framework for a commitment to mutual assistance. Organizational activity has intensified the involvement of member states, while tending to change the terms on which it has occurred. Initially, it was the lesser allies who were more anxious to commit the United States to leadership; they also wished to secure preferred treatment in comparison with other parts of the world and other states in a region. The point is manifest with regard to NATO; the original driving force behind SEATO was at first Britain and then Thailand; and, least decisively and forcefully, Iraq and Turkey contributed the impetus behind the precursor of CENTO, the Baghdad Pact. As advantages failed to materialize or as the liabilities of the connection became more apparent, the initial ardor of the lesser allies cooled. At the same time, the desire of the increasingly vulnerable United States to keep the lesser allies involved has grown, as a matter of deliberate security policy as well as one of prestige and sheer routine.

Such partial reversals in wooing and winning are common.

They contribute to the difficulty of developing collective force and policy, as leading allies fail to have their unfolding performance supplemented with the lesser partners' contribution to joint security. Somewhat like the Axis alliance with regard to co-ordinated offense, the defensive Inter-American system and the Middle East Alliance (now the Central Treaty Organization—CENTO) have remained very much in the stage of propaganda myths.[2] SEATO has progressed somewhat beyond the stage of a composite paper tiger toward co-ordination of interallied contributions, and NATO may have attempted too much by trying to bypass the phase of co-ordination in favor of integration.

It has become customary to evaluate Western alliances against the partly fictional model of NATO as a highly integrated alliance. Thus assessed, what is the standing of the main alliances?

The Inter-American system is hardly a collective-security or collective-defense system at all. The Rio Treaty organization has produced neither a joint command nor meaningful joint planning; and individual Latin-American members have neither been assigned nor did they accept a determinate role in international—as contrasted with internal—security. For the United States, the invocation of collective security made it easier to implement a unilateral security guarantee and conclude bilateral agreements; the agreements concerned bases and military assistance in kinds and amounts which, it was hoped, would minimize domestic and intra-regional violence. Most of the time, the United States kept its own counsel regarding the use of American and joint resources in an emergency.[3] The Latin-American governments were expected, in return, to observe at least benevolent neutrality

[2] See D. C. Watt, "The Rome-Berlin Axis, 1936–1940: Myth and Reality," in *The Review of Politics*, No. 4 (1960), pp. 519–43. Watt's findings apply to the Berlin-Tokyo Axis as well, to a large extent.

[3] E. Lieuwen, *Arms and Politics in Latin America* (1960), pp. 193, 214 ff., and *passim*.

in limited wars of collective security outside the region (such as the Korean War) and to resist the lure of neutralism in the politics of cold-war peace.

There are two main reasons for the non-integration of the alliance of the Americas. For one, the system is close to the idea of a regional arrangement for security applicable to disputes between members as well as to extra-regional threats. As such, the alliance shares the inhibitions of the collective security macrocosm with regard to integration and other things. For another, the system has been relatively remote from the Soviet bloc and, for the most part, from advanced bases of Communist power. It has consequently lacked the impetus of an immediate and manageable threat.

The case of SEATO has been more ambiguous. On the one hand, the principally guaranteed countries are close to the potential aggressor, perceived increasingly in the shape of Communist China. This has encouraged a measure of integration within the limits set initially by the non-Asian allies. On the other hand, non-Communist regional and domestic threats have been excluded from the American commitment in particular. This may have progressively reduced the interest of the lesser, local allies in integration. Thailand, initially the most ambitious, was at a later stage most anxious to retain subsidized national forces for relatively unrestricted use against non-Communist regional and domestic foes. The result was an early demise of SEATO's peculiar founding myth, that of a NATO-like integrated command. Instead, SEATO has inclined toward a dual-purpose integration: one which would leave open the choice between independent national action and collective action.

The SEATO allies sought to co-ordinate advance national planning, periodic joint military exercises on land, sea, and in the air, and the development of communication and supply facilities in the treaty area to promote mobility of allied power in an emergency. Constituent military forces retained their national character, however, as did the staffs of the permanent organization. The greater non-Asian powers have tended to be secretive *vis-à-vis* the lesser allies as well as to be often at cross-purposes among themselves. This has placed a great burden on the basic kind of integration—through common purpose and resolve in upholding the most acutely threatened countries, Laos, South Vietnam, and Thailand.[4]

The Atlantic alliance too has not been spared an unfulfilled myth. An early hope was for integrated, or balanced, collective forces based on interallied specialization in tasks and contributions. Integration under joint command went up and down as the allies wavered between treating the alliance as a façade for an American guarantee, a new form of military organization of proportionately contributing allies, or a conventional coalition.[5] Side by side with selective integration in command, communications, consultations, and specialization, there have been unilateral, national approaches to the nuclear sword as well as to the conventional shield. Here belong balanced national, rather than collective, forces, non-standardized weapons production and equipment, and national ownership of home-based components of the "integrated" infrastructure—not to speak of unilateral policy decisions suspending or limiting agreed-upon contributions. The alliance leader's secrecy with respect to other partners has been limited, but limited to the vital area of nuclear weapons; and the survival of bilateral implementing agreements has facilitated differential treatment of allies in such things as interallied control over IRBM's stationed on the territory of Britain, Italy, and Turkey, respectively.

The secrecy which an alliance leader maintains toward different allies is an irritant to the less privileged ones, while being often necessary in the security interest of all. What-

[4] On SEATO matters I owe much to parts I and III by George Modelski in Modelski, ed., *SEATO: Six Studies* (1962). See also his "Australia and SEATO," *International Organization*, No. 3 (1960), pp. 429–37.

[5] R. E. Osgood, *NATO: The Entangling Alliance* (1962), pp. 28 ff. and *passim*. In this case, as in that of George Modelski, my great debt to the author antedates the publication of the book.

ever may be the effect on cohesion, different degrees of secrecy constitute a suggestive index of real integration. So does the ratio of bilateral to multilateral implementing agreements, when the bilateral agreements accord differential treatment.

No peculiar virtue inheres in multilateralism. It may debase to the level of the least willing party the allies' readiness to act, as the impossibility of united action becomes a ready excuse for inaction by any power singly. Or multilateralism may induce laggard members to raise their national efforts to a higher common level, not least by enabling members to invoke allied pressure to justify politically unpopular sacrifices at home. The major ally garners some advantage from multilateralism when collective and, as it were, anonymous allied pressure lessens resentment against any one partner. In the area of intangibles, multilateralism contributes the comforts of the collective-security label. This may consolidate already existing support for an alliance by fitting it into a group's collectivist security ideology or into a member government's anti-colonial ideology. For non-members, on the other hand, it is bilateralism that may be less objectionable ideologically, since it creates less of a "bloc" and is less suspect of being intended to attract neutrals.

For more or less valid reasons, faith in multilateralism has been probably on the decline; the same may be happening with respect to integration. The military case for far-reaching integration had originally rested on the precedents of conventional total wars of the first half of the century; the case was reinforced by the massive character of Soviet land armies and by the growing speed, range, destructive power, and cost of weapons. It is too early to say whether developments in strategic and tactical nuclear weaponry, and desired increases in the mobility of forces, have weakened or strengthened the over-all need for integration, or whether they have merely transferred it to new areas of command and control. But it is apparent that the so-called military necessities of integration have had some difficulty in asserting themselves against the technological possibilities of military self-dependence. The difficulty is compounded when political requirements become predominant because overt conflict has neither preceded nor followed soon upon commitment.

In the political realm, the practical experience of fifteen years of the cold war has revealed two major disparities. One is between "permanent" (that is, long-term and renewable) alliances and impermanent regimes; the other is between a continually operating, farflung alliance organization and haphazard delimitations of the alliance's scope and the allies' solidarity. In such conditions, the ideal maximum of integration gives way to its irreducible minimum; and the concern not to duplicate functions of other organizations, typical so far of NATO, is matched with the urge to delegate to national control hitherto joint or novel functions and weapons. Inspiration of national morale through self-dependence comes to rate higher than economy and efficiency through integration and interdependence.

Deterrence and Auxiliaries

Selective or dual-purpose integration would permit both individual and collective action. What are some of its possible implications for the main functions of a defensive alliance? As already noted, the functions comprise restraint of the adversary, with the object of discouraging or at least confining conflicts. In achieving these objectives, flexibility in implementing alliance commitments and co-operation may work as a substitute for diminished flexibility in alignment.

Nuclear weapons have aggravated the problem of effectively deterring the adversary and protecting allies through unprovocative measures. What constitutes "provocation"? The query is no simpler to answer than that regarding "intervention." In a strict sense, adopted from the code of the duel, provocation is an act which unmistakably invites an adversary to take counter-measures or forfeit prestige and honor. In a looser sense, alignment itself might be regarded as a provocation of states which are not included. It challenges the rightness of their stand and limits the range of policy options left open to them. By converting an issue into a test of strength, an alignment must be expected to provoke a commensurate response: a diplomatic response if the alignment is merely of that kind; or a military one if the alignment receives a strategic implementation.

In actual fact adversaries aim the charge of provocation most frequently at a specific way of implementing alliances in peacetime. Such a charge is a commonplace weapon of psychological warfare, when adversaries and non-aligned countries decry inoffensive and necessary measures of deterrence and precaution. The adversary does so in order to foster dissension among allies and opposition among non-aligned countries; and even dissenting allies may cry "provocation" to justify non-co-operation. Partly due to her earlier eviction as the dominant power, France has been least anxious to contribute to the protection of the SEATO area. At the same time, she has inclined to regard the alliance's periodic military exercises as being unnecessarily provocative, overlooking the possibility that such exercises have been a necessary substitute for a more "provocative" standing military presence of the Western allies in the forward area.[6]

Viewed objectively, two kinds of provocation are particularly grave. One is primarily political: when a state's alignment spells defiance of a traditionally dominant power and

[6] Royal Institute of International Affairs, *Collective Defense in South East Asia: The Manila Treaty and Its Implications*, A Report by a Chatham House Study Group (1956), p. 127. Significantly, the SEATO exercises in British North Borneo at the height of the Laos crisis in 1961 were not treated as a "provocation" by the Communist powers, whatever may have been the utility of the exercises as a demonstration and, consequently, a deterrent. For a description of these exercises, see *New York Times*, May 3, 1961, p. 2.

asserts the state's independence from the protector. Here belong such examples as defections of the Dutch in the sixteenth and the seventeenth centuries, the Balkan states in the nineteenth century, and many formerly dependent countries, such as Cuba, in the mid-twentieth century. As a rule, the state anxious for emancipation defects from the previously dominant, conservative power to an apparently rising power. The Dutch defected from Spain to England and from England to France and back again; Rumania and Bulgaria from the Ottoman Empire to Russia and from Russia to Germany; and Castro's Cuba from the United States to the Soviet Union. The new protector may be able to restrain the deserted power's drive to retaliate and his own urge to merely replace the dominant power. As a result, a realignment may be permanent (and gradually cease to be regarded as an intolerable provocation) or it may constitute merely an interlude which leads to a more egalitarian implementation of the original connection.

The other and, perhaps, more serious provocation arises from a military posture which threatens the target state without erecting an adequate safeguard against its counter-measures over an indefinite period of time. The target state has valid reason for considering such a posture offensive to its prestige and security. The offense to prestige is the greater, the less adequate is the military posture of an adversary power or alliance for either defense or offense. The threat to security is decisive, when the military posture is more suitable for a preventive-aggressive action than for deterrence and defense. Bismarck pretended to be provoked (into the Austrian alliance) by Russian horsemen near East Prussia in 1879; the Russians displayed similar feelings about American missiles in Turkey. When a power is provoked mainly in its prestige, the decision-makers will be tempted to demonstrate that they cannot be easily frightened by forcing the antagonist to back down and reveal his inability to act. When the threat to security is real, the decision-makers will be actually fearful and under a pressure to act so as to prevent an aggravation of the threat. They will seek to diminish the ability of the major antagonist to protect both himself and allies from retaliation.

The conjunction of psychological, prestige, and security factors is most provocative when the implicitly threatening forces are located close to the enemy's heartland, in areas which history or geopolitics allow him to claim as his legitimate orbit. This has meant Western forces close to the Sino-Soviet bloc, but it may come to mean Communist-controlled weaponry in the Western Hemisphere as well. When the major ally becomes apparently unable to protect such advanced positions against punitive measures by the target state, local fears of being too provocative grow and undercut the otherwise morale-building effect of allied guarantee and presence. The issue has become somewhat less critical for the West, since its deterrent can be withdrawn to the Western Hemisphere and to the depths of the seas, if necessary. Pending such a costly retrenchment, however, allied presence, ability to protect, and avoidance of manifest provocation are key elements in the equation of defense and deterrence.

Insofar as it connotes terror, deterrence implies possible use of strategic-nuclear weapons as, in the past, it implied wholesale demonstrative devastations of enemy territory. Loosely speaking, the term "deterrence" may be extended to cover less destructive instruments of warfare, which can be more effective actually in defending a position and denying fruits of aggression. In the contemporary phase, the conditions of mutual deterrence, based on the two major nuclear powers' capability to return a strike have come to be virtually identical with the requirements of "mutual assurance," demonstrating their will *and* freedom not to initiate a first, preventive strike. However, conditions of mutual assurance between nuclear adversaries and, *a fortiori,* mutually supervised arms-control measures, cannot but undermine the sense of confidence *within* a defensive alliance system.[7] Such conditions further reduce the always low credibility and feasibility of "active" deterrence, which presupposes the nuclear ally's readiness and capability to strike first strategically in retaliation for an otherwise irresistible major attack or ultimative threat of attack on his allies.

The issue concerns so-called stability on the strategic-nuclear plane. As stability (and, still more of course, adverse instability) increases, mutual deterrence of the core-powers exposes a widening range of lesser allies to destruction or abandonment. To parry the danger, some lesser European allies have begun to think of the advantages of having an independent "passive" nuclear deterrent; and some American planners have come to regard protection of the U.S. deterrent and population as necessary for restoring credibility to the American deterrent's "active" employment (on behalf of allies). And to avoid the danger that an irresistible conventional attack might reveal the dilemmas which both nuclear stalemate and diffusion create for alliance cohesion, allies on both sides of the Atlantic have been re-emphasizing conventional forces. A conventional build-up may only accelerate decline in the credibility of the nuclear deterrent; but it also offsets the trend for stability on the strategic-nuclear plane to merely shift instability onto the sub-strategic plane of conventional warfare.[8] Effectively or not, any adjustment will aim at preventing the two mutualities between the

[7] Views differ on these matters. See H. Kahn, *On Thermonuclear War* (1960), p. 239, and R. E. Osgood, *NATO: The Entangling Alliance*, pp. 187 ff., also for the concept of mutual assurance. The issue is beclouded by the ever-expanding meaning of "arms control." The term has come to encompass everything from reciprocal surveillance of antagonists, intended to make a surprise attack impossible, to unilateral reassurance of the enemy, intended to make a surprise attack unnecessary.

[8] The model of instability-displacement can be extended if one posits a spectrum of conflict techniques, extending from nuclear to unconventional, paramilitary forms. See R. Strausz-Hupé, W. R. Kintner, and S. T. Possony, *A Forward Strategy for America* (1961), pp. 98, 139. Stability on any one level tends to unstabilize the immediately lower level of conflict techniques until the initially handicapped adversary develops a corresponding capacity.

core-powers—in deterrence and assurance—from undermining the defensive alliance system.

The quandary for an alliance like NATO is greatest when the threat is against one or several countries—as distinct from a wholesale challenge to NATO *en bloc,* which creates fewer problems for decision-making. The allies can follow alternative courses. They can respond in the spirit of solidarity and generalize the conflict. If they are manifestly ready for solidarity in action, the distinction between passive and active deterrence loses meaning. Or the attacked power may be left to shift for itself, if it has nominal capability to do so and the formulation of the challenge and the nature and history of the dispute make it morally possible for its allies to suspend their liability. The power's capability for separate war may then produce separate surrender as an alternative to solitary annihilation.

There may be an intermediate response. This would be one in which less directly involved allies would act as auxiliaries of the belligerent ally or allies with the tacit consent of the adversary. Both sides would have to share interest in keeping the conflict limited, and the total environment stable, to the highest possible degree. The prior requirement is a politically determined, selective integration of alliances on both the strategic-nuclear plane and, as both a supplement and extension of the idea, on the sub-strategic conventional plane. The object is to keep open the option of improvising agreement on a separate retaliation or other form of action by a sub-grouping of the alliance, while the formally unengaged remainder of allies continues its restraining function over the uninvolved capabilities and members of the adversary combination.

The idea can be applied to the proposal for a NATO

The level of conventional weaponry remains crucial, however. Equality in conventional capabilities may unstabilize the level of unconventional techniques; but the contestant who has been proven inferior on the less orthodox plane is more likely to raise the level of confrontation to the conventional plane than to pass from that plane to the thermonuclear one.

deterrent. According to one version of the plan, control over the deterrent would be joint and decisions unanimous; each power, including the United States, would have a veto. Now if the Atlantic allies could merely prevent the United States from using a small collective deterrent, which only supplemented the much larger nationally controlled American deterrent, and could not compel the United States to authorize its use, the situation would remain much as it was before. There would be genuine novelty only if, for the purposes of the integrated NATO deterrent, the United States would act as a NATO power-in-Europe.[9] This would entail three things. First, the United States would have to be willing to forego its veto in the face of an overwhelming determination of the most directly affected European allies to strike. Second, the United States would have to be both prepared and able to withhold in such a case the support of the strictly American deterrent for the NATO deterrent. And third, the enemy —presumably the Soviet Union—would have to respect the dissociation of the United States *qua* NATO ally-in-Europe from the territorial United States in the Western Hemisphere.

As, traditionally, an auxiliary lent his sword to a belligerent without himself formally challenging the adversary (or resorting to the fiction of volunteers), the United States would make its part of the NATO "sword" available to the allies while eschewing a state of war with the Soviet Union. The fact that involvement is only partial need not substantially lessen the deterrent effect on the adversary; it limits the scope of conflict and may facilitate peacemaking; and it preserves the possibility of interallied control.

The auxiliary's part in all this rests on his ability either to commit or to continue to withhold the uninvolved national-power reserves. As a restraint on the spiralling up

[9] A similar principle was contemplated in the original Norstad plan. American officers entrusted with the custody of nuclear weapons would be expected to act in compliance with NATO directives as agents of the alliance rather than of the American government. *New York Times*, November 12, 1960, p. 28.

of the modalities of conflict, the distinction between prepositioned alliance forces and the national forces of belligerents might supplement the distinction between conventional and nuclear forces. As an additional restraint on the nuclear deterrent, the only partly involved powers might continue mutual assurance through surveillance in the non-belligerent areas of the two alliances. Since the damage inflicted on the two sides would be presumably limited and symmetrical, the threat to stability of the total environment would be correspondingly less. This would reduce the danger of a nuclear exchange triggering any and all parties anxious to equalize destruction and postwar capabilities of actual as well as potential rivals. The symmetry of the damage would also be qualitative if, as is possible, the scheme deflected the exchanges to the territory of allies of both superpowers—Western Europe and Eastern Europe respectively.

The fear that the superpowers might hit only each other's forward areas in a conflict has been one of the reasons why France and probably Britain set out to develop an independent deterrent. It is apparently absurd to outline a scheme under which the Western European countries would co-operate in the devastation of Europe and immunization of the extra-European wing powers, as an alternative to still larger destruction or submission to satellite status. However, the idea is applicable both ways; NATO-in-Europe could just as well act as a mere auxiliary of belligerent United States, facilitating communications and warning, for example, but withholding use of the joint deterrent in return for Western Europe's immunity to devastation by the Soviet Union. Both superpowers would keep Europe as a whole inviolate, to serve as the reward of victory, contributor to postwar reconstruction, and counterbalance to uninvolved extra-European powers, such as China.

But mutual deterrence and mutual assurance in the thermonuclear sector are not enough. They can merely help disintegrate the defensive alliance, as the more aggressive side is encouraged to nibble away at points of local weakness instead of being forced to co-operate in the subsidence of mutually provocative activities. To avoid the pitfall, the defensive alliance must also dispose of conventional and dual-purpose forces which can move swiftly to relieve countries threatened by non-nuclear, conventional or unconventional, challenges. New techniques of mobility may come to resolve many an alliance dilemma by tying together different sub-areas of an alliance system, while primary or initial responsibility for particular areas is divided among allies. For the West, this form of integration means tying together the threatened rimlands and off-shore islands close to the Sino-Soviet heartland with the Western core-area: the continental-island base in North America and its advance base and bastion in the central NATO area in Europe.[10]

The main requirement of such integration is mobility rather than multinationality of the fire brigades.[11] Not only may essentially national task-forces be more suitable to cope with the exacting technical problems of organization and mobility. They might also have greater political mobility. Being relatively neutral as regards their allotment to a particular alliance, the mobile forces of the greater powers in

[10] A. Wolfers, "Stresses and Strains in 'Going It with Others,'" in *Alliance Policy in the Cold War* (1959), pp. 5 ff. The chief sea, air, and land communications to be assured relate North America and Europe, the central European sector with its northern and southern flanks (the latter extending to North Africa), and the Western core-area with the more remote allies and wards—as well as these among themselves.

[11] Both NATO and SEATO have been considering from time to time the setting up of integrated, multinational mobile forces. It is likely to prove more practical, however, to develop ever more interchangeable but essentially national, homogeneous mobile forces, with standardized equipment and training. Among possible models are the United States strategic reserve forces in the Pacific and in North America, the Commonwealth countries' reserves in Malaya and Australia, and the Canadian mobile brigade in Europe. See. A. Buchan, *NATO in the 1960's: The Implications of Interdependence* (1960), pp. 92 ff; M. D. Taylor, "Security Will Not Wait," *Foreign Affairs* (January, 1961), p. 181. For a pertinent description of the United States' semi-alert in connection with the crisis in Laos, see *New York Herald Tribune*, January 3, 1961, p. 8; SEATO exercises in May, 1961, are described in *New York Times*, May 4, 1961, p. 3.

particular could be moved more easily between alliances and in support of non-aligned countries without involving more actors than necessary and desirable. Mobile reserves insure dispatch when needed to check sudden probings—e.g., against NATO flanks and by airborne forces elsewhere. By contrast, military mobility facilitates deliberate phasing of political strategy in other conditions, which require speed only in the last stage of a crisis. This is true of politically sensitive areas where difficult terrain inhibits military surprise, such as in the Asian rimlands.

When individual and collective responses to an emergency can be improvised, provocative postures and activities of allies on both sides can subside at an even rate, possibly in conjunction with a concerted enlargement of non-aligned buffer areas and compensatory expansion of non-military alliance functions.

Contemporary "permanent" alliances are novel only in being implemented through continually operative military-political organizations. Their nearest kin are the permanent alliances of ancient Sparta, Athens, and Rome; they served as agencies of political control for the major ally, in Rome's case reinforced by dual citizenship, at least as much as agencies of common security. As associations for military co-operation and policy co-ordination, contemporary alliances have long to go before matching the record of longevity of such fixtures of classic diplomacy as France's Family Pact with Spain and her alliances with Turkey, Sweden, Poland, and client-states in Germany. Being periodically activated for individual campaigns, these attachments were only superficially different from the long-term, renewable alliances with periods of dormancy in the thirty-five years before World War I. It is almost as correct to speak of a permanent Franco-Swedish alliance in the seventeenth century as it is to speak of a set of Franco-Russian alliances between 1892 and 1917, differing in intensity and geographical scope of co-operation and the ranking of allies as primary movers and needers.

To have the potential for periodic dormancy and reactivation can be a source of strength and durability for an alliance. This is true notably for a combination in which a hard core of identical interests is beset by not so identical concerns, and compulsively continual activities threaten to pile up internal strains and external provocations to the point of disintegration or atrophy.

In the West, even the North Atlantic alliance has undergone periods of stagnation and heightened activity.[12] The spells of activism have been also periods of transformation, as the allies groped for a coherent response to increasing vulnerability (when Soviet ICBM's supplemented the Red Army and Air Force) and expanding challenge (when the danger of a Germanic kind of invasion under Stalin gave way to the threat of "socialist encirclement" by methods of partly American origin). A future adjustment might be to increase the allies' capacity politically to deactivate sensitive areas by developing national and joint, home-based and foreign-based, mobile forces, capable of swiftly reactivating a dormant sector of the enemy's choosing in ways of one's own choosing. The demonstration of such a potential in crises is apt to deter the adversary's probing operations without validly "provoking" the adversary and embarrassing or alienating neutrals.

Selective or dual-purpose integration makes possible varyingly intense co-operation of particular allies. In an emergency, allies can act as mere reserve, as auxiliaries, or as outright co-belligerents. This presupposes great mutual confidence; without it, fighting allies would hardly allow other members to act as mere auxiliaries. But the sense of solidarity is also likely to deepen when individual members have the capacity to act together as they wish rather than because they *must* act together or not at all.

Implicit in much that precedes is concern with limiting

[12] Buchan places the stagnation period in 1954–56, the periods of greater dynamism in 1951–53 and again after the Suez low in 1956. *NATO in the 1960's*, p. 35.

conflicts, whenever this is compatible with restraining the adversary. Although a conflict is limited in the types of weapons employed and in the contestants' objectives, it still need not be localized. And a localized conflict may involve any number of belligerents within a confined area of operations. To reduce the number of belligerents is a legitimate concern only if the uninvolved parties act as a check on both belligerent sides toward limiting the instruments and objectives of conflict. Next in importance to capability and the will to use it is the nature of the commitment; it will affect both ally and adversary.

Politically as well as militarily, the important thing in a conflict is the entry on either side of the first ally who can raise the level of confrontation above the means of the original contestants; it is not the entry of the third or the Nth ally with less or equal capacity. What conditions make it more likely and necessary for a third power (i.e., the first ally of one side) to become belligerent? The entry of another power is, on balance, most likely when the ally has the more individual obligation of a bilateral alliance and when the commitment is to mutual assistance; and it is more necessary when the resources available to the adversary of one's ally are vastly superior to his. It would have been more difficult to limit the Korean War (if perhaps easier to win it), had American prestige been engaged by a bilateral, mutual-assistance commitment to South Korea. For the same reason, it would have been difficult to keep the conflict in Indochina limited if the United States had an unconditional commitment to assist France against any Communist action anywhere; the conflict's limits would have likewise broken down had the United States irrevocably denied, withdrawn, or been manifestly unable to implement, a *de facto* guarantee of France against massive participation of Communist China.

A commitment intermediate between the two extremes, which was roughly the American one in the Indochinese crisis, aims deliberately at limiting a conflict. In its classic form, designed to limit the number of participants, it was described earlier as the guarantee against coalitions, or alternately, against two or more powers. As long as the ally's adversary receives no greater support, the guarantee stipulates benevolent neutrality and may entail non-belligerent assistance short of coalition support. In contemporary conditions, the guarantee can be adjusted to restrain all kinds of additions of superior power on the part of the ally's adversary, such as massive assistance with volunteers and matériel and the use of mass-destruction weapons on the territory of the guaranteed party. The commitment can be unilateral or bilaterally or multilaterally mutual, depending on which form makes performance more certain when it is necessary and less likely to become necessary in the conditions of the relevant area.

The main object is to insure approximate balance between belligerents. Therefore, the commitment to offset expansion of adversary resources will be most efficacious when the chief guarantor fulfills the conditions of successful deterrence by an outside party in a conflict of two.

What are these conditions? One is that the guarantor must be strong and determined, but also selfless and discreet. That is, he must be able to deny to the other side any advantage from enlarging the conflict and must be committed to limiting the conflict without specific gains for himself. Russia served Prussia well in all these respects, and her partial alert effectively pinned down Austro-Hungarian forces. By comparison, the series of American semi-alerts in 1960 and 1961 was less successful in stemming the more-than-equalizing Soviet assistance to the "rebels" in Laos. Public warnings to the target-state are especially fruitless when they are accompanied by propitiatory diplomatic activity in private—such as Britain's on behalf of the United States in the just-mentioned contingency.

Another condition is that the guarantor be free, in two

ways. One is practical only in a relatively flexible multipolar system. It means that the party to a guarantee against the expansion of conflict by coalition or analogous means should steer clear of more exacting commitments, such as assistance against any one aggressor. A commitment to immediate assistance presumably induces equivalent advance assistance to the aggressor himself; moreover the two types of commitment are potentially incompatible. The second, more immediately relevant, way for the guarantor to be free concerns his ability to use his military capability on behalf of the ally, if not necessarily on his side. The forces to underwrite such a commitment would have to be kept in readiness and include small-scale forces for limited conflicts as well as strategic nuclear forces, though not necessarily big conventional forces.[13] On the other hand, the formula rules out intimate advance integration of allied forces, which might be desirable if the commitment provided for instant assistance.

Let us look again at the Indochinese war. It can be said that the United States stood in a relatively selfless and discreet *de facto* alliance with France to guarantee her against an overtly belligerent Sino-Vietminh coalition. On the other hand, the United States was deficient in the requirement of freedom. In terms of commitment, as a defensive ally of France against Communism in Europe, the United States was not quite free to withhold from France all forms of support in the colonial war, or to make support absolutely conditional on an early grant of independence to the Indochinese states. As regards military capabilities, the United States could threaten massive retaliation in the event of a significant increase in the scope of Chinese intervention; but America did not have the capability to match Chinese involvement on all levels. For military and political reasons,

---

[13] The guarantee formula commended itself in the late nineteenth century as a means of avoiding the need for constant readiness of mass armies. J. Y. Simpson, *The Saburov Memoirs, or Bismarck and Russia* (1929), pp. 55–56.

the United States was unwilling to expand its economic and military assistance to the point of intervening directly. Still, the possibility that it might reverse itself and intervene against an all-out Communist drive must have been a factor in the decision of the Communists to limit their objectives and agree to terminate the war while they were winning.

Britain refused to participate in a "united action" in Indochina before sounding out the Communist powers on a settlement. Her attitude illustrates another restraint which, in a radical form, can go beyond denial of support. In 1871, some Russians would have switched the use of Russia's reserve power—from deterring a coalition against Prussia to restraining unified Germany—when German claims on vanquished France threatened the European balance. In a case like this, the stabilizer no longer restrains the side hostile to his ally by the threat of adding his resources to the conflict. By denying his power to the ally he strengthens the adversary's posture in diplomacy; and in principle he might commit his power to either side on the battlefield depending on which party's unreasonable demands frustrate the limitation of the conflict.

Restraints among Allies

In themselves, alliances neither limit nor expand conflicts any more than they cause or prevent them. As just discussed, modes of integration and commitment can help restrain both the adversary and the scope of conflict. And they can help allies restrain each other.

This is not to say that the economy of integration and commitment can concern itself only with maximizing interallied restraints and restricting the scope of conflicts. Allies grappling with a particular challenge do not welcome restraint by those from whom they expect support. Tolerance for restraint will be least when allies try to prevent each other's effective action for fear of the adversary's (or third powers') reaction. The cost of such restraints can be particularly high, when the adversary's strategy is to break up or erode an alliance, rather than fight it. When restraints are unequally distributed within and between alliance systems, international stability, too, can be impaired. One major source of such derangement is dogmatic interest in alliance, placing the alliance's preservation over all other considerations.

A dogmatic interest in alliance is qualitatively different from the particular interests which an alliance is to serve. When the two kinds of interest become too uncertainly related, the discrepancy between the alliance's outward front and its inner reality grows. This will annul in practice much of the predictability and stability which alliances introduce into international relations in principle—by identifying friend and enemy, specifying conditions of assistance, and roughly predetermining the relationship of forces in the early stages of a conflict. The derangement is still more acute, when only some allies develop strong interest in alliance as such. Any such inequality will vitiate a basic precondition of sound restraints—mutual, rather than unilateral, sense and acknowledgment of need; and it will interfere with the principal mechanism of restraint—the ability to withhold and recommit needed support.

Alignment itself may be subject to withholding; but particular forms of co-operation can also supply effective leverage. For restraint to be effective, the moderator must be trusted to seek neither disengagement nor gains for himself; but he must also be suspect of defaulting or deserting should his counsel be ignored. To gloss over the implied sanction, the restraining ally may match it with manifest compensation for the denial of support—no longer in territory, perhaps, but in other forms of material reward or in the form of intensified commitment for the future.

For full effect, restraints need time in which to be exerted.

The prevailing military technology and strategic concept may allow a leisurely unfolding of a crisis. Or they may put a premium on surprise and on acting first, with irreversible consequences. Such was the case in 1914, due to the presumed advantage of a mobilize-first strategy to expedite supposedly decisive pre-emptive strikes by the different contestants via Belgium, East Prussia, or Alsace, and due to the presumed impossibility to recall mobilization once it was started. The nuclear-weapons environment seemed to create similarly unfavorable conditions for interallied restraints in a crisis. Decreasing confidence in the decisive efficacy of a pre-emptive first strike has halted the trend, however. Once the advantage of surprise ceases to be manifestly decisive, delays for warning, negotiation, and renegotiation become possible.[14]

The requirement next to time is that of means. It concerns the existence of reserves in the international system. The urge to permit and back an ally's action "now or never" is less when an ally can be replaced by another state, or when the adversary's material advance can be counterbalanced with the developing resources of other states. The availability of alternatives enhances the ability to restrain; and alternatives themselves multiply with the increase in the number of relatively independent centers of power. Germany's will and capacity to restrain Austria-Hungary declined with the German statesmen's ability to stem the drift from multipolarity to virtual bipolarity, paralleling the shift of alliance-making intelligence from Berlin to Paris. Bipolarity reduces the scope for interallied restraints, especially on the part of a relatively declining power with self-assertive or apparently irreplaceable allies. To continue the parallel with 1914, it is a moot question whether the United States is now somewhat in Germany's position then, facing a Russia apparently favored by a shifting balance of prospective capabilities. But in any event Western Europe has not proved

[14] Kahn, *On Thermonuclear War*, p. 174 and *passim*.

to be America's Austria-Hungary after all, although a healthy ally can be as hard to restrain as a sick one if for different reasons. And there is now a lively sense of new powers emerging in the world at large.

In the age of nuclear weapons, the superpowers still need lesser allies; there is no fundamentally new balance of reciprocal need and, consequently, influence. The loss of even a small ally may be more painful in a nuclear situation than in a conventional one, despite the ally's insignificance in nuclear terms. For the core-power to lose such an ally may mean diminished capability to fight non-nuclear wars successfully; and the loss constitutes a political defeat which cannot be easily redressed by military or other counteraction. Moreover, nuclear weapons have multilateralized the international system in diplomacy; and they may do so in terms of effective power as lesser states acquire passive deterrents—to attacks on their own territory—and as the superpowers divert stalemated competition to the material build-up of lesser states.

Even pending substantial multilateralization, though, lesser states have been known to exert substantial restraints over greater powers in a bipolar context. This happens when no vital interests of a superpower or core-alliance are at stake or can be asserted, and the activated segment of a bipolar system acquires multipolar characteristics as a result. The diplomatic influence of lesser states, including allies, rises as they exploit the open embarrassment of the embroiled major powers. They can speak up and act for the powers' hidden desire to call off a stalemated test of strength; and they can help save the face of the contestants by acting themselves as conveyors of the adversaries' pressure on each other. In a limited conflict, the lesser states can even pose as armed mediators when they dispose of enough total military strength to balance the partial, limited resources which the superpowers can detail to the local conflict. Even the losing belligerent can accept limitation when he can expect that undue exploitation of gains by the adversary will set off a reaction in the *ad hoc* multipolar system.

One can compare in this regard the Korean War in the 1950's and the Crimean War of the 1850's. Both remained limited in committed resources, area of operations, and political objectives. In a situation which became quasi-multipolar for the purpose of the conflict, the United States was restrained, among other things, by the fear of exposing its allies in Europe and alienating the non-aligned countries of Asia. In the globally multipolar situation of mid-nineteenth century, the war aims of England and France had been kept limited by the desire to add Austria to their side, first as conditional ally and then as actual co-belligerent against Russia. To push the analogy further, while Napoleon III and some British statesmen, notably Lord John Russell, were, like the Truman administration a century later, primarily concerned with the global implications of the conflict for alliance policy, the first concern of the British Foreign Secretary, Lord Clarendon, like that of General MacArthur, was with military success as a precondition to effective negotiations and formulation of war aims. Whereas Clarendon sought to preserve the Crimean coalition while dictating its strategy, MacArthur was ready to act alone rather than accept policy dictation by weaker allies in the name of alliance unity.[15]

MacArthur's position was more consistent, and a valid one for a powerful state in a fundamentally bipolar situation. There very well may be a point at which the major ally should turn the tables on the lesser partners and confront *them* with the prospect of isolation from the indispensable protector.

The most direct basis for restraint is an explicit stipulation

---

[15] On the Korean War, see J. W. Spanier, *The Truman-MacArthur Controversy and the Korean War* (1959), esp. pp. 266–67. On the Crimean War, see the essays "The Eclipse of Lord John Russell," "The Diplomatic Revolution of 1854," and "The Two Interpretations of the Four Points, December 1854," in G. B. Henderson, *Crimean War Diplomacy and Other Historical Essays* (1947), and the other sources cited above, n. 28, Chap. I.

in treaty. Provisions for prior consultations before going to war have been as common in treaties as were provisos against separate peace once hostilities were on. There are other possible clauses. The membership of West Germany in NATO and in the Western European Union, for instance, was subject to various limiting stipulations and understandings. For other reasons, the Manila Treaty setting up SEATO required explicit invitation by the governments of South Vietnam, Cambodia, and Laos before the allies could intervene in their favor. The clause was introduced into the pact at British insistence;[16] it may have been intended to appease India, deflate charges of neo-colonialism against the treaty, and equip both wards and allies with a basis for restraining too eager American interventions, should they be forthcoming. In the 1930's, when Britain was the leading ally, her government employed a somewhat different formula for a similar purpose against another feared interventionist. It insisted that Soviet assistance to Czechoslovakia be conditional on prior assistance by another ally of Czechoslovakia, France, who was highly unlikely to act without prior British approval.

In the absence of explicit stipulations, forms of integration matter even more. As a rule, a low level of integration is apt to enhance the freedom of all, including the least powerful, allies to deny active or passive co-operation—as well as to accept or refuse assistance. But allies may be able to use factors *of* integration—rather than freedom *from* integration —to exert restraint and impose limitations.

An example between roughly equal allies is the French-made distinction between "forward areas" of NATO and the "rear area." According to this idea, only forces in the forward area, including all West Germany, should be integrated for effective defense; forces in the rear area, including France, should remain under national responsibility.[17] The main reason for making the distinction between "forward"

[16] Art. IV (3), R.I.I.A., *Collective Defence in South-East Asia*, p. 14.
[17] See *New York Times*, October 11, 1960, pp. 1, 3.

and "rear" areas was to justify to Bonn the exclusion of most French forces from NATO integration. But the distinction also served the purpose of selective integration, as a means of restraining a forward Germany. The purpose was further promoted by locating West German supply and training bases in the French "rear area" rather than in the uncontrolled Spanish hinterland. The arrangement was believed to make it virtually impossible for the Germans "to embark on a military venture not sanctioned by France and other allies in the North Atlantic Treaty." [18]

More commonly in contemporary conditions, "foreign bases" offer an opportunity for restraint by lesser allies over major ones. A host country may impose a ceiling on the kinds of forces and resources which an ally can deploy from a base, as a means of restraining the ally and limiting the conflict. Or, for fear of retaliation by the adversary, the host country may deny the use of a facility completely. This may remove the host country from the number of passive participants in a conflict and may even confine the theater of operations; it is more doubtful that such a veto would help limit the kind of weapons used and objectives pursued. Foreign bases have become primarily useful as means for deterring and fighting limited wars in adjacent areas. The denial of their use by a lesser ally might therefore only compel a major belligerent to resort to more powerful, longer-range weapons from remoter bases, notably if the denial of use was unexpected and the restrained ally had to fight or forfeit prestige in the region. A suddenly denounced integration must give way to improvisation, for which there may have been little previously fostered capacity. It is probably safer, therefore, for a power like the United States, remote from likely areas of conflict, to concert in advance the exclusion of bases from use in particular circumstances than to have an ally require the right of prior consent in an emergency.

The terms under which a power can use bases in other

[18] *Ibid.,* October 26, 1960, p. 11.

countries must conform to the prevailing technological conditions of weapon's range and mobility, to the political conditions of the greater power's commitment, and to local tolerance for its presence. Three main types of foreign bases may perhaps be distinguished: integral; contingent; and potential bases.

A base is "integral" when it can be used both for local defense and for strategic deterrence and retaliation. The typical location for an integral United States base is on American or American-controlled territory and on the territory of highly reliable and co-operative allies. By contrast, a "contingent" base is one which may be used only for the defense of the host country and, possibly, an adjacent ally or non-aligned country. To the extent that a strict separation is possible, the range of locally stationed weaponry and the terms of joint control must insure that local facilities would not be used for deterring or punishing an attack on the national territory of the major ally, i.e., the United States. And finally, a "potential" base would comprise essential facilities for land, naval, and air operations, without harboring any United States personnel and United States controlled matériel prior to actual intervention. Such facilities might be located even on the territory of formally non-aligned states, without infringing upon their status; the power which had built the facilities—or another power—could use them only at the invitation of the local government.

The range of base forms corresponds to a policy of graduating the major power's commitment in support of differently oriented and situated states. The different kinds of bases would be linked together by the mobility of the major power's resources; they would, moreover, fit a sensitive political climate by permitting transmission of locally tolerable forms of military power in differing conditions.

When they tolerate them at all, host countries will demand ever greater control over the use of bases and facilities on their territory. As the risks of provocation grow, the influx of assets into the domestic economy as a result of foreign presence weighs less in the scales. Pressures from and on the government of Japan when renegotiating the American security treaty have been matched by the pressure of the Labour opposition (or Conservative right-wing opinion) on the British government, by the posture of the de Gaulle government in France, and by the attitude of most or all new nations toward American or French and British bases.[19] The mixture of concern with security, status, and domestic stability may be slightly different in each case; underlying all is the desire not to become a lightning rod or to serve as mere real estate.

The concern of host countries is legitimate; but too exacting controls can only reduce the major ally's ability to help protect his partners. The modest feasibility and credibility of active deterrence is not increased when lesser allies insist on the right of "veto" or "decision" regarding retaliation, or when they demand the right to veto provocative reconnaissance of enemy targets and dispositions from their territory. Too restrictive allies may not only hamstring their own defense by the major ally; they may encourage his eventual withdrawal into a less confining strategy.

In seeking too much control against separate provocation of war, lesser allies may furthermore help realize their still greater fears: separate understandings between the major contestants. The irony is compounded by the fact that a

[19] The requirement of consent constitutes political control over bases; outright physical control as well may have to be conceded in touchy conditions. See H. W. Baldwin, "Kremlin Cloud Over Our Bases," *New York Times Magazine,* October 9, 1960, p. 107. General de Gaulle would go beyond "consent" to the use of nuclear weapons anywhere and claim the right of "decision" when nuclear weapons were to be launched from the French soil. If consent means "veto," it is tantamount to decision when preventing action, although it cannot compel action. See *New York Times,* October 8, 1960, p. 1, for de Gaulle's pronouncement; and *ibid.,* October 26, 1960, p. 1, and December 2, 1960, p. 5, respectively, on the Labour party's concern over the government's right of "veto" over United States reconnaissance flights from British bases and the Conservative right-wingers' opposition to the stationing of United States fleet ballistic missile submarines in Holy Loch in Scotland.

lesser ally may embrace the chief precaution against such danger—the development of an independent national capability—in order to withdraw himself from the kind of interallied controls he seeks in relation to the more powerful ally.

Negotiations between Alliances

Outright defection by an important ally is an unlikely occurrence in merely political warfare. The adversaries' strategies aim at eliciting from members of the opposing alliance mainly token acts of abated solidarity. Allies are never immune to fears of separate deals as a result of separate negotiations by others. Separate or not, negotiations in themselves tend to be disintegrative. In wartime, negotiations bear on the conclusion of peace as a preliminary to new configurations; and in peacetime they aim at removing or controlling sources and instruments of the very conflict that inspired partners to join and stay together. Whether in war or peace, negotiations aim at a barter of the military power of parties against alternative forms of security in settlements which, ideally, would leave no party so dependent on another party as to deprive it of the freedom of alignment in the future.

A truly negotiated settlement entails concessions and compromise. It is the golden age of negotiations when demands and concessions are made and traded while the test of arms is readily available, is still going on, or can be resumed by all parties. In our time, the Korean truce negotiations were of this kind, as were the negotiations over the first Berlin crisis in the late 1940's. In the absence of credible employment or threat of force, demands are part of a war of nerves and concessions are made with reference to the deity of neutral opinion rather than the fortunes of war. They are correspondingly unreal. Disarmed diplomacy merges with disarmament diplomacy when territorial and political demands and concessions are made, stepped up, or withheld in the hope that sooner or later one side or the other will prove to need a reprieve in the arms race. It might then be willing to "give"—that is, reduce its demands and increase its concessions—in the political and territorial sphere also. The same may be true the other way round, should a deliberately intensified political crisis make one side more pliable in negotiations over reduction and control of armaments.

As regards armaments themselves, their disposition induces concessions and compromise when adversaries reach two main conclusions: first, that the deployment of one's military force in peacetime both deters the use of force by the adversary and attracts adversary force into a countervailing array for a like pacific purpose; and second, that the amassing of military force cannot pressure the adversary combination into retreat or dislocation in one-sided, unilateral concessions. Serious negotiations and *bona fide* settlements are often foiled by the fact that especially the second conclusion is reached by adversary sides at different times.

Attitudes are easiest to synchronize when readiness to negotiate depends on third-party pressures; harder, when it depends on success in war, in an arms race, or in political warfare; and hardest, when, in addition, the adversary parties are associations of allies. The very pluralism of alliances hampers each ally in freely disposing of his part of interdependent military power in the barter for settlements; and it restricts the gains which the adversary can expect to make as long as allies successfully assert a stake in each other's security and integrity. Moreover, members of an alliance tend to be divided over when to negotiate and how much to demand or concede. The division may coincide with that between acquisitive allies, with ambitions to satisfy, and satisfied allies, with disputed possessions to confirm. Or, hardness and softness may be merely tactical devices to hamper or accelerate negotiations, so that a government may negotiate from the strongest possible international position or strengthen its domestic position by international negotiations.

Divisions between allies who are ready for serious negotiations and those who are not are among the causes of subalignments within an alliance. Disagreements over negotiating strategies aggravate quandaries peculiar to all negotiations. There is, to start with, the question of sequence in which to raise and try to resolve issues. On the one hand, a power may desire to show loyalty to an ally most interested in an issue and place the issue highest on the agenda; on the other hand, it will fear losing the ally's support once the issue has been decided to his satisfaction—or dissatisfaction. This problem used to be paramount in the procedural wrangles of classic diplomacy. It is, possibly, less delicate for the Western side in cold-war negotiations, when interconnected issues only reflect a deep-seated antagonism shared by all allies and the adversary himself tends to determine the sequence in which the issues become critical. Still, the matter of sequence survives in questions such as: what first, "disarmament" or a political, and specifically German, settlement? It is apt to reappear in serious negotiations and then may or may not be eased by the related quandary: whether to enlarge or limit the scope of negotiations, and whether to try to settle issues piecemeal or only in a grand over-all settlement.

Neither procedure is, however, likely to dispose of a central dilemma: that of the first serious offer or proposal. Always grave on grounds of prestige and tactics, the dilemma is doubly grave if a serious proposal entails some weakening in the commitment or capability to implement a commitment to one or more allies. The requirements of interallied cohesion are then at variance with those of efficacious negotiations. And not infrequently, as the positions of allies are brought closer together on substance and strategy, the position of the alliance as a whole moves away from that of the adversary. The concentration of parts entails polarization of the whole.

Such inhibitions are not decisive when negotiations unfold alongside more material contests, whose outcome is not yet conclusive in the eyes of one or both parties. The inhibitions of alliance may then be positively beneficial. They remove from any one contestant the odium of blocking a negotiated settlement while merely pretending to negotiate in order to distract the opponent. They may even gradually promote between adversaries with serious interest in negotiated adjustments a sense of affinity based on impatience with unaccommodating allies.

The potentially disintegrative effect of negotiations on alliances will make allies wish to retain an independent military capability for all contingencies. Despite appearances to the contrary, this may still be true in both extreme conditions: when fruitful negotiations and long-term settlements between East and West are impossible, and when they become possible in fact or in appearance.

Fruitful negotiations are impossible when, against the background of unimaginable total war, they bear on intrinsically insoluble isolated issues. Plausible arguments can then be marshalled for and against a number of strategies and solutions; the presumption is consequently in favor of immobility covered up with feverish diplomatic activity. Moreover, the form and style of diplomatic action become more immediately significant than its substance; in fact, form becomes substance, and style becomes strategy. The terms of a provisional *modus vivendi* may matter less than do the conditions set for attempting it and the circumstances of reaching it. The more formal the negotiating style, the greater the gap between the consequences of a miscalculation and the apparently petty formalism of method. The more informal the style, however, the greater is the danger that the initial gap between the adversaries' positions will be closed by concessions to the more aggressive, demanding party.

In traditional diplomacy, much of the art consisted in making the other side commit itself first. Negotiators were commonly instructed to maneuver their opposite numbers into stating demands or making offers which the instructing sovereign desired but did not wish to formulate himself in the form of demands. Various tricks of the trade can be used to achieve this. The main one is for negotiators to simulate interest in a solution other than the actually desired one; like oarsmen, they must turn their back on the goal in order to reach it faster. It was considered poor negotiating tactics to speak before knowing the opponent's mind or before knowing him to be ready to yield. To speak too soon might supply weapons to the opponent with which to attack one's carefully protected reputation for loyalty, restraint, and will to peace in the minds of third parties. It also meant committing the prestige of the sovereign, and having to back it with undesired initiatives in the face of unexpected resistance.

Contrary to this canon of diplomacy, advantage now goes apparently to him who commits himself first: in propaganda, by making a spectacular offer; in serious diplomatic business, by making a new demand. To make a demand is to engage one's face; since neither side wants war, the opposite side has reason to help the demanding party disengage itself from his self-created predicament. It has reason to make concessions, in other words, and may expect some help from the demanding party in making them.

The play can be quite elaborate. Twice in succession, the Soviets attached a time limit to their demand for a change in the status of West Berlin in order to dramatize their public commitment; they apparently had to act unless the West gave them some satisfaction. When the psychological impact of a war scare had been registered, however, the Soviet leader himself helped the West to help him; he allowed the start in negotiations to suspend the time-limit. This safeguarded the prestige of the West after its agreement to negotiate legitimized the Soviet grievance, and its apparent readiness to make "binding" counterproposals and tolerate *faits accomplis* insured the Soviets' "vital interests." Assuming that the Soviets did not expect to get all they asked for, or get it at once, they could expect to get a satisfactory compromise settlement by pretending to turn their back on it.

What is the assumption behind the tactic? Both sides fear-ing a clash, the more reasonable side is expected to give way to the more forward party. The simile is brought up to date if the oarsman becomes a reckless taxicab driver having his way regardless of the right of way. But the simile so stated is incomplete. When the situation is serious, the professional driver is only apparently reckless: he relies on his superior skill to slow down or swerve when the gentleman driver refuses to be cowed; moreover, he is covered by insurance against the consequences of miscalculation. Both parties to the East-West conflict fear violent clash; it is fatal for the more cautious party to pass up opportunities for demonstrating that it is no more fearful than the other side. When the demonstration is convincing, the question of prestige, or face, remains a crucial one but ceases to work to the advantage of the more forward party only. Both sides are compelled to examine whose prestige is more seriously jeopardized in a particular case.

Rather than reverse a traditional diplomatic precept about negotiations, one might supplement the theory of military deterrence. The way to deter unilateral demands for changes in the *status quo* is to commit oneself in advance to diplomatic inaction rather than counteraction, to refuse to respond at all rather than respond massively. To decline to negotiate before the day after a time limit has expired or refuse to take up any newly generated issue pending adjustment of old ones is a policy in itself under such circumstances. The policy's proponent need not—as he would have to in normal circumstances—propose at the same time a substantive policy for dealing with the consequences of his formal policy. He does not have to say what he would do if the demanding side acts in response to his procedural intransigence, on the assumption that the reaction would be so designed as not to force the conservative side into physical conflict.

Close military integration necessitates a concerted negotiating strategy for the alliance as a whole, without guaranteeing it. Integration inhibits the most resolute members materially and morally, when a firm negotiating stance might involve also the dissenting allies in possible military consequences. On the other hand, integration strengthens politically the ally resisting negotiations. The material and moral inhibitions will hamper the major ally when he is the one who takes a hard line; the political aspect will tend to make any ally obstructing negotiations into the *ad hoc* leader of the alliance. This may not be a bad thing in a particular case; it is not, however, a desirable norm for interallied relations in general.

Some independent military capability may also favor the opposite of negotiations over intrinsically "insoluble" isolated issues, such as the German question in its various aspects. These are negotiations for mutually desirable overall settlements. The dialectic of such negotiations is exemplified in the diplomatic activities which terminated protracted conflicts in the past. In concluding the Thirty Years' War and the Napoleonic wars, as well as many lesser and shorter ones, broadly acceptable settlements were advanced by individual allies moving to avert, anticipate, or rally to, their partners' separate understandings with the adversaries. The resulting untidy scramble may be a sorry model; but it often proved to be structurally superior to the stately progression of two perfectly co-ordinated alliances toward a common ground on which allies remain allies and adversaries cease to be enemies. The pattern is not unlike that of progress toward greater intra-alliance cohesion and integration, wrested from responses to the unilateralism of particular allies. Maintenance of cohesion, or advance in integration, may actually require prior assurance, by individual soundings of the adversary, that they continue to be necessary; and individual explorations are relatively harmless and may be profitable so long as they remain within the limits of the allies' essential loyalty to each other's vital interests.

The procedurally first question in separate negotiations is, "with whom?" As already noted in the discussion of separate peace, the choice of the partner is opportunistic and depends on the relation of success and failure, winning and losing, in minor or hegemonic contests. In a stalemated cold war in which neither of the major contestants is sufficiently triumphant to set off a stampede, the choice of a partner depends on the objective.

The objective may be primarily tactical, to weaken the counter-alliance. The most promising target of such an approach is the ally who constitutes a weak link in the adversary combination: sufficiently well placed strategically to be worth buying off and sufficiently vulnerable or dissatisfied to be receptive. Perhaps as part of a tactic to condition the United States for serious bilateral negotiations in due course, the Soviets have in the past given encouragement to a few lesser allies without really testing their allegiance to the Western alliance. They have experimented alternately with Britain, playing on her fear of war, and France, playing on her jealousy of Britain, fear of Germany, and colonial embarrassments. The French may have received somewhat favored treatment in Indochina and Algeria in return for (or coincidentally with) their thwarting the European Defense Community, stalling on the Western European Union, and impeding the integration of NATO. On the other hand, despite occasional baits, the Soviets have not so far substantiated the hopes (and fears) of those who visualize West Germany's negotiating her NATO membership for a separately agreed upon reunification.[20]

When negotiations are meant to be serious and lead to a major settlement, however, the logical partners are the strongest members of the adversary alliances.

A strong ally, for this purpose, is one who possesses a crucial asset, who can carry with him the lesser allies, and

[20] See R. J. Guiton, *Paris-Moskau: die Sowjetunion in der auswärtigen Politik Frankreichs seit dem zweiten Weltkrieg* (1956), pp. 257–60; F. R. Alleman, *Bonn ist nicht Weimar* (1956), p. 230; and on a Soviet approach to West Germany, *New York Times*, May 8, 1961, p. 1.

who, possibly, can enhance the status of the adversary by negotiating and settling with him in an exclusive transaction. The bonus of confirmed status may be a decisive inducement for a rising, upstart regime and for a nation that has an ambivalent attitude toward the more prestigious adversary. The alternative to reducing a half-envied, half-admired adversary to equality or less by conquest in war is to gain equality by way of an intimate agreement with him. The upstart Emperor of the French harbored such ambivalent feelings toward the Tsar of all Russias; ascendant Germany toward Great Britain; and rising Japan toward the United States. In the current struggle, the leaders of Soviet Russia have been obsessed with catching up with America one way or another. Missiles and industrial capacity may have taken the place of dynastic lineage, navies, and colonial possessions as the indices of status and objects of competition; but "alliance" consummating a division of spheres has persisted as a remote (and rarely feasible) alternative to military conflict which might prove profitable only for others.

For a power with assured prestige, material conditions are not only decisive but solely determining. When, in the protracted negotiations over a peaceful division of the so-called Spanish succession, Louis XIV gave up negotiating with his peer in both claim and status, the Habsburg Emperor, and shifted to William III of England, the French king was not concerned with status. He had enough of it to impart some to the half-legitimate new negotiating partner. The grand monarch's deliberate choice was determined by William's greater ability to rally the other members of the anti-French Grand Alliance to the settlement, if only by withholding from them the vital asset of Anglo-Dutch monies and navies.[21]

[21] A convenient survey of the great negotiations may be found in H. Reynal, *Succession d'Espagne* (2 vols., 1883). For more detail, see F. A. Mignet, *Négociations relatives à la succession d'Espagne sous Louis XIV* (4 vols., 1835–42); A. Legrelle, *La diplomatie française et la succession d'Espagne* (4 vols., 1888–92).

In contemporary relations, the vital asset is substantial nuclear capability under national control. The more manifest the capability, the more muted one's moves can be in the realm of separate negotiations. Neither allies nor adversaries can forget one's existence in their diplomacy any more than in their military strategy. It is, therefore, not surprising that fear of American negotiations with the Soviet Union has been an important reason and rationale for the development of independent nuclear deterrents, discreetly on the part of the British, vocally on the part of the French. The French were unsure of only one thing: whether to fear more lest France and Europe be crushed physically by the two nuclear superpowers sparing each other's homeland in a kind of particular peace in the midst of a nuclear war, or to fear more lest they be maimed politically by a separate agreement between the two superpowers united in dividing the world to avoid destroying each other.[22]

It is immaterial that such fears may have little solid basis and may be self-fulfilling. So far, they can feed on only a few instances of post-World War II Soviet-American diplomacy, notably in the U.N.; on speculations about the effect that even a partial military and political disengagement in Europe would have on the deployment of American forces and resources; on historical precedents of shifting foci of fears and enmities in long-lasting conflicts; and, last but not least, on the inclination of both superpowers to keep their diplomatic hands as well as their nuclear swords free of allied interference in decisive encounters. To lay to rest the fear of a separate "deal" may require interallied pooling of control over the crucial asset. The alternative is for resourceful lesser allies to develop independent nuclear capability, on the assumption that certainty or probability of being able to retaliate outweighs the hypothetical possibility of bring-

[22] Among his many statements, see President de Gaulle's pronouncement at a news conference on November 10, 1959, in *New York Times,* November 11, 1959, and Premier Debré's echo, cited in Buchan, *NATO in the 1960's,* p. 67.

ing about the feared event: a weakening in the major ally's commitment.

In the meantime, national control over a nuclear asset strengthens a country's position in cold-war diplomacy. It increases the likelihood of the country's inclusion and strengthens its voice in serious negotiations. And it increases its ability to frustrate separate negotiations. The major ally is no longer able to guarantee adhesion of dependent allies to a general settlement separately arrived at. This reduces the adversary's willingness to make concessions or to negotiate separately at all; or he may shift to the lesser ally for the purpose of partially pacifying a sector of the contest. The lesser power will be most receptive when a request for support in a crisis has not been met by its allies. We have seen this happen in the seventeenth century, on the part of Savoy; it can happen again over a future Suez. The adversary is more likely to offer agreeable terms when the ally has an independent capacity for either waging separate war or triggering his reluctant allies' capabilities despite themselves. Short of negotiations, a national deterrent makes more credible one's disregard of the enemy's nuclear blackmail in political warfare; and it makes it questionable that one has actually yielded to such blackmail when making concessions. It may be argued that so intangible a gain is more than offset by the fact that blackmail is more likely, or appears to be more legitimate, when its target is in possession of nuclear capability. But, so far at least, Soviet blackmail has been primarily due to a state's membership in the adversary alliance. The alternative to having nuclear capability, and being able to stare down such blackmail, would accordingly be a change in alignment, as a precaution against nuclear blackmail rather than as a result of it.

PART II:
Trends and Policies

Introduction:
The Contemporary International System

TO BE EFFICACIOUS, alliance policy must fit the prevailing environment and the trends perceptible in it. A major feature of such environment is the structure of the state system. The contemporary system is a mixed, bipolar-multipolar, one with respect to different forms of power; and it is tripartite in policy, in function of two dominant conflicts. There is a more than usual interpenetration of domestic and international politics.

Pure bipolarity exists when preponderant material power is concentrated in two core-powers; pure multipolarity obtains when more than two powers are capable of independent military action against any one other power. Immediately following World War II, each of the two superpowers was superior in capability to the sum of both its allies and nonaligned countries. It is more accurate to say today that NATO makes up the Western pole and the Sino-Soviet alliance plus the Warsaw pact make up the Eastern pole. Either of the core-alliances (with or without peripheral allies) is superior in capabilities to the nonaligned countries; the disintegration of either core-alliance would disturb the equilibrium between the two core-powers more profoundly than the adhesion to one of them of all the nonaligned countries. Such extreme developments are unlikely; but implicit assumptions of this kind affect policies to different countries and classes of countries. The question bears, among other things, on kinds of capabilities and on degrees and patterns of polarization.

As regards capability, the contemporary system is a mixed one. In the last resort—represented by strategic nuclear weapons—it is still bipolar. The two-power situation will continue as long as only the Soviet Union and the United States have a major self-sufficient nuclear capability—or can entirely and reliably control the deployment and use of nuclear weaponry distributed among their allies. The stalemate on the nuclear-strategic plane increases the political significance of the second plane, that of diplomatically and militarily more readily usable capabilities—chiefly conventional-military and economic. In that regard, the international system is now finitely multipolar, that is, it consists of a limited number of powers with substantial capability, whose dealignment or realignment would significantly affect the global balance of readily usable power. And finally, strategic-nuclear inhibitions on a free employment of even the usable capabilities heighten the significance of a third plane in the inverted pyramidal structure of world equilibrium. On the broadest but not any more solid plane, the international system is infinitely multipolar in political-diplomatic influence: a great and growing number of states, and groups within states, behave as if they were independent "poles" in the politics of the state system. To sum up, the system is quasi-multipolar in behavior and mixed bipolar-multipolar in the structure of capabilities; the pattern of behavior predominates over the pattern of capabilities whenever a balance neutralizes conflicting capabilities on one or the other level.

The strategic nuclear level is bipolar; the quasi-multipolarity on the political-diplomatic plane is diffuse. Between the two, the multipolar level of usable capabilities is polarized by alliance ties.

The polarization of a multipolar system can be more or less complete, depending on the ratio of aligned and nonaligned states. And it can be more or less tight, neat, and symmetrical. Tightness has to do with the degree to which it is possible for individual powers to dealign and realign without jeopardizing the survival or security of the state, regime, or social value-system; by the same token, tightness is a function of the possibility to force states out of an alliance system without warlike disruption of international stability. Polarization is geopolitically neat when solid blocs of adjacent states confront each other. When treaty ties create groupings of states that outflank and encircle one another, the pattern is not neat; it is symmetrical, however, if both groupings do the outflanking (or none does in a "neat" pattern), asymmetrical if only one of them does. In the contemporary system, the tightness of polarization has tended to diminish up to a fairly definite point determined by intra-alliance coercion or inter-alliance hostility and deterrence; and a hitherto asymmetrical geopolitical pattern has shown a potential for evolving toward the symmetry of two solid core-blocs, each outflanking or "encircling" the other through its peripheral members.

As patently usable economic and military capabilities became more widely dispersed and diplomatic influence was diffused without apparent limits, the typical pattern of policy became tripartite. There tend to be three parties to any conflict or situation: two directly involved principals and a third merely interested party, to whom the principals may or may not explicitly accord the right of interference. The third party may be interested as a potential sufferer from a conflict between the adversaries; in such a case, its typical role will be that of a moderator. Or the third party might be interested as a potential beneficiary of a split between allied and other powers; in such a case its typical role would be that of abettor. In a tripartite system, principals must forego satisfaction in the basic, bilateral relationship if the satisfaction would entail alienating a third-party neutral or friendly power, or if it would mean pleasing an unfriendly one too much. By contrast, in a strictly bipartite relationship between adversaries, between allies, or between an ally and a neutral, third parties are eyewitnesses without the power to sway actors one way or another.

If and when nuclear weaponry is diffused into the possession of ever more countries, tripartism will increasingly affect not only policy but also military strategy. Multilateral, rather than mutual, deterrence will then constrain extreme behavior in a system which will have become multipolar also on the strategic-nuclear plane. Inequality in the nuclear capabilities of greater and lesser states will accentuate their division into two tiers, likely to modify, if not cut across, the then existing polarization due to formal alignment and non-alignment.

In an interdependent system, tripartism is more common than bipartism. It is consistent with any structure except hegemonic unipolarity and pure bipolarity, in which two powers tower over all other states. In the two exceptional instances the stronger powers' control over the weaker actors is a relatively direct one, backed by the capacity for coercive sanction; the control is institutionalized in an empire, informal in a hegemonic alliance. In a tripartite system, controls are indirect, reciprocal, and depend on inducement and suasion at least as much as on sanction.

A tripartite system of policy is more likely to obtain in a structure ordered by at least two dominant conflicts. The postwar international system has witnessed the gradual rise of a second major conflict, as the demand for economic progress and political independence in new nations has grown and evolved concurrently with the nuclear stalemate between the two industrial giants. The two conflicts or issues have elements of identity; they interpenetrate in the politics of cold war; and they carry in them the seeds of rivalry over which is the truly dominant one.

As for the element of identity, both conflicts are originally domestic in their concern with the institutional forms of individual and collective welfare and freedom. The older confrontation of Liberal Capitalism with Marxian Socialism has long since lost its mystique to the domestic and international politics of the East-West contest. The South-North conflict is more recent and less sharply drawn ideologically; it retains more of its essentially domestic character. The two global issues interpenetrate in practice as the stalemated powers seek decision in the East-West conflict by methods peculiar to the South-North issue: competitive economic growth for themselves, and competitive support for the economic development of the less advanced countries. In (for them) favorable conditions, the countries of the South play the superpowers against each other and stay more or less aloof from both. It is often the superpowers that seek to move closer to the lesser countries if only to capitalize on their competitive investments of effort and treasure, which tend to cancel each other out in terms of political influence. In so doing, the superpowers foster the misleading impression of subscribing to the Southern concept of the dominant issue of the day.

The latent controversy over which global issue is *the* dominant one has been obscured so far. The North lacks a separate identity as a fourth pole; it consists of the industrial nations of both East and West, and these seek varyingly to identify themselves with the South for some purposes. But the North as a political entity might disintegrate any time into its component parts if peaceful coexistence of East and West gives way to warlike confrontation, with lessened tolerance for non-alignment of third countries; or, as a remote possibility, the North may be unified in opposition to a too demanding, or reinforced, South. The first development would subordinate the South-North issue to the East-West conflict; the second would do the opposite.

In the meantime, preoccupation with economic and political development has affected another kind of priority. The domestic requirements of the politically less developed countries have been determining their foreign policies and through them international politics, including that of alignment. And as the balance of reciprocal determination shifted against foreign policy primacy, a kind of reciprocal assimilation took place between the methods of international and domestic politics. The politically less integrated countries have tended to conduct domestic politics as a matter of relations among "sovereign" groups with the right of international alliance for use in both peaceful and civil-warlike contests. We are reminded of the right of alliances assured to non-sovereign entities in the Holy Roman Empire by the Peace of Westphalia. Conversely, the developed and powerful countries have set the tone in conducting international politics on the pattern of domestic politics, as they have been forced to look for functional substitutes for a suicidal use of decisive force. Propagandistic overstatement has become a quasi-parliamentary alternative to diplomatic understatement, reducing the credibility of threats and warnings. In an attempt to make ballots do the work of bullets, powers have resorted to quasi-electoral campaigns, advertising both philanthropic intent and scientific and cultural achievement; to voting coalitions in international organizations; to bargaining before "neutral" umpires and against the background of available fatal sanctions; and to judicious allocation of patronage for supporters who have been and still might be brought over to one's side.

In themselves such partisan contests would be futile were they not in some way related to underlying factors of decision. Foremost among these are politico-military capabilities and strategies, which affect a doubtfully stable balance of nuclear power of destruction, and politico-economic capabilities and strategies, which affect an indubitably dynamic equilibrium of economic growth. Especially when politico-military crises subside or embarrass one or the other side, economic growth looms large; it appears then to be *the* successor to territorial aggrandizement serving as yardstick, symbol, and determinant of victory between antagonists and of equality among allies. Although no lesser ally equals either core-power in the level of economic development, many can equal (and some can better) the superpowers in the rate of economic development, while virtually all can match their status as industrially developing countries. Moreover, both core-allies have come to need their economically developed or reconstructed allies to help with foreign-aid activities in non-aligned countries.

The consequence is something of a paradox. Both the United States and the Soviet Union have held their distance or grown militarily stronger relative to their allies since the late 1940's. But both of them have declined in prestige and influence, partly as a result of material assistance to the currently strongest allies—in Western Europe and mainland China.

4
The Dissolution of Alliances

AN INTERNATIONAL system does not maintain a particular structure of alignments indefinitely. Transformations may be deliberately promoted by negotiations or by the build-up of lesser states by larger powers. Alliances break up or, much less frequently, consolidate into new political communities. The ever-present element of the unintended is greatest when alliances facilitate a transformation in the process of preventing another—by allowing new challengers to arise in lieu of the thwarted ones.

Speculation about the contemporary international system opens up two major perspectives: the diffusion of power in another spell of multipolarity; or the repolarization of power as the two alliance systems congeal in closer-knit entities and possibly expand as well. Should it be forced to unite for freedom by external or internal compulsions, the West would have to discount the immediate political effect of such a consolidation on the anti-colonial, non-aligned countries; and diplomacy of maneuver would wane before an intensified contest of achievement and attraction between the polar blocs, punctuated by tests of economic and politico-military strength. In retrospect, the renascent flexibility and multipolarity of the late 1950's and early 1960's would appear as a last fling of nationalism in industrialized countries before the triumph of multinationality in the two industrially developed world systems. Such a development may prove to be the last best hope for the West and for international equilibrium, notably if the Sino-Soviet bloc progresses toward an integrated "supra-society." [1]

This study is concerned primarily with alignments, not with community building. Therefore, discussion in this chapter will enlarge upon tendencies toward break-up and realignment; the succeeding two chapters will deal with challenges to contemporary alliances in the form of neutralism and new power centers, respectively.

Parallels and Differences in East-West Alliances

Despite decline in cohesion and in primacy abroad, the adversary alliance systems remain the key factors in the contemporary international system. They can be compared with respect to the political, economic, and military conditions of cohesion and integration. To correct somewhat the preceding emphasis on the Western system, the following section stresses the Eastern bloc. Its theoretical interest grows whenever the bloc seems to be evolving toward an alliance system in fact as well as in name.

The Stalinist order was at best one of hegemonic alliance; it was typified by direct and coercive, if largely informal and partly self-imposed, political controls over satellite regimes. Increasingly meaningless bilateral treaties of friendship and mutual assistance constituted the formal framework. The order was subject to two main transformations. A formal change occurred when a multilateral Warsaw Pact was placed alongside the bilateral Sino-Soviet alliance. The pact may

[1] Z. K. Brzezinski, "The Organization of the Communist Camp," *World Politics* (January, 1961), p. 209, uses the term "supra-society."

have been meant to counteract the progressing erosion of Soviet controls. A more basic change resulted from the climactic upheavals of 1956. They made out of the bloc a kind of system of states, subject to some of the strains and tensions of an alliance. A major and apparently enduring development was that controls became more indirect and partly reciprocal.[2]

There are both similarities and differences between the Soviet system and other alliance systems, including the Western one. The fundamental difference is probably in the role played by a specific ideology and a single political party in promoting the frankly expansionist objectives of the "socialist system of states." A crucial, if tactically mutable and consequently controversial, aspect of the ideology concerns the outside world and the chief enemy of the moment. The third, non-aligned parties have been alternately identified with the capitalist enemy in a two-camps world view or else treated as actual, potential, or "objective" allies of the socialist camp. Such ideological fluctuations are, on balance, an element of strength in that they alternately intimidate and encourage outsiders. On the other hand, the West may have been better off in two other areas of ideology. For one thing, the recurrent contest over the identity of the Communist system's ideological leader has had no counterpart in the Western alliance, which is less preoccupied with ideological differences and systematization. For another thing, the Sino-Soviet bloc has failed to evolve a specifically socialist ideology of interallied relations which would go beyond references to a "socialist commonwealth" and incipient systems of collective security. On their part, Western allies find it easier to accept, conform to, and institutionally adapt to traditional postulates regarding interdependence and equality of allies and the rights and duties of the alliance leader.

[2] In much of the following section I am adapting to my purpose the salient findings of Brzezinski's *The Soviet Bloc: Unity and Conflict* (1960). See also G. Modelski, *The Communist International System* (Research Monograph No. 9, The Center of International Studies, Princeton University, 1960).

The leadership question is vital for both alliance systems; so is that of status for individual members. As physical coercion moved into the background in the Communist system, contests over formal ranking of its members moved to the fore. The Soviet Union was alternately described as the "center" or the "head" of the socialist camp, its "leading" or merely its "first" state; Communist China ranked alternately as the first ally of the Soviet Union or the prime challenger of its paramountcy in the bloc; and among the lesser countries, Poland saw herself as the second Communist power in Europe and the third one globally. Like that of the United States most of the time, the leadership of the Soviet Union has depended from time to time on the ability to follow lesser partners with a more forceful viewpoint and to balance groups and viewpoints from a position of weakness. The lesser states in the Communist bloc inclined increasingly to respond in kind, by play-off tactics with respect to the two leading powers, Russia and China.

The attitude of Communist China toward the Soviet Union has varied. Sometimes it has resembled that of the United Kingdom toward the United States: acceptance of the major power's leadership as a cover for the first ally's influence in a united alliance. At other times, Mao's China has behaved toward Russia more as de Gaulle's France toward America: she has questioned Soviet leadership and used recalcitrance to satisfy particular grievances and to make the leader embrace courses he did not favor. On the other hand, the lesser Communist allies have been less united in desiring the greatest possible autonomy than are the lesser partners in the Western alliance most of the time on most issues. The internally insecure Communist regimes in particular have opposed attempts by more self-confident regimes to enhance their status by "independent" behavior, following Yugoslavia at least part of the way. In both alliance systems, the status of individual members has reflected somewhat the degree to which they realize the particular system's ideal polity—socialist and communist in the East, liberal-democratic in the West. In both camps the advance toward the ideal has coincided by and large with the degree of industrialization. The major exceptions have been mainland China, with communes in advance of industrial progress, and West Germany, with industrial progress in advance of proven liberal-democratic tradition.

After Stalin, the Soviet bloc discovered consultations as a means of adjusting the demands and grievances of allies. It is rather commonly assumed that lesser states always prefer multilateral arrangements. Actually, preference for bilateral dealings with a much stronger power is not uncommon. A lesser state, Communist or non-Communist, may wish to get a special deal from the great-power ally and prefer the status of the unequal but distinct partner to that of being absorbed in an apparently equalizing multilateral mass. In the Soviet bloc the most ardent advocate of post-Stalinist bilateralism was anti-Stalinist Gomulka. The Polish leader feared being both absorbed and isolated in an anti-revisionist majority of satellite states, which might legitimize Soviet pressure by the myth of democratic centralism—the Leninist form of controlled consensus. By contrast, the Soviet leadership has developed a new preference for multilateralism. Stalin's bilateralism isolated the satellites from each other and subjected them separately to Soviet hegemony; the new multilateralism would isolate merely the deviant or recalcitrant members, such as Poland and China, and confront them with a "democratic" majority grouped around the Soviet Union.

As long as a preponderant Soviet Union remains able to control the votes of most small-state allies, it will couple multilateralism with lipservice to equality, while China's lipservice to Soviet leadership will continue to aim at Chinese co-determination. The Western alliance is not substantially different in this respect. Only when a leading ally cannot count on support or sympathy in a multilateral conclave, will he incline to unilateral or bilateral action. Unilateralism tempts most when national capability is equal to a challenge, and allies rate the challenge unequally. Being committed to seek consent, the United States faced the problem most acutely following the military successes of the American-controlled U.N. command in Korea and the military failure of the American-sponsored invasion of Cuba. Bilateralism is attractive to a leading ally when he can effectively coerce or when he must hope to persuade his partners one by one. To be defeated in the more informal and private bilateral negotiations is less fatal to leadership than to lose both case and face in a multilateral conference. When the Soviets negotiated with the Yugoslavs for political support, and the Americans with the Germans for financial support, both core-powers preferred a *tête-à-tête*.

From occasional transactions there is only a step to subalignments within an alliance system. To date, intra-bloc politics have brought the Soviet leadership into spells of tactical alliance with Tito against Stalinist and Maoist forces; Yugoslavia was treated as part of the system of socialist states, though not of the Sino-Soviet bloc. The Chinese have responded with an intra-bloc alliance for orthodoxy and militancy, associating themselves with Yugoslavia's local enemy, Albania, and other momentarily like-minded lesser Communist regimes and hopeful parties not yet in power. When a subalignment including China did not support but defied the Soviet Union as the fountainhead of ideology and policy, the socialist system of states suffered from strains. Cohesion was then expected to occur on the plane of a new and higher consensus, comprising concessions to the more extreme grouping. The equivalent in the Western alliance has been the uneven advance of particular groupings toward military or economic integration and policy co-ordination.

Such mobility within an alliance may keep the alliance politically alive and get it moving. But intra-alliance strategies must not endanger the alliance's military posture and requisite economic integration. On the military side, the Chinese challenge to Soviet leadership posed fewer problems for the militarily unintegrated Communist alliance than de Gaulle's challenge did for NATO; on the economic side, the Soviet bloc has converted strains into impetus toward more integration, as the Soviet leadership sought to supplement its military veto over the lesser countries' unilateralism with ties of reciprocal trade and planning plus economic specialization of all allies but the leading one. The bloc has so far displayed less interallied competition over trade with neutrals and enemies than the Western grouping. But only the future will show how adaptable the two systems are in the economic sphere, and how effective are their evolving agencies and institutions of co-ordination. Both alliance systems include states with high rates of economic growth; the Western system is economically stronger but more dispersed than the Sino-Soviet. A self-contained "world socialist market" could probably maintain itself indefinitely in a hostile environment, and the bloc members can hope to expand beyond present confines by combining paramilitary infiltration in adjoining areas with overt mobilization for trade and aid campaigns abroad. Any loosening of the bloc, in itself undesirable, has in that regard the advantage of permitting superior division of labor; the lesser bloc members can be assigned a disproportionately large part in the bloc's political and economic strategies.

Such practical matters do more for the Sino-Soviet bloc than does a complementary strategy: that of making a virtue of the necessity to practice economy in formal alliance commitments with non-Communist states, while picturing Communist alliances as open-ended islands of "collective security" in contrast to war-producing "military blocs" Western-style. In suitable conditions, such formulations might become useful as ideological justifications for presently unaligned regimes and countries, drawing closer to the bloc for compelling material reasons.[3]

[3] On Soviet-bloc economic techniques, see J. H. Wszelaki, *Communist Economic Strategy: The Role of East-Central Europe* (1959), Part IV; on Soviet security ideology, see W. Welch, "Soviet Commitments to Collective Action," in A. Wolfers, ed., *Alliance Policy in the Cold War* (1959), pp. 271–300.

The Communist bloc's affinity for economic ties is manifest also in the field of military integration. It is greatest in the area of weapons production and quite limited in the field of operations below the highest levels of command, even in the Warsaw Pact. The Soviets may not need more visible integration to secure adequate control; and they may be inhibited by the need for secrecy with respect to lesser allies, by the apprehension that satellite armies might prove infectiously unreliable in combat, and by local hostility to a too widely dispersed Soviet military presence. Integration with Communist China, on the other hand, may have run into Chinese suspicion of Soviet control and Soviet apprehension lest military integration come to mean nuclear sharing without compensatory control over a militant ally. Or, finally, military integration in the field may just be a Western specialty, an expression of the economizing approach of only reluctantly armed democracies.

Strains and Symmetries

Given the structure of the two adversary alliance systems and the nuclear stalemate, the great issue of the cold war has been whether one of them will disintegrate, and if so, which. In principle, the cohesion of an alliance rests on the relationship between internal strains and external pressures, bearing on the ratio of gains to liabilities for individual allies. An ally's liabilities and gains are relative to his partners', his goals, and his alternatives. Even without coercion or inducement from the outside, an alliance will be severely strained and may break up when allies can no longer compensate or redistribute unequal gains and liabilities.

The principal strains in the alliance systems of East and West have to them a certain symmetry. German unification within or outside the Western alliance and the growth of West Germany within NATO have greatly preoccupied the West; the critical counterpart for the East has been China's unification with Taiwan and the growth of mainland China within the Sino-Soviet alliance. The lesser parts of the two great countries created supplementary, and likewise comparable, problems for the two alliance systems. In the immediate present, Germany and China illustrate a function of alliances which is also a possible source of their disruption—restraint between allies. We have seen that selective integration is one means of interallied restraint. Its utility as a material safeguard can be supplemented by explicit legal stipulations and by the political restraint of relaxing protection or withdrawing support from the party to be checked.

Rightly or wrongly, West Germany has been the ally most prominently singled out for restraints on the Western side. Britain's position has been closer to France's in the concern over German economic and military resurgence; and closer to America's in the concern lest controls over Germany confound Western defense for the sake of satisfying French anxieties and ambitions. Seen from the European continent, the role of Britain has remained the traditional one within a newly defined area, encompassing only Western Europe, on the one hand, but also the United States on the other. As a European power, Britain has continued to be sought out as a balance-wheel between France and Germany; as a global power trying to combine Commonwealth preference in trade with a preferential alliance with America, Britain would remain an anti-European influence to be balanced by means of a continental combination around France and Western Germany. To bring about such a combination, France has exerted a not altogether original initiative: as Bismarck's and, more fitfully, Emperor William's Germany before, she has tried to compensate a truncated "historical enemy" with new opportunities in and outside Europe in exchange for the renunciation of reconquest.

In both instances the truncated partner was curtailed in his eastern provinces. Western Germany was severed from Eastern Germany and lost originally Slavic provinces to

Poland and Russia. In the period following World War II, this has divided France and Germany less than did, prior to World War I, France's loss of the originally Germanic provinces to Germany. However, in neither case was the truncated continental power willing to let go of its connection with the principal maritime power in the West. This meant Britain for France and both Britain and the United States for contemporary Germany. The overseas connection was too necessary as a diplomatic counterpoise and a makeweight in a bid for eventual reunification. Moreover, to avoid complete dependence on the maritime ally, and to comply with powerful economic interests, both pre-World War I France and post-World War II Germany kept ajar the door to an accommodation with the despoiler to the East —Imperial Germany in the first case and the Soviet Union in the second.

This being so, and the relation of actual and potential forces between France and Germany remaining unfavorable to France, any regime in Paris was constrained to cultivate, however discreetly and intermittently, the traditional option in the Russian East, as well as to experiment with direct or circuitous restraints on the German partner.

Explicit restraints on West Germany have borne upon both political objectives and military means. They were built into German membership in the Atlantic alliance and the Western European Union, respectively. On the political side, the Atlantic allies (and in particular the successive French regimes) inclined to view West Germany's membership in NATO as the product of a compromise, comprising allied support for the unification of Germany and Bonn's willingness to renounce territorial and other claims east of the Oder-Neisse line. Such a resignation, conjointly with the limitations on armaments, would keep in balance the assets (in the realm of protection) and the liabilities (in the realm of provocation) accruing from German membership; they would also reduce other than self-imposed dependence of any regime in Poland and Czechoslovakia on Soviet protection. Conversely, the West Germans sought to offset continuing ambiguity in their ultimate political objectives in two main ways: they renounced the use of force in attaining any such goals; and they scrupulously observed their limitations in the production of weapons of mass destruction.

If anything, it has been the other allies who countenanced the gradual lifting of less essential restrictions (e.g., over rockets and warships) and toyed with the possibility of diluting the vital ones for the benefit of various schemes in the realm of strategic deterrence. Plans such as those for a French-centered or WEU-controlled European nuclear force had one thing in common. They would relax legal restraints on West German production of nuclear warheads just enough to release German financial and scientific resources for assistance to other European countries producing nuclear weapons. Selective integration would take the place of sweeping prohibition in plans like the one reserving to France exclusive control over a jointly developed deterrent to be integrated into NATO's Central European theater of operations.[4] Should West Germany come to insist on sharing control over tactical nuclear weapons as part of a new deal, other forms of selective integration would become important. Among them we have already noted superior integration in the forward (i.e., West German) area of NATO and location of West German supply bases in the non-German rear.

West Germany's growing concern over an equal status in the alliance was not confined to Bonn's interest in the most modern, that is, tactical nuclear weapons for the Bundeswehr, and the demand for more NATO commands for Germany to match growing contributions. West Germany also showed interest in securing supply bases from Spain, a démarche that actually touched off a reintegration movement toward accommodating her needs in France and else-

[4] See *New York Times*, December 5, 1959, p. 2, and December 28, 1960, p. 26, respectively, for the Western European Union and French schemes.

where within the NATO area. The possession of bases in Spain would have placed West Germany on a par with the United States with regard to a controversial non-member of NATO; and, by outflanking France in the West, Bonn would have gotten even with France for outflanking West Germany diplomatically in the East and taking Poland's side over the Oder-Neisse line. Concern with status has had even more patently a part in Bonn's opposition to discriminatory disarmament schemes—such as the British plan for limiting conventional and nuclear arms in a belt of Central-European territory encompassing West Germany and parts of the lesser Soviet satellites but not the greatest Communist power itself.[5]

It is not always possible to distinguish preoccupation with equal status from concern with greater security. The Bonn government cannot but try to insure the activation of the Western (or American) deterrent in defense of West Germany, for instance. From the viewpoint of the other allies, however, the Germans might either demand or receive too great a compensation for NATO's inefficacy in advancing unification. A major shift in the intra-alliance balance, in part due to such compensations, would threaten the cohesion of the association. To square the circle, the alliance had to stabilize the role and status of West Germany somewhere between those of a second-class ally and a preponderant one.

There has been a striking difference between France and Germany in this connection. Having first bartered the promise of military contribution to NATO for the status of a sovereign state and ally, West Germany has since allowed (with decreasing patience) her claims to an enhanced role within the alliance to lag somewhat behind her absolutely and relatively rising contribution. Underlying this attitude was Chancellor Adenauer's central foreign-policy precept: to act so as to make Germany's strength bearable and accept-

[5] *Ibid.*, March 14, 1959, p. 2; April 10, 1959, p. 2, on the Macmillan scheme; and December 18, 1960, pp. 1 and E 5, on the question of commands.

able to her (Western?) neighbors,[6] in the hope that they might learn to regard her self-restraint as a sufficient safeguard and one likely to last. In the meantime, the Germans acted like a great power while claiming to be still a weak and poor country: they built on military and economic performance. Their diplomatic influence was not lessened by their having to be coaxed into the performance by needy, if senior, allies.

Materially weaker France behaved differently. Before 1958, she was interested in having great-power status without assuming a corresponding role; under de Gaulle, she sought the role without making a corresponding contribution. To secure the role of a great power, de Gaulle adopted the tactic of a small state: gain influence by withholding resources from the alliance; but he also used the influence to gain time for France's power to catch up with her diplomacy.

The two attitudes have coincided with two contrasting concepts of NATO. Under a minimalist concept of the aliance's functions and integration, a French-controlled nuclear force would assure Western Europe's diplomatic and, in the last resort, military independence from the United States (and, secondarily, Britain); and it would offset West Germany's material superiority over France, in general, and in the councils of nations of Western Europe, in particular. A maximalist concept of NATO, on the other hand, entails a growing German role in expanding conventional and dual-purpose military forces and in stepping up economic and politico-psychological warfare; a revitalized NATO would entail more integration for all as an alternative to a so far infeasible and possibly no longer desirable supranational "little" Europe.[7]

The maximalist program's manifest appeal lay in promising more effective collective defense against the Soviet bloc

[6] L. A. Free, *Six Allies and a Neutral* (1959), p. 132.
[7] The ideas of the West German Defense Minister F. J. Strauss and of the political opposition are reported in *New York Times*, December 2, 1960, p. 3, and November 23, 1960, p. 10, respectively.

for the long pull; the minimalist program's more muted appeal lay in its minimizing the other program's possible dangers—provoking the Soviets, especially were West Germany's role to be also nuclear, and upsetting intra-alliance equilibrium, especially if Germany's role were chiefly conventional.

In a fluid situation, only one thing stood out: the test of any formula for NATO lay in its probable long-range effect on two major possible developments. Political differences among Western European allies might be gradually submerged, while the United States acted as an increasingly unnecessary balancer between individual allies and groupings of allies; or there might progressively emerge a dominant West Germany, while the United States would reduce its commitment and contribution as the input of Germany was rising. Should developments point in the latter direction, the propaganda charges of the Soviet Union—that Western European and Atlantic integration were instruments for removing limits on Germany's armaments production and economic predominance—would find growing echo in the fears of both West and East Europeans.[8] The policy of compensating West Germany for her frustrations as a second-class, front-line and partitioned ally might then have to be abandoned for the old policy of restraints. Henceforth unable to apply such restraints within the alliance, however, the Western European NATO powers might have to reimpose them through the political device of a rapprochement with the Soviet target state—possibly to forestall a dissatisfied Germany's move in the same direction.

Major realignments do not take place in response to strains and tensions on one side only. For alternative alignments to become possible, adversary alliances must give rise to parallel

[8] For the Soviet charges, see W. W. Kulski, *Peaceful Co-Existence: An Analysis of Soviet Foreign Policy* (1959), p. 159. The charges and the fears have some factual support, such as the reluctance of the West German steel industry to submit to "discriminatory" supranational controls which would restrict contractually banned forms of expansion. *New York Times*, May 3, 1960, p. 11.

or analogous grievances. And these must be perpetuated for so long that, together with changes in the relation of forces among allies, they make some parties on both sides ready for a change at about the same time. The East's parallel to the problem of West Germany has been that of mainland China. And, in addition, each camp has had to concern itself with the fragments of the two partitioned great states: Taiwan for the West and East Germany for the Soviet bloc.

The more powerful segments of the two partitioned countries created for their allies and alliance leaders somewhat different tasks than the lesser fragments. It has not been particularly difficult to restrain the Nationalist government in Taipei and the Communist regime in Pankow from making a separate deal with the main part of China or Germany, leading to some kind of coalition or confederation. The growth of vested interests within the parts and of disparity in strength between them inhibits such rapprochements, although it does not rule them out. The alternative danger is that the lesser regimes might attempt to involve their respective major allies by provoking a separate-war incident. The focus of America's dilemma has been in the off-shore islands Quemoy and Matsu, as points of access to and from the Chinese mainland; the Soviets threatened, and hesitated, to create a like dilemma for themselves by putting Pankow in charge of access routes between West Berlin and the main part of Germany.

Somewhat precariously, the protectors had to balance conflicting requirements. They had to extend to their protégés material assistance and guarantees against overt aggression or domestic subversion by adversaries; but at the same time they had to restrain possible misuse of the positions, resources, and rights vested in the protected regimes largely by their own making. The restraints themselves were weakened by a related ambiguity. The means of extra security and potential provocation were bestowed upon the dependent regimes in part to compensate for the principal allies' inability to help unify the divided countries on their terms; as such they were ends in themselves and essentially defensive. But the assistance and the guarantees were also symbols of a future consummation and instruments of pressure on the larger fragment and the adversary alliance; as such they had an offensive thrust.

The thrust can be directed within as well as outside the alliance systems. The complementary, smaller and bigger, parts of the two partitioned great countries within each alliance are the natural partners in a subalignment. They stand to gain from a tough policy of opposition to any formal or informal agreement on the basis of "two Chinas" and "two Germanys." Pankow can be expected to align with Peiping on ideological exegesis and policy practice whenever the Kremlin seems to falter. The parallel alignment is between a newly nationalistic West Germany and Nationalist China; it might materialize whenever the position of the United States toward its allies and enemies weakened, the foreign-assistance and other global responsibilities of West Germany grew, and a Bonn-Taipei axis within a Western system could hope to retaliate in kind against Sino-Soviet pressures and diversions without incurring devastating reprisals.

Subalignments of Communist China with individual Central-European members of the "Socialist commonwealth" may somewhat bedevil Soviet control over the satellites; they do not render materially more difficult the task of restraining the thrust of Chinese power in Asia.

Chinese expansionism has a historical background vaguely similar to that of Germany. An early empire exerting suzerainty and influence over adjoining areas, it was in both instances gradually weakened by the contention of local power-holders in occasional alliance with outside forces. The fragments of empire were eventually reassembled in a nation-state, claiming total hegemony over the remotest confines of the previously feudal dominion. The West Germany of today is weakened by the scale of the Third Reich's drive for domination and dwarfed by the forces which it had conjured up. By herself she is less of a threat than mainland China to the equilibrium of the world and of the alliance to which she belongs. But both dissatisfied states naturally incline to employ their rising influence with allies to advance their primary, and in the eyes of past and prospective victims preliminary, national unification objectives.

One can only conjecture in what way and degree the Soviet Union has been trying to restrain its Chinese ally. Peiping has hardly been willing to offer the Soviets the equivalent of the Nationalist government's explicit pledges to *its* major ally, the United States, not to act without prior agreement and not to rely primarily on force in prosecuting the "liberation" of the missing part.[9] A measure of restraint may have been merely implicit in the Sino-Soviet treaty and in the subsequent extension of the Soviet commitment, which paralleled and offset American commitments to Taiwan in 1958. A major ally can exert restraint by explicitly reducing his actually operative commitment in a crisis; the idea is to exploit the lesser ally's fear of abandonment. Conversely, when the ally is strong and self-willed and the crisis looms in the future, the alliance leader may have to extend his commitment to defense and possibly offense; the idea is then to gain the right to restrain as a reward for the heightened risks of solidarity.

There has been some purchase, rather than enforcement, of restraint in Taiwan-American relations from the beginning; in Sino-Soviet relations the barter of restraint for backing is likely to have grown in importance within the limits set by a "revisionist" ideological exegesis. Unwilling to trade missiles over Chinese objectives, the Soviets have come to deprecate war unless it was one of revolutionary or subversive "liberation"; and Peiping's displeasure over the Soviet ver-

[9] On Taipei's assurances in 1954 and 1958, see R.I.I.A., *Collective Defence in South-East Asia*, pp. 68, 69; H. D. Barnett, *Communist China and Asia: Challenge to American Policy* (1960), pp. 411–13. On the Sino-Soviet relationship, see *ibid.*, p. 118.

sion of coexistence was kept in check by the inability of the Chinese to face American nuclear power alone. But restraints from a dialectical ideology are no more stable than restraints depending on progressive expansion of commitment. A change in the relationship of forces within the Sino-Soviet bloc and between the bloc and the West can abruptly reverse both kinds of restraint into incentives to risk-taking.

So far the decisive Soviet restraint over mainland China has been the physical one of Peiping's dependence on military and other assistance. The Soviet Union has been about as reluctant to supply its Chinese ally with rockets and nuclear weapons as the United States has been to assist Taiwan with military hardware chiefly usable for offense. But physical restraints will lapse as Communist China develops her own resources, including nuclear ones. And in the meantime, she is likely to go on exerting pressure on the Soviets to relax any existing ideological restraints over nuclear blackmail and subversion. This would eliminate two kinds of indirect restraint which the Soviets may have been able to employ so far. One is implicit in preclusive diplomatic support for targets of Chinese expansionism, such as India with regard to the frontier regions. The other indirect restraint might be lost only after a period of increased, last-resort use. It consists of pre-emptive politico-military Soviet support for spearheads of Communist expansions in countries like Iraq, Laos, and Indonesia, displacing or moderating the more aggressive, provocative, and largely counter-productive methods of the Chinese.

National Unification and Diplomatic Revolutions

As the balance of capabilities, or of sheer influence, between the two major Communist powers undergoes a shift, co-operation between them becomes hard to distinguish from competition. The cost of cohesion may ultimately rise so high as to invite separation.

To date, speculation in the West has identified two main

sources of tensions within the Sino-Soviet alliance. An earlier school of thought drew attention to China's historic differences with Russia over such places as Korea, Outer Mongolia, Port Arthur, and Dairen; the idea was to alert a presumably dependent satellite to the injury of its "national interests." A later hypothesis, trying to explain China's more bellicose posture toward the capitalistic world, stressed the difference in stages of material and political development of the two Communist allies. Like Soviet Russia in the early 1930's, China was being drained by a gigantic economic-development effort; Peiping indulged in verbal bellicosity to cover up military and other weaknesses.[10]

Proponents of the earlier view did not doubt that the West would gain by luring China into "Titoism"; since then it has become apparently less advantageous for world peace and the West to see China break away from the Soviets into war-minded Stalinism. But a reversal in Western attitude has hardly been justified. China's bellicose words have been diverting attention from much more cautious actions, and have been making up for weakness relative to the Soviet Union as much as relative to the United States. Ideological intransigence has been a way of offsetting China's inferior status as a non-nuclear "great" power within the Communist alliance; and of impeding an understanding between the two superpowers before Communist China matches the Soviet Union as a militarily *and* geopolitically nuclear power, with both rockets and political satellites of her own. China's position in that respect has not been analogous to Soviet Russia's in the early 1930's, but to that of the pre-nuclear Soviet Union in the middle and late 1940's. Unable to wage a nuclear war, Mao, like Stalin before, has had to emphasize the inevitability of war in order to disguise its avoidance and forestall a premature "settlement."

[10] See, for instance, G. F. Hudson, "Russia and China: The Dilemmas of Power," *Foreign Affairs* (October, 1960), pp. 2, 9. The earlier theory was variously formulated and probably affected official United States policy prior to Chinese intervention in the Korean War.

While it lasts, the disparity between the two Communist allies might make it tactically easier to promote strains between them; and a Sino-Soviet split would be almost certainly safer for the West before Communist China acquired nuclear weapons. Until such a time, Soviet restraints are necessary chiefly for the Communist powers themselves: for the Soviets, to spare them the choice between losing a major ally and having to "win" a major war over secondary interests; for the Chinese, to spare them the choice between fighting a major war and admitting their inability to do so. For the West, Soviet restraints merely supplement the largely self-sufficient checks imposed by America's nuclear monopoly in relation to China. And from the perspective of Western interests in non-aligned countries, the show of apparent Soviet restraints is positively harmful insofar as it facilitates a confusing division of labor between the tough and the moderate Communist allies.

Another argument, stressing ideological aspects, has held that a Sino-Soviet split would be dangerous because it would force the Soviets themselves into more radical policies. They would have to outdo militant China's superior attraction for other Communist parties and powers.[11] This line of reasoning is diametrically opposed to the previous one: a split would now do away with the restraints which allied China's militancy unwittingly exerts on Soviet policies by way of contrast and reaction. If so, a split would do away with the division of labor we have just deplored. But a contrary prognosis might be made just as convincingly. A relatively moderate faction in a revolutionary movement, responding to the challenge by an ideological competitor, may behave in roughly the same way as does a relatively satisfied power defied by an upstart power in inter-state relations—seek a conservative alliance. Confronted with a schismatic and expansionist China, the Soviets might have to do exactly that.

[11] Brzezinski, "The Challenge of Change in the Soviet Bloc," *Foreign Affairs* (April, 1961), pp. 441–42.

The debate is illusory. At no time has the West been able to do much in promoting or preventing a split. Even when there are no ideological bonds between them, major allies do not part, or allow themselves to be parted, at the outset of a promising partnership when a split would weaken both of them in prosecuting their maximum objectives. The conditions for a parting of the ways ripen only with time, when the ways of implementing the alliance have left one ally worse off in relation to the other ally, the adversary alliance, or an alternative alignment. The reservation applies to both of the main non-coercive techniques of alliance splitting. One technique is to entice a chosen adversary away from his ally by the prospect of unilateral gain as a reward of separation; another is to press two allies together as a means of enhancing the liabilities of the alliance.

The policy of enticement is not an easy one to practice. The United States discovered this when it tried to draw Peiping away from Moscow prior to the Korean War; the Bandung powers, when they followed suit with a similar policy some years later. Specific rewards for a favored adversary are likely to be payable by friend or ally—be the gains for China in the Far East or for the Soviet Union in Eastern Europe. And even more than territorial or other specific concessions, inducements of a general kind can have highly unpredictable consequences, and may strengthen rather than weaken the adversary alliance as a whole. For example, it might be argued that concessions to the Soviets in the area of disarmament would permit the Soviets to divert resources to private consumption, improve standards of living, and thus unwittingly increase the strains due to differences in the stages of development in Russia and in China. But even if resources were actually saved and diverted, this might only decrease a consolidated Soviet regime's fear of popular disaffection in a war with the West, deprive the economically stronger West of the outside chance to bankrupt the regime under the armaments burden, and enable the Soviets to channel more resources to Communist

China; the latter shift might increase the combined strength of the alliance through investment in areas with superior marginal productivity. A comparable argument could be made for and against Western material assistance to an economically distressed China.

There are no more certain criteria for deciding which of two allies to single out for preferential treatment. One criterion is that of momentary attitude: which adversary is or seems to be more conciliatory and less aggressive? To apply the criterion might well encourage co-ordinated allies to elicit gains by alternating in the role of the friendlier adversary. Another, more objective, criterion is that of relative strength and likely future rate of growth. Of the possible combinations, the correct policy would probably be that of favoring the weaker but more rapidly growing adversary. Only at the last moment, just before he is overtaken and supplanted, could the hitherto dominant partner be bought off successfully. The policy would merely accelerate a presumably natural process toward disruption.

In view of the costs and the uncertainties, the safer way of dealing with an expansionist alliance is the less artful one. This is the policy of denying significant gains to all of its members and making them responsible for each other's behavior. The United States followed this course whenever it made the Soviets accountable for Chinese behavior or for proxy acts by satellites while threatening retaliation at the focal point of the alliance. Even without "massive retaliation," a policy of undifferentiated pressure can be superior to that of differential treatment, if only because it corresponds to the internal autonomy of a self-contained, if ideologically perhaps strained, alliance. A marginal effect on an adversary alliance is more likely to flow from policies toward third countries, designed to tax the antagonists' capacity for co-ordinating response; in direct relations between the Western and the Eastern alliance systems, the most promising policy for each has been to deny to the other any success on the way to unification of China or Germany, and thereby to increase the need for restraints and compensations as time goes by.

The interplay of restraints and compensations bears directly on the ratio of gains and liabilities for individual allies. A serious crisis within an alliance is apt to originate when compensations that would effectively satisfy the restrained ally become in one or another way impossible.

An effective compensation is physically "impossible" when material assistance to the lesser ally has ceased to suffice and the adversary is strong enough to deny significant external success to the allies regardless of the way they share or deploy their capabilities. The ally which suffers most from such inhibition may be a self-confident regime in a big and growing country—such as the regime in Peiping or in Bonn; or it may be an unstable regime in a country with limited potential for growth—somewhat like the regime in Taipei and in Pankow. The critical stage for rupture is reached when the regime seeks to shake off restraints and employ the militarily unusable capabilities in a political transaction. On the Western side, any of the regimes succeeding Chiang-Kai-shek's in Taiwan or Syngman Rhee's in South Korea might come to experiment with short-cuts into national unity; the impetus would probably be not only the failure of unification but also of stabilization and development within the controlled fragment. The incentive of internal failures will probably remain absent from the West German scene. In the Communist camp, the dissatisfaction of relatively weak Communist regimes and parties becomes a threat only when it is combined with the dissatisfaction of China.

The dissatisfaction of a strong ally like Communist China and West Germany is likely to grow when compensation is withheld for reasons of political as well as physical "impossibility." The merger takes place when in an expanding international system the major ally is realizing gains in an area which is (or is made) inaccessible to the lesser ally. In an earlier age, the area inaccessible to Austria was the extra-European realm of colonies and commerce; partly by Britain's making, Austrian Netherlands could not serve as a basis for compensating overseas the efforts and setbacks in Central Europe. In our time, the "inaccessible" realm encompasses a new type of weapons and new worlds in space. The superpowers' reluctance to share gains in these areas has antagonized America's Western European allies and mainland China alike. Immediate concern with international stability has played a role in the superpowers' reserve; but their control and preponderance over allies has also been at stake. Success for one of the two alliance systems reduces the outside pressures which make for cohesion. The very success may confront a core-power of the winning combination with a strengthened ally-competitor, while possibly depriving it of the possibility to counterpoise the rising ally with the aid of third states.

Such concerns will be minimized by those who assert the ideological unity of contemporary alliances, or those who expect break-up from ideological differences alone. But the issue does point to the last form of "impossibility" to compensate a dissatisfied lesser ally. This is the strictly political one of the compensating ally's reluctance to nullify the alliance's purpose. Allies may covet the same territory or be primarily concerned with different enemies. In order to satisfy Austria in the mid-1750's and preserve the "old system" from the "diplomatic revolution," Britain would have had to match Austria's assistance in curtailing France by extending the alliance to the destruction of Prussia. The undertaking would have defeated Britain's global strategy by mobilizing Prussia against Britain's holding operation in Europe. Some such conflict of interests and strategies might come to strain Sino-Soviet relations in Asia, although another reason of political impossibility to compensate may be more important. Austria's success might or might not have removed the basis of Britain's commanding role in the Austro-British alliance;

but it is always possible that continued compensation for failure in one place may shift the balance of power within the alliance against the compensating ally and shatter his political controls in the process.

The burden of decision is then on the initially more powerful, restraining partner. He can relax the weakening restraints before they are completely lost in the reversal of capabilities; in doing so, he may hope that the ensuing international conflict will set back the turbulent ally. Or he can switch the employment of his independent capability and other vanishing assets from compensating and restraining partners to securing favorable terms of accommodation from the adversary.

Once the critical stage for rupture is reached within the alliance, the relationship of forces outside it assumes decisive importance. The relatively declining major ally will be disposed to trade his realignment potential when the adversary side is both strong and, for its own reasons, receptive. If it is strong, the penalty for the alternative course of relaxing restraints on the more aggressive partner is likely to befall the major ally, too. And if the adversary side is receptive, due to its own problems in interallied balancing and restraining, the dealigning power will not be expected to pay a higher price than would be the cost of saving the overstrained alliance. Roughly the same is true for a dealigning weak ally, with the difference that the former adversary's strength is now necessary to guarantee the defector against sanctions by the deserted alliance leader.

It is too early to say whether the Chinese alliance has turned into a liability for the Soviets, as Peiping threatened to divide the bloc, alienate non-aligned countries like India, and involve the Soviet homeland in an unwanted war with the West. It is less doubtful, however, that a major nuclear war would probably turn the Sino-Soviet balance much more devastatingly against the Soviets than did their military assistance to China in the Korean War or than would the most successful development of China's industries in the foreseeable future.

What China is to the East, West Germany is to the West. But China presents her ally with the keener problem, if only because no regime in West Germany can reasonably hope to gain unification and improve its standing relative to its principal allies by precipating a major war. The Sino-Soviet alliance would be most likely to fall apart if the most advanced country of socialism were faced with major sacrifice for the aggrandizement of a retrograde but pushing China. If the actually dealigning partner were the regime in Peiping, it would probably retreat into temporary isolation in an attempt to save itself internally, retain its positions in the Communist Asian countries, and mend fences with the non-aligned powers of South Asia. If it were the Soviets who took the first fatal step, they would be more likely to take also the next toward a novel configuration.

Any such changes are unlikely to take place today or tomorrow. Epoch-making reversals of alignments flow from conditions which mature with time. As they transpire, fundamental changes create both alternatives and opportunities for adopting the alternatives.

Three stages may be required. There is, first, the period of rigid enmity and single-minded contest over predominance, when the power of at least one of the contestants is growing relative to both the adversary and other states. The intermediate period is one of fluidity, initiated by one side or both recognizing that the enmity is becoming obsolete and serves new, third powers which are the "natural" future enemies. Awareness of a common interest in the *status quo* grows, at least relative to the revolutionary ambitions of the third powers; but it has to contend with a surviving sense of hostility and with the apprehension of alienating present allies by drawing closer to the traditional enemy on particular issues. In the second period of fluidity, *ad hoc* diplomatic cooperation alternates with conflict. Rivalry can terminate completely in a realignment only when a new big issue overshadows diffuse hostility and compels adjustment of surviving conflicts on specific interests. The typical ideology of this, the third, phase proclaims a conservative condominium for general security, which would perpetuate the distribution of power as it emerged from the preceding period of conflict.

That is how secular rivalry evolved between the Habsburgs and the Bourbons. Intense hostility lasted two centuries until European Spain passed to France, who thus ceased to be encircled by Habsburg powers. The shorter period of fluidity extended from the Peace of Utrecht (in 1713) to the reversal of alliances (in 1756). While the struggle over the Spanish succession was being slowly liquidated and positions were being prepared for the contest over succession to the Central-European domains of the Austrian Habsburgs, the two land powers experimented with occasional co-operation against maritime Britain and, secondarily, Spain. In the final phase, the impetus of the struggle against new principal enemies (Britain in the case of France and Prussia in the case of Austria) compelled Versailles and Vienna to draw together more intimately. A major price of alliance was greater reserve in the new partners' continuing rivalry over the balance of power in the Holy Roman Empire—the in-between world of European diplomacy.[12]

With modifications, a like phasing and pattern of action can be discerned in the maturing and passing of another traditional enmity, between France and England, under the impact of rising German might and, not yet fully or definitively assured, the passing of the hostility between the two Western nations and Germany, under the impact of new forces in an enlarged, global structure of powers and conflicts. Ideological dogmatism may long hamper the unfolding of a similar process between East and West, but might also

[12] In German, *das Land der Mitte*. For detailed discussion of the history of the Austro-French rapprochement, see M. Braubach, *Versailles und Wien von Ludwig XIV bis Kaunitz: die Vorstadien der diplomatischen Revolution im 18. Jahrhundert* (1952).

precipitate it in a major crisis that would jeopardize "socialist achievements" in say, the Soviet Union together with the national interests of Russia.

Alignment Alternatives and Transnational Union

We can only speculate about new alignments which might follow upon the breakup of existing constellations. To give some basis in reality to the logically possible variants, some of the historical alternatives to NATO and within NATO can be referred to. Every alternative presupposes a conflict that divides and in a way links major adversaries, which are target states for each other and core-powers for their lesser allies. Every possible configuration, moreover, entails a primary area for strategy and integration and relegates third states to the role of secondary target states or merely peripheral outposts.

The nominal target state toward the close of World War II continued to be Germany, variously involved in the issue of American withdrawal from Europe as both a feared and desired event. Among the by-products of this concern was the still-born Franco-Soviet treaty, on the pattern of the earlier Anglo-Soviet wartime alliance, and the Soviet alliances with the East European countries. By the time France and Britain came together again in the Dunkirk pact, the real target state of the traditional anti-German allies was the Soviet Union in Europe and, up to a point, the rising anti-colonial forces outside Europe. In such a construction, the United States would figure both as a reserve power backing the allies *vis-à-vis* the Soviet Union and, alongside the Soviet Union, as something of a secondary target in its anti-colonial capacity.[13] Once the Soviet Union manifestly replaced Germ-

[13] It may be that only the aftermath of the colonial question has been driving the two Western European powers into closer partnership since the late 1950's, when the emancipated Afro-Asian countries continued their campaign beyond independence. For one instance, see *New York Times*, December 18, 1960, p. 16.

any as the chief threat to international stability, the identity of the Western core-power changed, too. The United States took the place of Britain and Britain that of France as the first, but junior, ally of the principal island power of the West. The primary area for strategy and integration came to be the Atlantic world, while Soviet bloc activities elsewhere became the secondary target. A major change occurred with the diversion of the main Soviet pressure to non-Atlantic areas, paralleling the rise of Communist China. The threat's global diffusion only intensified the interest in a continental-European association, extending to parts of North Africa if possible. The grouping would still have the Soviet bloc as its principal security target in Europe, while the secondary targets would be a revival of militarism in rearmed Germany and the hegemony of the maritime powers within the Western alliance. Western European confederation or, more accurately, a French-centered Franco-German partnership enjoying the diplomatic support of lesser—notably Latin—countries, would act as an intermediary between the Anglo-Saxon powers and the Soviet Union. Should the concept fail, and the United States prove unable to withstand the Soviets in Europe without promoting Germany's resurgence in NATO, the alternative might be another traditional anti-German combination: that of France with Russia. It is noteworthy that wartime diplomatic flirtations of the French with the Soviets took place before the demonstration of American nuclear power in Japan; they might resume in earnest with a demonstration of that power's insufficiency. In contrast to what they did in the early 1940's the Soviets would then have to treat France as a privileged great power at least in form. The possession of nuclear capability would place the two continental-European wing powers in the same category and above a merely conventionally rearmed Germany—somewhat as the possession of standing armies was previously supposed to set them apart from the Anglo-Saxon sea powers. Also unlike almost twenty years ago, France would adopt the Soviet option as a merely European power, no longer vulnerable to American ill will in her overseas possessions.[14] France and the Soviet Union would be the unequal core-powers of the European system; a resurgent, perhaps unified, Germany would be the principal target and the European continent the primary area of strategy. From the viewpoint of the continental European system, the Anglo-Saxon powers and Communist China would be in the same category, if possibly playing momentarily different roles, as reserve powers or secondary targets. The logical consummation of such a pattern would be a global system of outflanking alliances, matching the Franco-Soviet alliance with one between Germany and China or the United States against their respective neighbors and principal enemies.

The counterpart to a Franco-Russian rapprochement is a Russo-German arrangement, in the tradition of Bismarck and Rapallo. As a practical possibility, the combination suffers from the absence of a logical target state and, consequently, of at least a partial makeweight to Soviet predominance in a partnership with adjacent, and thus doubly vulnerable, Germany. A diplomatic revolution might foreshadow a social one; to run the risks, West Germany would have to be both considerably rearmed and insufficiently backed by the Western allies—as well as be unwilling to use her own military power unilaterally on a vital German issue in a pinch. And on their part, the Soviets would have to be ready to pay a high price (in all kinds of safeguards) for neutralizing Germany in a bilateral deal.

In global terms, finally, the United States might supersede France in a renewed alliance with the Soviets. The principal target of such an alliance of equals would be Communist China (conceivably allied with Germany on the issue of unification and expansion), while control over other states with actual or potential nuclear capability would be the

[14] In this connection, see de Gaulle's conversation with Vishinsky in November, 1943, reported in his *Mémoires de guerre*, Vol. II (1956), p. 605.

allies' secondary object. The Pacific area and the European area would share primacy as foci of strategy co-ordination, with a possible edge for the Pacific theater.

The West European nations face a dilemma. To relax the rigidity of contemporary alignments on the Western side only, without a parallel development on the Sino-Soviet side, would merely open a new field for Soviet tactics of division and domination. Should, however, a Sino-Soviet split make the Soviets seek an accommodation with the West, the Soviets would probably seek contact with the United States directly. This would downgrade the position of individual Western European powers, even if it did not produce a feared division of the world between the giants. Only union might put the old continent in a stronger position to participate in shaping the international system.

In the movement toward European union, the issue of whom to include has overshadowed the issue of what kind of authority to superimpose on the nations. Two main positions can be taken. One is to rely on the attractive powers of cumulative integration. Only by pushing ahead with integration on a narrow front will lagging nations be induced to rally. The United States might eventually find herself in the position of Britain with regard to the Community of Six, and might have to go beyond verbal support for the idea of an Atlantic Community. At variance with the belief in attraction and cumulation is the second position, stressing the danger that more intimate smaller associations will disrupt larger entities. To unify the Six economically is accordingly to disrupt Western Europe both economically and politically; to institutionalize co-operation of the Six in political and defense matters could alienate both Britain and America and disrupt the Atlantic alliance; and to formulate political and economic strategy-making within the Atlantic framework would alienate the uncommitted nations and disrupt the "free world."

Actual developments in a specific case are a matter of alternatives—mainly of the nations and groupings temporarily left out of a successful combination. Following the establishment and early success of the European Common Market, the decision between cumulation and conflict of integration hang in the balance of individual fears and expectations.

The inner Six and, in particular, the all-out continentals among them, feared that the accession of Britain with her non-European ties and anti-Continental traditions would frustrate the smaller grouping's confederal purpose. The proponents of a larger grouping and, in particular those with a maritime tradition and outlook, such as the British among the outer Seven and the Dutch among the inner Six, were less concerned with the long-range political purpose. They were more preoccupied with the risks and objectives of a European combine in the shorter run, being on the whole less ready to correct past failings with a formula for the future than to question the formula on the basis of past disasters. The endemic instability of France and Germany, it was feared, might spread into the larger body politic by way of an uneasy condominium of the two populous nations or through an acute struggle over predominance between them. And the immediate diplomatic objective attributed to the smaller combination, that of posing as a third force in world affairs, only increased the desire of some to have the British in, and of others to keep them out. The British, while offsetting the Germans, would also check any tendency on the part of the French to apply the principle of balancing to American-Soviet relations. Such a check would not be undesirable to the Germans, if only because they are unlikely to agree with the French on the specific objectives to be pursued by a policy of balance.

As for Britain, as part of a Western European bloc she would forfeit her key position between the continent of Europe and America, and weaken her special ties with America and the Commonwealth; but she might recover stature as the leader of Europe. If she stayed outside, along with the independence she would retain the liability of her position as America's exposed bridgehead and, along with trade, would lose political influence relative to the European grouping as well as over it. Even the old Commonwealth would increasingly gravitate toward the larger centers of trade and security; little England might soon regret the risks Great Britain feared to take.

As a thing of the future, a Western European grouping, in whatever shape, could still be all things to all men. It could be seen as a new weight in the Western scale, equal to the United States; as a counterpoise to the non-European giants, balancing them through comparable power and superior political intelligence; and as a magnet for the weak in Central-Eastern Europe, enlarging the area of freedom by a combination of attraction and non-provocative pressure. If, concurrently with consolidation in Western Europe, the pressures of rising China grew on Soviet Russia's Asiatic frontiers, the Soviet Union might be moved to relax its hold on the satellites to facilitate accommodation with the West. The terms of a new deal in Europe would largely depend on two things: on the degree and form of American involvement necessary for underwriting an equilibrium between the Soviet Union and a Western European Union disposing of major industrial and nuclear capability, but deprived of the North African equivalent of the Soviet hinterland in Central Asia; and the terms would depend on the formula for Central-Eastern Europe itself. If the formula were military non-alignment, the area might be kept in place—in addition to any treaty stipulations and guarantees—by the pull of economic ties with the Soviet Union and the uncommitted nations outside Europe, on the one hand, and by the contrary pull of indigenous nationalism and cultural and political affinities with Western Europe on the other hand.

So much for possible structural realignments in the future; contemporary actuality has been of a more tactical kind, as Western diplomacy wavered between two approaches. One approach was toward an implicit acknowledgment of Soviet "vital interests" in Eastern Europe in return for like consideration in areas of concern nearer home—the Middle East for the British, North Africa for the French, and the Caribbean for the Americans. The other approach was to re-emphasize the right of the captive nations in Central-Eastern Europe to self-determination as part of diplomatic counter-offensives, keyed so as to appeal to the non-aligned countries in the newest world of Africa and Asia.[15]

[15] On the policy of the British government, see *New York Times*, March 17, 1959, p. 14, and March 24, 1959, p. 1. The traditional British view toward European integration has been restated by H. C. Allen, *The Anglo-American Predicament: the British Commonwealth, the United States and European Unity* (1960). De Gaulle formulated his grand design most succinctly in a speech before the United States Congress (*New York Times*, April 26, 1960, p. 18): "Through the organization of a Western Europe ensemble, facing the bloc built by the Soviets, it will be possible to establish, from the Atlantic to the Urals, some equilibrium between those two zones which are comparable, both in populations and in resources. Alone such a balance may, perhaps, one day, enable the old Continent to bring a reconciliation between its two parts, to find peace within itself, to give a fresh start to its civilization and lastly to have the possibility, together with America, to help, in an atmosphere of serenity, the development of the unfavored masses of Asia and of the awakening populations of Africa." See also *Mémoires de guerre*, Vol. III (1959), pp. 369 ff. On the American position, see *New York Times*, July 17, 1961, pp. 1, 3.

5
Non-Alignment and Neutralism

THE WAY the lesser states' position evolves in Central-Eastern Europe is significant for lesser countries elsewhere; the significance will increase as new larger powers arise amidst them. The basic choice may be between satellite belts and buffer belts of militarily non-aligned states.

Both patterns have disadvantages. A satellite belt brings the core-powers into direct contact with each other through the most sensitive, because always potentially seditious, outer rim. A buffer belt keeps the greater powers separated. But as the buffer states and factions within them seek closer ties of support with different great powers, the belt may become highly unstable and contentious.

In the abstract, the danger is roughly equal. Domination over satellites by one major power gives rise to a permanent moral and political pressure on the adversary great power to intervene. This threatens to set off a major conflict on the occasion of a flare-up, which may be carefully avoided but is eventually unavoidable. If and when satellite nations are subdued, the belt will serve as the marshalling ground for further expansion. When there is a buffer, interference by the larger powers tends to incite a perpetual state of frictions. Actual clashes are less explosive than in the former case, however, since no paramount power's prestige is at stake. Consequently, a buffer zone is, on balance, more likely to serve the cause of stability, notably if both the great powers and the in-between states gradually assimilate rules of self-restraint which make for genuine non-alignment. As this happens, the small powers become less anxious to make themselves secure against one local great power in alignment with a remoter or safer one.

The conspicuous practitioners of non-alignment have most recently been non-European states with little or no foreign policy tradition. It will in part depend on their behavior whether present and future greater powers look upon non-alignment of lesser states as a temporary expedient or a desirable long-term formula.

The Rationale of Non-Alignment

The growing number of non-aligned countries have been the most frequently noted "third party" in the contemporary triparite system of policy. What are the main characteristics, the motivations, and the rationalizations of non-alignment and its militant variety, neutralism?

Non-aligned countries avoid alliance, refusing to add their power to that of others. If it were merely a matter of withholding their power from others, they would pursue a traditional policy of neutrality. In wartime they would remain aloof, except when asked to mediate; under cold war conditions they would maintain an equally aloof posture. Not all of the non-aligned countries have been pursuing such a neutral policy. The militant neutralists have not been content merely to withhold their power from others, as did the traditional neutrals, such as Switzerland and nineteenth-century Belgium, and countries that have been more recently neutralized by treaty, such as Austria, or that have tried to virtually neutralize themselves, as Burma. The "positive" neutralists have instead engaged in an active policy of play-off and unsolicited mediation between the great powers.

The smaller is the margin of capability that favors either of two contending parties, the greater is the bearing of the total power of an intrinsically weak third party. Such power need not be greater than the net balance of advantage favoring one of the contending major powers, and may be incommensurate in kind. Short of—and sometimes even despite—its manifest abuse, third-party influence is greatest with stalemated contestants. They are more than usually inclined to display respect for the forms of independence and the fictions of impartiality or superior morality, upon which non-belligerent or non-aligned countries base their claim to protection, function, and authority in the international arena.

There are two main counterparts to contemporary neutralists in the annals of traditional diplomacy. One is the league of armed neutrals, actively seeking to prevent forms of warfare, mainly naval, injurious to its members' interests, mainly economic. The other counterpart is the former ally bent on separate peace. The validity of this latter analogy may be affirmed or denied, depending on how one judges the "defection" of the neutralist countries from the Western system following independence, despite continued adherence to the main values and aspirations of the West in many cases. The analogy in actual behavior is less controversial.

The similarity between separate peace and neutralism is quite pervasive. It bears, first, on the salient reasons for separate peace in war: reaction to inferior status within an association, the compulsion of material inability to cope with the adversary, and the desire for a special advantage for oneself rather than for a more successful ally. On the part of neutralist groups in firmly aligned and manifestly threatened countries, the desire for release from struggle—typical of separate peace under duress—is aggravated by the apparent impossibility of leaving the alliance. On the part of neutralist regimes situated in the zone between the two core-alliances, the ease and profitability of the policy magnifies the desire for special advantage, typical of separate peace under inducement. The characteristic strategy of separate peace is demand for an impossible performance by the partner to be deserted, so that the anticipated failure to comply may legitimize defection and reduce the danger of sanctions. The principal demand of the neutralists has been for instant and complete withdrawal of all and sundry vestiges of colonial control; a secondary demand has been for disarmament and diversion of resources into economic assistance. The latter demand coincides with the separate-peacemaker's typical ambition: to pacify the general conflict in such a way as to retain and consolidate previous gains. The characteristic technique is unsolicited mediation. Such mediation may be in good faith, when it is armed with the threat of behavior favorable to the co-operating side; or terms may be so defined as to insure an apparent compliance of the favored party.

The attitude of neutralists to presently contending blocs is one thing; another is their position toward the institution of alliance as such. Traditionally there have been two kinds of policy; neutralism has added a third. The three policies range along a spectrum of increasing hostility toward alliances.

The first type of anti-alliance policy rules out alliance with a particular country while approving or condoning policies of alliance generally. Thus France, after 1871, would not consider an alliance with Germany unless the latter returned the conquered provinces. The rejection of this particular alliance, however, only intensified France's search for allies against the German enemy.

The second type of anti-alliance policy consists in abstention from all alliances. Such a policy may be adopted after a dispassionate weighing of the gains and liabilities expected from all feasible alternatives. Abstention was the policy pursued by England and the United States in periods of "splendid isolation," and has remained the policy of traditional neutrals. The abstaining country is not opposed to alliances among other countries, for these often insure its own position of aloofness. For instance, in the pre-World War I period, neutral Belgium could not but favor an Anglo-French alliance which, at different periods, served as a restraint on France, as a counterpoise to Germany, or both. And when Great Britain became antagonized by Germany's *Weltpolitik* but remained anxious to avoid commitments on the continent, she stopped opposing the alliance between France and Russia, her colonial rivals. Similarly, early American statesmen did not extend their philosophy of nonentanglement to imply opposition to alliances among European powers. A change in American outlook did occur, however, in the twentieth century as the environment and prevailing ideology changed. The United States, for a while, adopted an anti-alliance policy of a third type, similar in nature to that pursued or advocated by neutralists.

The third or neutralist anti-alliance policy opposes all alliances including those among other powers. Anti-alliance ideology holds that competition for allies is a cause of tension and war. Alliances are concluded in anticipation of a test of strength; they increase the total power which statesmen can wield and encourage them to use it while the alliance holds together. Alliances might partially substitute for national armaments, but they also exacerbate an armaments race as states seek to attract new allies and to disrupt the adversary alliance. Armament efforts have at least the merit of absorbing national energies domestically; the race for allies takes place between countries and puts a high premium on prestige. Prestige is born of success, and the diplomatic success of one state entails the humiliation of another, which then seeks retribution. Since alliances are built on shared antagonism rather than amity, they tend to fall apart. War is then welcome as an alternative to disintegration of the alliance and isolation. The fear of isolation is viewed in the anti-alliance ideology as the *reductio ad absurdum* of the rationale for alliances. In the absence of alliances all nations would be isolated and as such more amenable to universal law and its sanctions.

The realities of non-alignment and neutralism must be viewed in a double perspective, since they themselves flow from closely interwoven responses to external factors and domestic conditions. Non-alignment can be adopted on the basis of rational estimates of the conditions required for national security and domestic stability; but a policy of militant neutralism in particular is likely to be strongly affected by non-rational ideological preoccupations and by an almost too pragmatic quest of aid and status internationally.

We have seen earlier that there is no single reason for alignment; there are also many traditional motives for non-alignment of smaller powers. If only one issue or conflict is dominant and the smaller state does not wish to be identified with the policy of either power center in a bipolar structure, it may elect to rely on almost automatic protection, assuming that one power group balances the other. In such a case the danger of provoking one side by aligning with the other may well appear greater than the need for, or possibility of, protection. When more than one issue dominates the international system, a smaller state's leaders may hesitate to determine alignment on the basis of only one of the issues. They might make common cause with the West against the East on the issue of Communist expansion, but not with the industrial, residually imperialist North against the ex-colonial, pre-industrial South on the other dominant issue of today—economic development and political independence for the less developed countries. Likewise, as the number of particular conflicts increases, so does the fear of the smaller states that alignment may involve them with new antagonists. The political cost of alliance becomes extravagant when it entails not only an initial compromise with the ally but the liability of adding his enemies to one's own as well. Such considerations would suffice to keep Afghanistan or Burma out of an alliance that included Pakistan and, consequently, antagonized India.

While following traditional anti-alliance patterns of thought and action, the non-aligned states and neutralists have been stressing two new factors in contemporary international relations to justify opposition to alliances. The first has to do with the character of modern weapons of mass destruction. According to the neutralist school of thought, no individual or collective effort by a small country can significantly increase that country's security if security means capacity for defense against a nuclear power. So-called deterrence requires actions which are indistinguishable from provocation in the eyes of the enemy. To parry the provocation, each great power will try to demonstrate that its nuclear opponent is unable to protect the small ally. The safest course for a small country is therefore to do nothing to attract the contending giants either as allies or as enemies. It should instead rely on the nuclear powers' reluctance either to initiate a major conflict over a small country or to antagonize other small countries by using force against any one of them. Spontaneous solidarity of non-aligned countries for the purpose of opposing great power encroachments is the most effective "alliance" at the small country's disposal in a nuclear environment.

The second factor in the contemporary world which has worked against alliance is the alleged relationship between Western alliance policy and Western colonialism. From the anti-colonial viewpoint, the West has had two kinds of alliance. The more objectionable kind associates former colonies with former metropolitan or other Western powers; the other kind does not involve ex-colonial nations. The immediate victim of neo-colonialism, which perpetuates Western presence and control, is the allied small country itself. The prototype of the neo-colonial alliance is the Anglo-Iraqi alliance, which replaced Britain's League of Nations mandate in the 1930's. Its military and political clauses can be read as so many devices to keep a pliant oligarchy in power, aligned with British interests and supported by the major ally's residual presence in the country. The government of the dependent ally cannot conduct its own foreign policy, and the people are not free to change the regime by force if need be.

According to the same view, the dangers of neo-colonial alliances may be only indirect but no less real for other countries in the region. Colonialism thrives on conflict between indigenous forces. As long as smaller countries depend on their own resources, the argument might run, conflicts are nonexistent or inconclusive. Things change when lesser countries align with a major outside power, even if ostensibly against another major power. The ally acquires new resources and believes, rightly or wrongly, that it has gained additional support for pressing its claims on neighboring small states. In the eyes of Nasser and his followers, the Baghdad Pact disrupted the common front of the Arab League against Israel and, under the guise of an anti-Soviet front, intensified the ambitions of the Iraqi elite with regard to Syria and Egypt; from Nehru's viewpoint SEATO has enabled Pakistan to be tougher toward India and Afghanistan, and Thailand to press her ambitions against Cambodia. The affected states cannot but react by aligning with another power or giving a militant slant to their non-alignment, so as to enhance their nuisance value, penalize the great power ally of their local adversary, and secure countervailing outside assistance. In one way or another, the great power adversaries secure new avenues of influence to the lesser states. By introducing arms and discord into the region, the alliance of a small state with a great power constitutes in Nehru's words a "reversal of the process of liberation."[1]

The other kind of Western alliance is that which does

[1] F. R. Moraes, *Jawaharlal Nehru: A Biography* (1957), p. 452.

not include a former colonial dependent. NATO is such an alliance. The neutralists have objected to NATO only to the extent that it helped the metropolitan members resist the trend toward "decolonization," at least indirectly by reducing a colonial metropole's defense burden against the Soviet bloc in Europe. Alliances like NATO and, on the Communist side, the Warsaw Pact are least "provocative" because they associate countries which are close to each other geographically and do not encircle the principal target state. And they are not "colonial" alliances for they associate nations kindred in culture and color. Affinity in ideology and political organization among the members makes such groupings even more acceptable to the neutralists. They have been inclined to overlook the fact that such affinity has been forced upon the lesser allies in the Warsaw Pact, so long as the ideology can be considered "progressive" and the dominant Soviet ally manages to avoid overt repression within the alliance.

Seen from the neutralist viewpoint the above criteria for differentiating between acceptable and unacceptable alliances have certain advantages. A big unaligned country, such as India, may acceptably enter into security arrangements of her own with a small country like Nepal. And, as long as the areas included within the alliances of the major powers are kept at a minimum, the in-between or unaligned area will be large. The fly in the ointment is the Sino-Soviet alliance. At first it ran afoul of the anti-colonial principle, because China was weak and racially different from Russia. After the Bandung powers failed to dissuade Peiping from coveting China's former "protective" belt of dependencies, the security aspect became critical. Instead of growing, the unaligned area might be progressively reduced, and reduced near the homeland of non-alignment at that.

As reconstructed so far, the neutralist position on alliances has ignored the objective requirements of international equilibrium and security. The omission is not serious if one holds that a strategic parity would remain in existence between East and West even if the West withdrew from all bases in former dependencies. All that is necessary is that the United States retain links with Japan, Australia, Turkey, and a few small island bases; it would need neither SEATO nor CENTO. Some such beliefs may have permitted neutralist governments to feel that their countries could enjoy the best available protection at little cost and risk to themselves. An imaginary neutralist might go so far as to postulate a natural division of labor between non-aligned countries and the West, if only the West suffered this partnership to be disguised by anti-Western tirades. The fear of adverse repercussions among non-aligned countries might be relied upon to restrain the Sino-Soviet bloc from small-scale military and paramilitary penetrations by land; and the fear of a Western deterrent could suffice to restrain the Communists from an all-out assault. Such a complementary politico-military deterrent, our imaginary neutralist might conclude, would reduce the Sino-Soviet bloc to truly peaceful competition.

In short, flexibility in diplomacy and avoidance of provocative policies insure short-run security. In the long run Soviet imperialism will not replace that of the West, the neutralists seem to believe. In this respect neutralist opposition to peacetime commitments can be bolstered with assumptions about the character of the two chief contestants and about the winners in the cold war.

The neutralists have inclined to discount the Western thesis that Communism is inherently aggressive; on the contrary, they have largely adopted the theory that internal expansion will absorb Communist efforts and that the Communists' bellicosity will subside when they have attained Western levels of mass consumption. The assumptions regarding the West, and particularly the United States, have been in many ways complementary. The United States may be deemed capable of deterring all-out war even without bases or allies on the Sino-Soviet periphery; but America has not been credited with the ability to defend small countries without destroying them, especially if these countries are close to the Sino-Soviet bloc. The neutralists have also seemed to assume that within the limits of American capability and resolution, the United States is tacitly committed to defend any country that is threatened by a Communist power, regardless of that country's previous policy. Therefore, it would be absurd to undertake the material and political liabilities of alignment.

Assumptions regarding "victory" in the cold war have likewise militated against alignment. The leaders of many non-aligned countries remember the two World Wars; their independence movements triumphed largely as a result of the second. In that conflict the Western nations suffered initial setbacks but finally defeated the totalitarian states. Japan's totalitarian expansionism in the Second World War was temporarily of great service to the cause of anti-colonial nationalism in Southeast Asia. For the neutralists this recent history has set the guidelines for the long-term perspective. The West was likely to win over the Communist bloc in the end and therefore needed no assistance; and the methods used in gaining independence could be revived for consolidating it. Japan had once proved useful; the neutralist should stand ready to garner any incidental advantage from the more recent cold war conflict. The long-range neutralist ideal is the decline of both contending sides' power and influence relative to the new nations. This is what happened in both World Wars, and unless a third destroys everything, it will, so the neutralists hope, happen again. The basic requirement is that the cold-war substitute for war be waged by means of a competitive economic build-up of the less developed nations.

Meanwhile, however, fear and concern about voicing fear have been very much a part of the universe of non-alignment and neutralism. There are non-aligned leaders who will privately admit that they fear Communist encroachments and resent Soviet "nuclear terror," but the dogmatic neutralist rejects the very thought that he is swayed by the fear of anything and anyone. Fear makes for caution and has been a paramount reason for non-alignment of Burma, Afghanistan, and Cambodia, countries close and vulnerable to the Sino-Soviet bloc. Absence of fear may be put forward as the reason for non-alignment when remoteness or natural protection and vast size of a country like India apparently give the country immunity.

Fear of an external threat often stimulates very pragmatic calculations. These may produce alignment or non-alignment. The option will be affected by such intangibles as historical experience and political culture as well as by the nature of specific, tangible threats. Thailand, for instance, chose alignment despite and partly because of her proximity to China. Burma chose non-alignment. Unlike the Burmese, the Thais have long been independent and are impressed by the limitations of neutrality. And unlike the Cambodians, the Thai elite is familiar with the pitfalls of a play-off policy. The Thai propensity for active diplomacy led, therefore, to initiative for and within a Western alliance. The Burmese tendency to withdrawal found political expression in non-alignment. Moreover, the specific threat to Thailand came from a "Free Thai" movement based in Communist China, while the Burmese were beset by incursions of Nationalist Chinese. The case of Iran is similar to that of Thailand. The difference between India and Pakistan is less complex. West Pakistan is peopled by war-like races; more importantly, India thought of non-alignment first, thereby leading Pakistan to do the opposite. Afghanistan in turn took a line contrary to that of Pakistan. Controversy over Kashmir and Pushtoonistan loomed larger than either the Soviet Union or China.

Much in the neutralist ideology of international security seems based on an optimistic degree of confidence in automatic protection. But seen in a second perspective, as a politics of compensation, reflecting concern with internal problems, neutralism combines deep-seated emotions about the past with crudely pragmatic methods for coping with the present.

Many new nations have instituted a priority which the liberal democratic West has more consistently preached than practiced—that of domestic over external conditions as determinants of foreign policy. This is not surprising. Domestic concerns tend to be preponderant in societies that are free from external security dilemmas or helpless to cope with them, and whose central authority is subject to factional opposition rather than being freed for action abroad by equipoised pluralism at home. In addition, many of the new states have incurred a tendency towards internationalization of domestic politics, in the essentially feudal pattern of internal factions aligning with and receiving moral and material support from different outside powers. Even if the politically less developed countries manage to contain the internationalization of their internal troubles, their domestic politics still tends to resemble international politics. Factional leaders fight to survive in governing positions, and other factions strive to conquer such positions, without accepting the arbitrament of a successful performance of functions associated with the modern state.

The policies of non-alignment and neutralism are a means for counteracting these tendencies. Non-alignment presumably enhances the international status and, consequently, domestic authority of "national" leaders. This promotes short-run stability. And the isolationist bias of non-alignment appeals to both traditionalist and nationalist factions, at the same time that it helps to insulate factional and regional struggles from the strains of outside interference. The graver the internal troubles, the greater the temptation for leaders to go beyond non-alignment to militant neutralism. Indonesia's militancy has intensified as internal tensions increased. And underlying Indian "positive neutrality" is the leaders' concern with preventing division of the country into a number of quarreling states.[2]

This fear of domestic division is one of the reasons for the militancy of the neutralist governments in relatively non-integrated new nations. Neutralism as an active foreign policy provides a focus for domestic cohesion and silences opposition to the government. Moreover, militant neutralism appeals to governing groups in many new nations as a reaction against the passivity of former colonial status. The hallmarks of dependency—lack of a separate foreign policy and of diplomatic access to third states which could counterbalance the metropole—seem perpetuated in today's "unequal alliances." The neutralist leader of a new nation is determined to avoid a relapse and to demonstrate his freedom and ability to create and use foreign-policy alternatives.

In contrast, the neutralism of opposition groups in well-integrated societies such as Britain and Japan stems from different experiences. Such groups covet withdrawal and passivity in reaction to the government's active policy of alliance and involvement; their concern is less with independence, which seems assured, than with immunity to the danger of nuclear destruction, which appears acute. Their pacifism is a delayed response to wartime exertions and deprivations, unlike the pacifism of some non-aligned countries which is influenced by their prevailing religion and world view. Neutralists in opposition share, however, with neutralists in power the desire to remove domestic politics from the pressures attending a permanent alignment. The socialists in Japan, West Germany, and even Britain would probably fare better if, wittingly or unwittingly, the American alliance did not work in favor of the more conservative regimes. The protest vote, however intense, is too small to offset the vote for continuing protection. By the same token, the Soviet alliance helped the Communist party electorally in Czechoslovakia in 1946.

[2] L. A. Free, *Six Allies and a Neutral* (1959), pp. 11–14.

Neutralists in and out of power are likely to develop along different lines in the future. Neutralists in well-integrated, allied countries may become increasingly militant as the level of the arms race rises. On the other hand, neutralists in positions of authority may progressively temper their militancy as they come to grips with concrete problems; and they may become less volatile as they realize that too frequent shifts in tactical alignment eventually debase the standing of the practitioner.

In the initial stages of independence, compensation has worked both as a psychological response to past dependence, and as a tactic to make up for present weakness. The psychological reasons for an anti-Western tone of policy are often quite subtly related to the colonial experience. A leader may fear that alignment with the West would degrade him in the eyes of his own and other ex-colonial nations. At Bandung, Nehru identified those favoring alliance with the West as "yes men," "hangers on," and "camp followers." Or a leader may adopt neutralism to make up for his Western formation and to disarm traditionalist strata in his society.[3]

Foreign policy serves the needs of "compensation" best when it can be changed more easily than basic domestic policies. That is eminently the case with neutralist policy. The basic international posture of a radical or socialist regime like Sékou-Touré's in Guinea merely extends domestic policies abroad; but occasional moves toward the Western position can help keep Communist influence within bounds. More conspicuous even is the utility of an anti-Western foreign-policy slant for an internally conservative government, hoping to undercut nationalist and leftist opposition groups, possibly with the aid of external claims known to be opposed by the West. While turning to the East diplo-

---

[3] The pertinent statements by Prime Minister Nehru at Bandung are reprinted in G. McT. Kahin, *The Asian-African Conference* (1956), pp. 64–72, 73–75. See also W. H. Wriggins, *Ceylon: Dilemmas of a New Nation* (1960), p. 467.

matically for internal reasons, the royal government in Morocco, for instance, stepped up its claims in the South— in Mauretania and in the Spanish Sahara. Likewise, Nasser's neutralism was originally the new regime's way of making up for the predecessor's alleged supineness *vis-à-vis* the West. Subsequent Western opposition to Egypt's objectives with respect to Israel and the Middle East generally consolidated Nasser's anti-Western policy.

In prosecuting regional ambitions, the neutralists force compensatory shifts by others. Unaligned countries such as Burma, Tunisia, and even potentially powerful Nigeria have been opposed to bids for regional dominance by local states no less than by outside powers. To counter such bids, leaders of threatened countries may move toward alignment with the West, if they can; or they may try to outbid their regional competitors in the pro-Soviet line, if they dare or must. The danger to the first line comes from radical nationalism; the risks of the latter course come from indigenous Communism. The relatively pro-Western non-alignment policy of Tunisia and of some of the former French-African colonies, as well as of Nigeria, was originally rooted in the personality of the leaders and in the relatively smooth accession to independence. Thereafter, the standing of the leaders and their policy has depended on their ability to steer a middle course—or balance opposites. They have had to withstand regional ambitions of neighbors and satisfy the hunger for prestige and progress of domestic nationalists and modernizers, securing just enough Western assistance to contain and construct without being compromised.

Non-alignment and neutralism are international policies inspired largely by domestic concerns. By the same token, they are political policies largely motivated by economic needs and interests. The leaders of new and some not-so-new nations are committed to economic development as a means to political stability which, among other things, would keep them in power. Many of them have come to believe that their countries cannot afford the cost in national unity or defense spending which a controversial alliance policy would entail.

The main reason, however, why the policy of non-alignment is economical is that it is profitable, when it brings in material assistance from both sides. The merely non-aligned leader seeks to demonstrate his impartiality by accepting assistance from both sides; the militant neutralist is seeking to prove his international importance in accepting such aid. When the neutralist leader has to accept the West's conditions of aid, he pays the price for extending the tripartite game into the field of economics. To have a Soviet alternative helps in relations with the West. And the existence of a Western alternative has enabled some neutralists, such as India, to place economic relations with the bloc on a sound monetary basis. Even when a neutralist country has had to put up with bilateral barter, as did the United Arab Republic, and has overcommitted itself economically, a chastened regime can presumably count on the West to bail it out in the last resort.

To sum up, the policy spectrum runs by way of strict non-alignment from biased neutralism to outright alliance-membership. Since the eclipse of the British-oriented ruling group in Ceylon, only some of the formally non-aligned French-speaking African elites have been openly critical of Sino-Soviet (and indigenous) imperialism; with such lone and, possibly, passing exceptions, the bias in neutralism has been against Western colonialism. The typical non-aligned regime is primarily concerned with internal stability and in some cases with security against proximate powers. The militant neutralist invokes anti-imperialist ideological precepts while working to profit from the contest between old and new imperialisms. Non-Communist Marxist that he often is, the neutralist actively seeks to employ the Soviet "antithesis" against the Western "thesis" in order to advance what he sees as the higher goal of his own national and socialist synthesis.

The differences between policies of neutralism and non-alignment are significant, though shadowy and fluid. They affect the influence which the uncommitted countries seek and which they actually do bring to bear on the international system; and they condition the strategic response of the cold-war contestants.

The "Blocs" and Stabilization

The self-styled "non-bloc" countries regard themselves as a third force for stabilizing international relations on a lower level of tensions between the adversary blocs. Can and do these countries perform such a role in fact, or is it a fiction impatiently tolerated by the greater powers for reasons of their own? I shall first examine some basic requirements of the role and then the performance itself.

To help stabilize the larger field, non-aligned countries themselves would first have to be reasonably stable and politically developed. This would mean for some or most militant neutralist regimes a delay in assuming an active international role. By contrast, mere non-alignment can ideally complement internal efforts to develop a national consensus capable of containing contests over fundamental foreign as well as domestic policy decisions, when a country is just emerging from dependence or division along tribal, ethnic, or class lines. Only as a coherent community forms, is the nation ready for gradual involvement in international politics at large and for commitments to other nations. Next to internal consensus, the country's leadership must first acquire an elementary sense of the reciprocity which truly equal states expect from each other whenever they relax the concept of self-interest and immediate need.

Colonial status is the worst possible school for international politics, when it comes to the acquisition of such a sense of reciprocity. For one thing, the responsibility of the metropole for foreign relations and defense isolated indigenous elites from the experience of relations with other states; such isolation could not but confirm the local elites' tendency to see their particular colonial power as the one and only embodiment of the hardships which actually mark relations among all states and collectives. For another thing, the colonial powers' monopoly of responsibility for internal order and welfare made all advances—such as the lessening of internal insecurity, disease, and poverty—appear unrelated to the performance of the "exploited" colonial society. And for a third, in many cases, and virtually in all cases most recently, outside forces had more to do with the attainment of independence than did the efforts and sacrifices of the indigenous elite.

Such colonial experiences have had one thing in common: they distorted the political vision of the new elites, especially by rupturing in their imagination the nexus between performance and consequences in relations among self-dependent actors.

Neutralism's effect is "neo-colonial" whenever it perpetuates the unreal world view under the new conditions of independence. The colonial experience shows when neutralist leaders neglect internal efforts, expecting aggrandizement from manipulating outside forces. And it shows also on the part of the more restrained non-aligned countries, when the attitude of non-responsibility is carried over into the question of national capability for defense.

For a poor country to delay acquiring such capability is apparently justified on grounds of internal development as well as external security. A non-aligned country derives a form of immunity from international configurations; and it may dispose of domestic substitutes for security-through-defense effort. One method is immunity through imitation of the potentially dangerous power. This may currently mean the adoption of much but not all of the disciplined one-party system of the Communist bloc countries. Another, and in a way opposite, mode of immunity is through irrationality.

This is the posture of a country which absorbs or deflects external pressures through chaos and anarchy instead of confronting them with organized strength. The attitude was allegedly Iran's in the past, and has been that of some more recently non-aligned countries.[4] When a country endowed with this kind of absorptive capacity aligns itself with an industrial power, the ally no less than the adversary tends to deprive it of the indigenous formless immunity without necessarily supplying an equivalent in rationalized means of security.

The trouble with substitutes is that they may be too effective. This may, at least for a time, be true of substitutes for self-made security. The decision to defer the burdens of a defense establishment—often prompted by the desire to avoid strains and imbalance in the structure of the developing nation's economy and political power—may actually retard both political and economic development. In many places a modern national army has been, and will continue to be, a major agent in welding together a heterogeneous society, imparting elementary acquaintance with modern skills and arbitrating factional conflicts. Not every country can have an Atatürk, to be sure, but even the Mobutus can be useful. They can temporarily "neutralize" rival politicians who are unable to master the range of intractable practical problems, decisions, and influences. Being the self-appointed guardian of national interests, moreover, the army is likely to discourage outside interventions, which feuding politicians sometimes elicit and are almost always prepared to exploit.

Unless it is relatively immune to intervention by greater powers, a country can itself hardly intervene with effect between such powers in the interest of stability or anything

[4] L. Binder, "The Middle East as a Subordinate International System," *World Politics* (April, 1958), p. 425. The posture recalls the strategy of confounding the adversary with apparent irrationality, failure to register demands and other messages, and inability to comply with threats. T. C. Schelling, *The Strategy of Conflict* (1960).

else. And truly effective intervention must be based on some independent capability. In contemporary conditions this capability need not be such as to permit an armed mediation; but the third party's influence must not derive only from the interplay of the powers which the party seeks to moderate. To the extent that it does so derive, the effect of third-party pressures is actually due to the greater powers' regard for the capabilities of each other. The leaders of the unaligned Bandung, and more recently Belgrade, powers are right when asserting that rightful influence is not merely a function of material strength. But "moral" influence cannot be—any more than can influence derived from the deadlock of contending forces—lastingly effective unless third-party pressures are such as to equalize great-power behavior even if they cannot equalize great-power capabilities. Much depends, therefore, on the meaning which the neutralist leaders attach to their other contention, to wit, that independence need not mean equidistance from the two materially strongest powers.

Before we evaluate the neutralists' influence, we may ask in what framework they might best be able to exert any influence. In order to enhance their individual bargaining power and capabilities, the neutralists could combine in a separate bloc organization of their own; and in order to enhance their moral authority as a group, they might prefer to act mainly or exclusively through the similarly authoritative world organization of the United Nations.

To abstain from "permanent" bloc organization reflects more accurately the attitude toward international relations of countries which build "independence" into a dogma. Moreover, a bloc-organization would be undesirable on strictly pragmatic grounds. It would probably reduce the bargaining power which the members have individually. The more conservative of the two superpowers, the United States, would shift onto the bloc-leaders the preoccupation with preventing defections from non-alignment; and the expansionist superpower, the Soviet Union, might let up on courting individual countries for fear of gaining less from any one of them than losing in bloc good will—or the good will of the bloc's leaders. The strength and influence of a loose and heterogeneous neutralist bloc as a whole might also decrease relative to the alliance systems, after it itself has helped consolidate them. In order to avoid being isolated between one enemy bloc and an expanding neutralist bloc, the alliance-leaders would have to reaffirm primary allegiance to their allies; and the governments of the lesser allies would have every reason for firming up the existing ties in preference to late-comer membership in a weaker grouping, subject to conflicting leadership ambitions.

Moreover, to add a neutralist bloc to the two alliance systems might well dissipate the greatest asset of the uncommitted countries. A neutralist bloc would debase the standing of the United Nations and decrease the unaligned nations' influence within as well as outside it.

Facts as well as official ideology have made the United Nations into an organization of the "non-bloc" countries for dealing with issues that are apparently separable from the struggle of the two adversary blocs.[5] Both East and West have countenanced the United Nations' evolution into a non-committed as well as non-committing organization, hoping to use it as the main forum for appealing to non-aligned countries in political warfare and mobilizing them for mediatory, supervisory, and policing functions in small-scale military clashes. The new ideology of the U.N. is, however, often discredited by the neutralist leaders themselves. They imitate the great powers whenever they transact a particular issue—such as that of the Congo in 1960-1961—outside the U.N. framework, hoping to gain a particular advantage, compose their conflicting interests, or merely escape the contrary pressures of the superpowers. More than a mere ideology, the very standing of the U.N. in the esteem of the

[5] See Introduction to the Annual Report of the Secretary General, in *New York Times*, September 13, 1960, p. 41. On bloc voting and membership, see T. Hovet, Jr., *Bloc Politics in the United Nations* (1960), p. 38.

great powers would be at stake if the neutralist countries went further and set up a "permanent" body of their own outside the global organization.

Within the U.N. itself questions relating to the role and composition of a neutralist bloc organization could not but interfere with the existing informal groupings. These diversely defined voting blocs and shifting alignments have proved to be the ideal mode of exerting influence. If mere membership in the U.N. raises a small country's status above that imparted by independence, as alliance with a great power used to, membership in one or several influential voting groups raises status above that imparted by membership in the organization and well above that implicit in material capability. The institutional arrangement has enabled the lesser countries to perform their part in adjusting global issues, while reducing to an approved scope and method the part of greater powers in local and intra-regional issues and disputes—a combination that has been an unattainable ideal for small states most of the time. But, if diplomatic influence of lesser states is contingent on great-power relationships, so is their diplomatic self-sufficiency. The contests of the two superpowers have not only enhanced the standing of the "third force" within the enfeebled organization; they have also increased its cohesion. The presumably U.N.-supporting non-aligned countries are not themselves a self-sustaining group. To the extent that a separate organization would lessen the need to react against great-power involvement, the group's cohesion and thus influence would wane.[6]

On balance, a neutralist bloc would probably decrease rather than increase its members' influence; but more im-

[6] In keeping with this analysis, if not necessarily for the same reasons, Prime Minister Nehru opposed President Nkrumah's agitation for a neutralist bloc organization during the 1960 United Nations General Assembly session. *New York Times*, September 28, 1960, p. 17. Since then, African neutralists have turned to regional organization, allegedly on the model of NATO; competing combinations have not failed to emerge. *New York Times*, January 8, 1961, pp. 1, 3.

portant than framework is the thrust of actual policies and their impact.

Given the necessary self-restraint of all concerned, mere non-alignment can reduce inter-bloc tensions and stabilize relations while favoring no contestant. On the regional plane, non-alignment counters the tendency for local states to divide between competing global powers. On the global plane, too, non-aligned states can be useful as insulating buffer states, mediators, and international policemen. The bigger non-aligned countries can serve as guarantors of the lesser buffer states; while a Laos might insulate East-West forces from each other, India might help guarantee Laos' immunity.

If non-alignment decompresses tensions between alliance blocs, militant neutralism injects pressures of its own into the field of forces. In principle, the effect can be none the less relaxing and roughly equal for each of the adversary sides. Third-party pressures do not ordinarily consolidate alliances, as do manageable pressures exerted by the adversary. The main reason is that third-party pressures are likely to bear on and activate secondary conflicts within the alliance blocs. They may be conflicts over substance, like those dividing the colonial and non-colonial countries in NATO, or over strategy and tactics, like those arising between the Soviet Union and China in the Communist bloc. The resulting intra-alliance policy debate has a positive incidental effect. It forces the publication of at least parts of the alliance's inner story. The revelations are especially valuable when they come from the totalitarian bloc, which relaxes secrecy about its intentions and commitments mainly by way of doctrinal disagreements.

A more far-reaching relaxation is within the realm of possibilities, however. As the neutralists attract attention, adversaries might moderate their activities and objectives. Head-on collision between antagonists is derouted into encircling movements; and reciprocal pressures mellow into enticements of third states. The adversary alliances, may, ideally, come to behave somewhat as rivals in a two-party system, competing over a floating vote of independents and being drawn to the moderate center in the process—while continuing all the while to stress their differences.

If this is a theoretical possibility, what has been the actual state of things? It can be argued that even pressures equal in force and kind would be disadvantageous to the Western side, because the basic security postures are not comparable. The Soviet bloc has a firm offensive and defensive base because of its central position on the Eurasian land mass. The West's security concept depends on bases in overseas islands and rimlands. Neutralist pressure on both superpowers to withdraw from advance positions and disarm tends to hamstring the West's strategic retaliatory capabilities. This might merely reinforce other compulsions to scale down levels of conflict to smaller-scale conventional and guerrilla-type operations; but a West disengaging and disarming under pressure would be handicapped in conducting the "limited" kind of operations in threatened areas. To be anything like equalizing, therefore, the neutralists would have to press both superpowers to withdraw into their respective national confines, following genuine self-determination of their wards and dependencies—a desideratum which would be unacceptable to the Soviets and might be distasteful to the United States in some cases.

Thus, with the best of intentions, impartiality would be difficult to attain. In actuality, the pressure of the neutralists has tended to be unequal; it has often been either coincident or openly co-operative with the Communists' pressure on the West. In the propaganda war, the neutralists have leaned toward adopting Communist meanings and attributions of categories like "deterrence" and "terror"; "disarmament," "arms control," and "arms race"; "aggressive" and "collective-security" alliances; "self-determination," "imperialism," and "neo-colonialism." Individually, a West-supported country has not hesitated to accept Soviet military assistance, even if it was capable of neutralizing Western positions scheduled for early evacuation by previous agreement.[7] Collectively, the neutralists have conducted a campaign against Western alliances and bases that has threatened first to upset a delicate balance of strategic power and then to necessitate a stampede toward the winning side—a last blow to the losing side that might exceed, and make unnecessary, the military effect of a first nuclear strike.

There has been no single reason or motive for the inequality of pressures—or, to put it differently, for the double standard applied to East and West. Apart from elements of short-term opportunism and personal rivalry, the primary reason could be either the greater fear of Soviet power or the greater familiarity with the West, compounding resentment of both deprivation and indebtedness with an ambivalent sense of familial identity. The fear has engendered a tendency to propitiate the Communist bloc and be receptive to its appeals and pressures; the familiarity has engendered a more critical attitude toward the West and the expectation that it be receptive to neutralist appeals and pressures. The actual mixture of motives in particular instances must remain obscure; clearer is the pattern of effects which the rapprochement between neutralist countries and the Communist bloc has had on the three multilateral Western alliances and the Soviet bloc itself.

NATO has been exposed to pressures chiefly from the Soviet bloc. The campaign against the Baghdad Pact, on the other hand, was conducted mainly by Middle Eastern neutralists. And SEATO has so far been saved from a combination fatal to the Baghdad Pact: intensification of neutralist opposition while Communist-bloc pressures apparently subside or are transmitted and legitimized by local non-Communist powers. The lesser intensity of local antagonisms

[7] Thus Morocco received Soviet military aircraft after the United States had agreed to evacuate American bases by 1963. The next step might be to concede a counter-base to the Soviet bloc. Guinea was reported, probably prematurely, to have granted a submarine base to the Soviet Union. *New York Times*, December 8, 1960, pp. 1, 6. On Morocco see *ibid.*, December 5, 1960, p. 13.

in Southeast Asia than in the Middle East has been a factor; moreover, after 1958, the bloc (and Communist China in particular) stepped up pressure on both the SEATO powers and the non-aligned countries in the area. Of the two main consequences, one was favorable for the West and the other less so. The Sino-Soviet bloc failed to subvert to its purposes the pressures beamed at SEATO by local non-aligned and neutralist states; but the resumption of Communist expansion also served to stimulate the fears of these states and their subsequent inclination to apply restraints on the West.

The new Sino-Soviet thrust for expansion had another significant consequence. It advertised the failure of the non-aligned Southeast Asian countries to loosen the Sino-Soviet alliance in such a way as to make it match and accelerate a like trend in the West's Asian alliances. When making the attempt, the Bandung conferees did not apply outright pressure in order to detach the Asian power, China, from the European ally, Russia; they relied on enticement, moral suasion, and verbal commitments.[8] The Bandung policy toward China was thus reminiscent of Anglo-French policy toward Germany in the 1930's. It differed, however, in that the object of neutralist appeasement was being simultaneously deterred by the Western alliance system. Ideally, the American strategy of deterrence might have supplemented the neutralist strategy of attraction; actually, American intransigence was no more effective than Asian wooing, and the former was not necessary to thwart the latter. In any event the Bandung operation in Asia was both a less deliberate and a less successful division of labor between neutralists and a cold-war belligerent than was the onslaught on the Baghdad Pact in the Middle East.

The neutralists and the West complemented each other no better in the unintended effect which Bandung had on the Soviet Union's European allies, mainly Hungary. There

---

[8] Kahin, *The Asian-African Conference*, pp. 67 ff.

the attraction of the neutralist model worked, but Western deterrence of Soviet counter-action did not. The events of 1956 showed the limits of neutralism as a force affecting both blocs. Domestic upheavals made some Communist leaders in the satellite countries receptive to the formula of non-alignment; but the Afro-Asian neutralists refrained from doing anything to enlarge the unaligned area at the expense of the Communist bloc. The Soviet Union was permitted to crush "counter-revolutionary" neutralism while retaining the ability to foster "objectively revolutionary" neutralism in the non-Communist world—both as a matter of "internationalist duty."

Following 1956, elements of both strength and weakness in the Western strategic posture have stimulated dealignment into neutralism in non-Communist countries, albeit for different reasons and to different degrees. On the other hand, Soviet technological and strategic successes have discouraged longings within the captive countries for their neutralization, and failed to encourage counterbalancing shifts in the position of the Afro-Asian neutralists. Even Titoist defection, the Soviet bloc's major failure to date in regard to neutralism, has worked on balance against Western interests. Receptivity has worked one way only. Tito has had some success in making Marxian-brand socialism attractive to the neutralists and in setting up Belgrade-brand neutralism as an alternative to the old-fashioned, self-liquidating anti-colonialism of Bandung. But Tito failed completely to have the Communist bloc accept non-alignment as a policy which could also be applied among "socialist" states.[9]

[9] W. W. Kulski, *Peaceful Co-Existence: An Analysis of Soviet Foreign Policy* (1959), pp. 118–19, 148. It must remain a matter of conjecture whether Tito has sought primarily to strengthen Yugoslavia vis-à-vis the Soviet Union and China, or whether, despite momentary disagreements with the bloc, he has been playing a part in the Communist strategy of dividing and neutralizing the non-Communist world. The two possibilities are not mutually exclusive. On the Belgrade Conference of "non-bloc" nations, see *New York Times*, September 7, 1961, p. 8, for final declaration, and P. Hofmann, "Bomb Jolts 'Neutrals,'" *ibid.*, September 3, 1961, p. E 4, for comment.

The imbalance that has so far marred the neutralist impact on the West and on the East has been too definite to disappear in the perspective of a few symmetries. Both sides in the cold war have learned that no amount of skill can reliably contain or master the neutralist wave. The Soviets' agreement to neutralize Austria boosted their new-look strategy outside Europe and, incidentally, added Austria to Switzerland as land barriers between NATO forces in Germany and Italy.[10] But the Austrian settlement also encouraged neutralist tendencies in Eastern Europe, which forced the Soviet Union into unpopular counter-measures. The West, in turn, has been ready to neutralize Austria's Far Eastern counterpart, Laos, albeit under the adversary side's military pressure. The readiness to do so threatened to strengthen neutralist tendencies among the Asian SEATO allies and to necessitate costly remedies in the future.

Frustration was shared by the cold-war adversaries most acutely in the area of foreign aid. Both superpowers have been uncertain about the likely course and outcome of alternative ways of rendering material assistance to non-aligned and neutralist countries; and both sought reassurance in largely analogous doctrinaire assumptions and beliefs about the ultimately favorable effects of such assistance on their respective goals. But it is hard to see how material assistance to less developed countries could serve to expand both the socialist commonwealth and the area of freedom; and for the Communist Chinese to oppose Soviet favors to neutralists has been as natural as for the Thais to deplore a like diversion of American resources. There have been more pointed divergencies on both sides. As a "neutral" in the Sino-Indian conflict over the borderlands, the Soviet Union has volunteered military supplies to India; and the Chinese have begun to dispute the Soviet monopoly of Communist influence in individual non-aligned areas, in remote Africa as well as in the traditional Chinese zone of

---

[10] See Kulski, *Peaceful Co-Existence*, p. 158, for the barrier argument.

influence. On the Western side, America has observed neutrality in the conflict between her ally, Pakistan, and India, as well as in a number of colonial contests involving European allies; and the French have contested American influence in formerly French-dominated Vietnam and Laos, both in "alliance" with neutralist elements in local upheavals and as part of plans for the neutralizing of Laos.[11]

It remains to be seen, however, whether the symmetries are real. The competition of the Communist powers in particular is hardly distinguishable from a deliberate division of labor, notably in its effects. Thus India's indebtedness for Soviet support against China may well have helped Communist strategy in Laos. The divisive impact of Bandung neutralism on the satellite belt has since been largely corrected, with the cooperation of the anti-colonial neutralists themselves. Their receptivity to bloc trade and assistance has helped diversify economic activities and outlets for the satellite countries and, consequently, has re-consolidated the bloc on a more substantial foundation than before.

Subversion versus Containment

The utility of the neutralists as self-appointed moderators is impaired whenever they distribute pressures and opportunities unevenly between the two alliance systems and elicit from them responses that are still more upsetting. The "responses" add up to the strategies of East and West toward neutralism, which implement certain designs and are impeded by certain dilemmas. The "designs" bear on the main strategic issue of the cold war: who contains or encircles whom by military, political, and economic means.

---

[11] See *New York Times*, October 5, 1960, pp. 1, 2, on Soviet military supplies to India; and Joseph Alsop, "The Yawning Drain," *New York Herald Tribune*, January 6, 1961, p. 18, on French support for Kong Le in Laos. Also see *New York Times*, May 24, 1961, p. 1, for a French proposal in Geneva, designed to restore French monopoly in military training and instruction in "neutralized" Laos.

An examination of the Sino-Soviet bloc's strategies must precede a more extended analysis of two main alternatives in the West's armory of responses.

The Communists' efforts to foster divisions among the members of the Western alliance as well as in the relations of Western allies with the non-aligned countries do not fit the model of two parties moderating their programs in order to win over the political center. The strategy is much more in keeping with the model of a multiparty system, with a revolutionary party seeking to disorder relations among all the other parties. The revolutionary party's objective is to impose its program of social transformation without concessions to anyone; its method is to divide and demoralize opponents by using "fellow travellers" to obscure and dissipate the straightforward character of the contest. The principal enemy of the moment is to be defeated with the help of a future enemy, or victim, which is singled out as a current ally for tactical reasons.

The Communist powers' chosen tactical allies have been the bourgeois-nationalist regimes in formerly colonial countries. The principal enemy, the West, is to overtax its resources and bring about its own division and isolation by ill-conceived responses to the provisional "alliance." Beyond this point, the Communists have seemed to hesitate. One possible direction for their strategy has been to try to subvert the less developed countries themselves one by one, as they were individually ready. Another has been to work for a stampede *en masse,* by eroding the non-Communist world as a whole and breaking up the West's "provocative" alliances; subversion in Iran, unlike subversion in Burma, would not so much alienate the non-aligned countries as bolster their conviction that their policy was the only right one.

The uncertainty over a key aspect of strategy has reflected the bloc's dilemmas in its relations with non-aligned countries. These dilemmas, now to be discussed in succession, concern the pace and the methods of Communist subversion on the one hand, and the revolutionary character of neutralism itself on the other.

The difficulty besetting the strategy of subversion in one country at a time has been the strategy's repercussion in other non-aligned countries. These countries' greater fear of the Sino-Soviet bloc serves the East best when the Communist bloc acts to intimidate the West or the world at large; but the dividends of fear decline into liabilities when the bloc encroaches on individual non-aligned countries themselves. Moreover, for the Communist powers to prevail at the center of authority in any one country, their real, subjectively committed, allies—the local Communist parties —must be able to prevent a last-minute reversal by the neutralist elite; and the Soviet Union must be able to deter a Western intervention on behalf of the chastened nationalists.

Most regimes in the less developed countries have been making skillful use of the distinction between the Soviet or Chinese state as an international friend, and the Communist party as an internal enemy. These regimes can be expected to resist the transformation of a tactical, limited-liability alliance with the Communists into full membership in the "socialist commonwealth." Such a transformation would be paralleled by domestic changes from a "national" to a "popular" democracy, and bring about the eventual liquidation of the nationalist elite. There have been few Castros willing to ignore the risk.

The increasing number of countries that combine the techniques of Communist-style one-party organization with radical-leftist ideology and policy are no exception. The authoritarian one-party system is efficient in mobilizing the masses; and it is less wasteful of scarce elite resources than is the alternative, born of an earlier, French, revolution: the combination of a centralized bureaucracy and a multi-party system. In addition to its internal economy, the one-party system has advantages in the international politics of the cold war. On the one hand, the one-party system may be the best available guarantee of internal security against a takeover, by imitating the Communist party's techniques for organizing mass support. Such a regime may, therefore, lean farther to the Sino-Soviet bloc than any other without danger of toppling over. On the other hand, should the global balance of power shift against the West, the non-Communist elite of the one-party system would find it easy to stampede into the Communist orbit. The smallness of the gap between the Soviet system and the local regime, which had so far immunized the indigenous authoritarian system, would then both predispose and qualify the regime to seek membership in the socialist "world system."

To promote such a stampede, the Sino-Soviet bloc must not prematurely alienate non-aligned countries by the pace and the techniques of subversion. To avoid loss of good will (from forcible takeover) and of face (from a successful counteraction) the Communist powers have been assisting neutralist regimes without daring to transform support into subversion. Only when the West has become too weak to serve as a rallying core for frightened neutrals does annexation become possible, but is no longer necessary for fighting the main enemy. In the meantime, the main difficulty besetting the strategy of progressively eroding the non-Communist world has been in the fitful interplay of countries and regimes at different stages of radical anti-Westernism and of maturity for Communist-style socialism.

Neutralism itself has in common with all revolutionary movements a pattern which confounds the outsider's attempt to harness such a movement to his ends.

The pattern is one of successive waves of radicalism and competitive thrusts of ambition, forcing most older and relatively satisfied revolutionaries into a more moderate, relatively conservative posture. Over the years, Nehru was first outdone by Nasser, and the two were subsequently brought into virtual unison relative to Nkrumah, as well as in reaction to him. To outdo the more radical newcomers to independence, and to reassert more than nominal leadership, the moderates will fitfully return to extreme postures; but this is unlikely either to last or be convincing. As a consequence, not many non-aligned regimes adopt an identical nuance in attitudes toward global issues any more than they are wont to adopt identical tactical stands on specific issues. The dynamic is unwittingly fostered by Communist-bloc policies. The bloc's special favors are highly unstable, as the bloc seeks out the most extreme champion of radicalism and anti-Westernism at any particular time and place; and the favors are limited. Not only does the bloc work with scarce resources; it can effectively support only so many rivals for finite prizes. The bloc could not back and favor simultaneously both Nasser and Kassim while they competed for leadership in the Middle East or both Nkrumah and Sékou-Touré in West Africa. Combined with the persistency of the Communist supreme command's "sympathy" for local Communist parties, the vagaries of bloc support for individual "bourgeois-nationalist" regimes cannot but advance the political education and moderation of the new elites.

The paucity of concrete results has increased the Communists' uncertainty about method; and this has made it all the more necessary for them to restate dramatically their ultimate intention—Communist triumph everywhere. Restatement was necessary in order to maintain unity and revolutionary ardor within the Sino-Soviet bloc;[12] but as a result the bloc's merely "objective" allies have become still more circumspect and more cynical about their own motives

[12] For such restatements see C. B. Marshall, *Two Communist Manifestoes* (1961), and the text of the draft program of the Soviet Communist party, in *New York Times*, August 1, 1961, pp. 13–20. Following an analysis of the vacillating attitude of the "national bourgeoisie" toward (Western) imperialism, the draft program concedes (p. 15): "The development of the countries which have won their freedom *may* be a complex multi-stage process." (My emphasis.)

for the alliance. The moment the Soviet Union felt strong enough to exploit the "general crisis of capitalism" on a broad front, Lenin's idea of "uneven development" began turning against Communist strategies in underdeveloped countries. Communist advances have proved to be reversible in countries which are not adjacent to the Communist heartland, like Syria, Iraq, and Guatemala, as well as in territorially adjacent countries like Iran—when the local Communist party rode the wave of Mossadegh's nationalism. The bloc registers failure whenever nationalist elites retreat from a pro-Soviet line, or when an alternative leadership displaces an elite which went too far without being able or willing to go all the way, or even allowed to do so by the global requirements of Communist strategy. Until and unless a major phase of expansion has run its course, the Communists themselves have to make necessity a virtue; they have to demonstrate the possibility of coexistence on the example of only half-controlled countries—Czechoslovakia until 1947, when Communist prospects in Western Europe collapsed, and probably Laos in the early 1960's, when that small country was being set up as a model of "neutrality" for Asia and Africa.

If militant neutralism is self-liquidating, and the Communist powers are beset by dilemmas, why should the West be preoccupied about militant neutralism? One reason lies in the capacity of the Sino-Soviet bloc to shift between strategies. Soviet nuclear terror can replace or supplement bloc wooing, producing superficially identical neutralist responses. This keeps the problem alive for the West and aggravates another reason for preoccupation, bearing on the Western response to neutralism.

Although directed at each other's weaknesses, the strategies of the cold-war protagonists have displayed a comparable pattern of concept and indecision. As the bloc has seemed to waver between seeking to subvert countries one by one and inducing a mass stampede at a somewhat later date, so the West has wavered between a long-term, country-by-country approach and one stressing the immediate requirements of the free-world system as a whole. And if the Soviets have seemed to be at loggerheads with the Chinese, the West has had even less of a unified strategy. The British have inclined to a long-suffering attitude, born of experience with ex-colonial countries such as America; the French, painfully decolonizing under neutralist pressure, have inclined to a sterner concept; and the United States has vacillated between courtship of the new nations and exasperation over them.

America's choice hung in the balance as her revolutionary myth and sentiment ran against two interrelated inclinations: cautious reformism for the free world and militant anti-Communism in the cold war. Her related, and partly contradictory, concerns have been to win the neutralists over and to maintain the West's alliances and vital security positions. The two concerns and emphases imply different assumptions and minimum objectives, and entail different dilemmas. As these are made explicit and the differences between them sharpened for purposes of exposition, there emerge two contrasting strategies—a strategy of conciliating all "neutrals" and a discriminatory strategy of containing the anti-Western "neutralists."

A major premise of the strategy of conciliation is somewhat as follows. The United States must identify itself with the anti-colonial position. It can sympathize with the growing pains of statehood, having itself passed through the stages peculiar to most "new" nations: colonial dependence, emancipation, fitful expansionism under the color of anti-imperialism—and economic growth. America too drew on the imperial conflicts of older-established powers while gaining and extending her independence—such as the conflict of the French with the British and subsequently of the British with the powers of the conservative Holy Alliance; and she used the reprieve to develop at home with capital assistance from abroad. In disputing the Soviet monopoly on anti-colonialism, therefore, America can and must act like an older brother who understands and humors the exaggerations of adolescence.

The conciliation strategy's key objective is for the individual non-aligned countries and regimes to uphold their commitment to independence. The commitment is taken to constitute the West's main political capital in the so-called uncommitted countries; its manifestations are of secondary importance. The strategy takes into account only one class of non-aligned countries, however called, and within that undifferentiated group it stresses each country's unique characteristics and individual needs. As the West meets these needs with properly adjusted policies, the new nations' spirit of independence is expected to come into conflict with Sino-Soviet imperialism, This will bring into the open the impartiality latent among the Westernized elites. Meanwhile, the West must foster an image of itself as a selfless friend and helper. The West can afford to take the long view, because it is both sufficiently strong and cohesive.

In the second, somewhat less optimistic view, Western policy should not only conciliate but also contain the apparently irreconcilable. It should be concerned with the contemporary requirements of the non-Communist state system as a whole, rather than with analogies from the American past, with utopias in the future, and with individual non-aligned countries in the present. The spirit of independence in less developed countries is valuable; but, like the stable growth of its material base, it cannot be prized regardless of its foreign-policy manifestations. The key, or minimum, objective is, therefore, not to foster commitment to independence *per se;* it is to contain both Communism and its neutralist "allies," so as to insure an elementary pluralistic order in the non-Communist world. Within such an incipient order, the developing countries must be able to progress *and* regress in their decolonization, politico-economic development, and foreign-policy attitudes at such uneven rates and in such a staggered phasing that at no time will all or most of them be ripe for simultaneous Communist takeovers.

The number of independent countries has been growing, and the greater powers' means for directly influencing their behavior has been waning at about the same rate. For both reasons, Western policies can have a desired impact only if they are consistent; hence the need to differentiate comparable types of behavior within the universe of non-alignment. Differently oriented elites interact and influence each other's behavior; to make their interaction orderly at any one time is as important as to promote individual countries' movement along successive stages of economic growth. The West is not infinitely secure; the global distribution of power is adversely affected by a particular type of neutralist policy, and it would be more substantially altered by the disintegration of the Western core-alliance than by the adhesion of all non-aligned countries to it. Hence the vital importance of repercussions of policies toward neutralism among Western allies. There may be occasional conflicts of interests between these allies and the genuinely non-aligned countries; but there is no fundamental conflict, since most of the alliances are still essential for shielding all of the non-Communist countries' "uneven development."

When material assistance is employed under the strategy of conciliation, it is ideally apportioned according to a country's need and absorptive capacity. The strategy of containment would employ assistance and other means in ways determined by the requirements of two vital and related balances. One is the balance of apprehensions, which has favored the Soviet bloc and channeled neutralist fears into one-sided restraints on the West; another is the balance of rewards and sanctions, which has apparently favored the more militant neutralists and made the West suspect of wooing them over against genuinely non-aligned countries and outright allies.

Before evaluating the two alternative strategies, I shall describe the two balances and outline the means of redressing them.

The balance of rewards and sanctions concerns support for stable growth and assured status of new countries and their regimes. It is unusually difficult for one government to impart status—in the form of prestige and influence—to the regime of another, weaker state. To give flagrantly is to detract; to impart conspicuously is to impugn. The difficulty is greatest in a fluid society, like the present international one, when status depends neither on tradition nor on accomplishments and inherent potential. Many past "diplomatic dictatorships" over the state system were the precarious expressions of some powers' monetary ability to manipulate their freedom of alignment. This freedom being now virtually foreclosed to committed states, it is incumbent upon the leader of a free alliance to contest the pretensions of "independent" neutralists; beyond that he may try to distinguish friendly regimes by well-advertised consultation and other means.

The task is easier when, rather than status, a great power dispenses material assistance toward stable internal growth. The criteria for allocating assistance among recipients are as important as is the fact of assistance, and they need not be left to inference from ambiguous statistics and coincidences in donor's and recipient's policy and conduct.[13] To encourage favorable alignment and concurrence of policy is not the same as to penalize impartial non-alignment; and the Western donor must be neither blackmailed into conspicuous assistance to anti-Western neutralists nor coaxed into it by

---

[13] These can be made to show, for instance, that the United States increased its assistance to the Asian members of SEATO and to non-aligned countries that did not shrink from expressing views paralleling Western ones—e.g., Burma and Ceylon on the subject of Soviet imperialism in general and its expression in Hungary in particular. See C. Wolf, *Foreign Aid: Theory and Practice in Southern Asia* (1960), pp. 198–99, 222–24. At the same time, American public spokesmen have been often at pains to deny favoritism or sentimentality toward allies and friends.

friendly recipients fearful of being too conspicuously identified. If the friendly regime in Senegal, for instance, needs large-scale American assistance to neutralist Ghana in order to appease its own opposition (while ignoring that to Nkrumah), it is unlikely to stay long in power anyhow. On the other hand, the United States was justified in continuing economic and military assistance to Morocco after it had agreed to evacuate American bases there under nationalist pressure; an attempt to use the occasion for serving a warning to other host countries might only accelerate demands for withdrawal from too patently "bought" facilities. It is less certain whether the decision actually to increase assistance to Morocco was wise in terms of its over-all impact, valid as may have been the desire to show good will for the hard-pressed and supposedly moderate dynasty.[14] But, without question, it must be advertised in advance that tolerance will stop (in Morocco and elsewhere) when non-alignment veers into opportunistic alignment with the Soviet bloc in support of regional ambitions.

When such an alignment materializes, a discriminatory policy of assistance may not suffice. It may have to be reinforced with the policy of graduated commitment, bearing on the second balance, that of apprehensions, which must be enlarged before it can be redressed. The West must be manifestly able and willing to help defend friendly countries with minimum devastation and prior "provocation"; but it must no less manifestly differentiate its commitments against Communist expansion as well as extend them to expansion by non-Communist states. Incipient expansion by would-be national or regional unifiers may not greatly threaten international stability in every instance; the same is not true of over-reliance on an apparently unconditional Western commitment to aid against Communist encroachments, regardless of a regime's prior disregard for the security needs of the West and for its own security risks. Supplementing the

[14] See *New York Times,* January 10, 1961, p. 78.

graduated deterrence which the West opposes to the Communist bloc, the policy of graduated commitment would also extend to neutralists the restraints which they would apply to the "committed" nations and which allies apply to each other.

The problem of communicating the policy and making it credible is still greater than it is with regard to graduated deterrence. The deterrent policy is implicitly communicated as the capabilities which are required to implement it come into being. By contrast, the principles of graduated commitment (as well as of discriminatory assistance) have to be enunciated, at least in general terms. Short of that, the possession of capabilities for making assistance possible and denial of assistance politically significant might merely confirm belief in an undifferentiated, universal commitment. The communication is heard by the potential major expansionist, too. This may call for some ambiguity, unless an explicit statement is part of a policy of pressure on an unfriendly non-Communist regime.

To compel choices from a position of weakness would result in permanently consolidating adversary alignments and creating new enemies, without compensating advantages. There are, however, two classes of reasons why a discriminatory policy is a credible one for the West to adopt. On one side are the dilemmas of Soviet-bloc strategy; on the other side is the discriminatory strategy's conformity with immediate Western requirements and its compatability with long-term Western objectives.

The West's dilemmas are not altogether different from those of the Sino-Soviet bloc. Both sides face an identical strategic quandary. They can seek subversion or stability, in the more or less remote future, by action concentrating on individual countries or on entire groups and classes of countries; they can adhere to a one-country or a one-system strategy. And both sides share the pitfalls inherent in dealing with a self-willed, faction-ridden revolutionary movement.

Regardless of which strategy it follows, the West's peculiar dilemmas are less intractable, because its designs are less far-reaching. The dilemmas have to do with the criteria and likely effects of the two alternative strategies.

The strategy of conciliation stresses needs and conditions in non-aligned countries; the discriminatory strategy of containment stresses their attitudes and policies. The two sets of criteria are fundamentally different and cannot be combined without producing some confusion; both have shortcomings. One criterion—that of structural needs and conditions—may contravene the immediate policy needs of the Western party when internal conditions apparently require the local government to pursue an anti-Western foreign policy. The other criterion—that of policy—may play havoc with the lesser country's economic needs and merits. The criterion of policy must, moreover, be combined with consistency in Western responses, if these are to influence comparable behavior in the system as a whole; but the policies of the local actors themselves are often internally inconsistent. A simple dilemma of this kind occurs when a regime combines an approved, anti-Communist, domestic policy with a disapproved, pro-Soviet or expansionist foreign policy. A more complex form of the dilemma is when one regime, say Nasser's in the U.A.R., clashes with Western interests in his foreign policy, while another, regionally rival regime, say Kassim's in Iraq, seems to be running counter to Western interests in his internal policies.

The dilemma is also one for the Soviets, which fact may help to make it only temporary for the West in individual cases. Thus Nasser, soon after being provoked by the Communists into repressing them internally, has moved to offset their ultra-revolutionary drive and his own failures abroad, in part due to Western opposition, by turning seriously to domestic reconstruction. And the dilemma's complicating feature likewise faded when Nasser's regional rival, the Kassim regime in Iraq, evolved toward a Nasser-like combination. The revolutionary regime's initial dependence on Communist support has given way to anti-Communism at home; and defensiveness abroad has given way to propagation of unifying regional designs (at the expense of Kuwait) —confined, again, to verbal expression by local opposition and British counteraction. While the dilemma lasts, however, it calls for a decision on priority and acceptance of the resulting liabilities. A strategy that is concerned with the international system as a whole logically assigns primacy to a regime's foreign-policy behavior over its domestic-policy behavior. It would destroy the rule-making and limit-setting impact of a consistent policy to try to combine the two criteria in an index of external-internal behavior to be encouraged or discouraged.

It is uncommonly hard to say which of the criteria—a country's needs or its policies—has more serious drawbacks. A general principle of evaluation may follow from a speculative question. Are gains in individual countries (and weak non-aligned countries in particular) capable of compensating for erosion of the non-Communist state system as a whole; and are they more, or less, capable of doing so than a resilient system of states is of absorbing and adapting itself to subversion and defection of individual countries? To answer, one must examine the likely effect of the two strategies (identified with the two sets of criteria) on the Western alliance system and the neutralists themselves.

Alliance members respond in a variety of ways to outside pressures. The allies' response to pressures from the adversary is divisive when the adversary is not blocked or repelled by the response; by contrast, an alliance may try to absorb, or deflect onto the adversary, the weaker pressures coming from third parties. A more flexible response is needed to absorb and deflect an outside pressure than to block and repel it; this is a point in favor of a conciliatory strategy toward neutralism. However, the response must be co-ordinated as well as flexible. Allies are mostly able to control each other's separate approaches to the adversary. When allies individually conciliate third parties, the resulting prejudice is likely to be against some member of the alliance rather than against the security function of the entire alliance; this will impede a unifying joint response. When the injured ally is unable to block intra-alliance initiatives which favor an outside party, he himself must absorb the combined pressure—from both allies and third parties—pending possible compensation by his allies for the loss suffered in the process.

The United States has contended with problems of this kind in its relations with the European allies over the issue of colonialism; and with non-European allies over local conflicts and jealousies. The bone of contention has been the distribution of America's political and material support. Two situations must be distinguished: one, when only the United States woos the non-aligned countries; the other, when several Western allies do so concurrently and may do so competitively.

The first situation may be the less dangerous one for the Western alliance. A Portugal, and a Thailand or Pakistan, are in the last resort less decisively swayed by what they regard as American courtship of neutralists than they are by NATO's and SEATO's ability to perform their functions. The two kinds of considerations can, however, be virtually indistinguishable from each other. Thus a relatively secure Portugal expects the alliance to safeguard its stability and status, intimately dependent on Portugal's extra-European possessions; and the security, status, and, possibly internal stability of countries like Thailand and Pakistan are intimately dependent on their standing relative to local non-aligned countries. Only in allied countries free of direct concern with non-aligned countries—like Canada and, decreasingly, Japan—is American policy toward neutralism definitely less significant in preserving or loosening ties than is the alliance's security performance and economic advantage.

The danger to the alliance grows with the number of partners that can and do nurse their relations with non-aligned countries without constant regard for their allies' interests. Many of America's allies can do so from superior past experience as they recover economic strength—thus West Germany; as they shed the colonial incubus—thus Britain and France; or as they atone for past aggressions—thus Japan. When competitive wooing in peripheral areas does take place, it may cause strains at the center of the alliance in the age of neutralism no less than interallied contests in such areas did in the age of imperialism.

Almost by definition, the discriminatory strategy of containing neutralism should have the clearest advantage over the more conciliatory approach when it comes to alliance cohesion. The great risk is that avoiding division may bring about the allies' isolation, no less than avoiding isolation may cause their division. The question of risks and one's attitude to risk-taking are at the root of any decision on strategy; the uncertain gains and liabilities of any course of conduct are notoriously hard to calculate.[15] The advantage of a deliberate risk-taking policy is that more of the risks are of one's own choosing in contrast with the unknown risks of an apparently prudent policy.

The two strategies incur different kinds of risks for the West, as they impinge on the non-aligned and neutralist countries themselves. The conciliatory strategy's risks are mostly speculative and are easy to underrate. The risks of the discriminatory strategy appear to be manifest and can easily be overrated. A reverse pattern seems to characterize the two strategies' advantages.

In the relations between the neutralist countries and the West itself, conciliation can easily lapse into appeasement and self-identification into condescension of "adults" toward "adolescents." To apparently condescend would augment

[15] C. J. Hitch and R. N. McKean, *The Economics of Defense in the Nuclear Age* (1960), p. 65.

resentment, to appease would forfeit respect. Intangible as they are, such matters govern relations between parties with highly unequal capabilities and inhibitions. More tangibly, the conciliatory strategy enables the courted countries to retain and compound gains from both sides, while leaving intact the imbalance in their fear-induced restraints on the two main parties to the cold war.

This makes things more difficult for the West. The West seeks to demonstrate the expansionist capability of the Sino-Soviet bloc; but it reduces the danger's imminence as it shows itself capable of dealing with the bloc. The neutralists can go on exploiting the East-West conflict and propitiating the bloc while claiming to have no fear of it. Moreover, if both the United States and the Soviet Union "reward" anti-Westernism, another premium is put on the most radical form of neutralism; the non-aligned and neutralist countries and groups then have no alternative course to tempt them. It is more difficult to contend with neutralism in allied Japan—and to apply strict criteria to the use of American assistance by allied Pakistan—when India gains from both sides; Senegal and Nigeria might not stay long on their relatively pro-Western course, were Mali and Ghana to receive equal or greater attention and support from the West; and a policy of indiscriminate conciliation would counteract the competitive interplay among neutralists themselves, an interplay which tends to confine extremism to a minority position.

The long-term risk of the non-discriminatory policy lies in the possibility of gaining no new friends and of losing old ones. The immediate risks of the discriminatory policy of containment are those of seeing one or several countries become positively hostile to the West, aligning themselves more closely with the Sino-Soviet bloc, or moving into full membership within it. The risks are those of any policy which presses two opportunistic allies together in the belief that enforced intimacy will reveal incompatibility—if kept up long enough, despite an initial rapprochement. The belief that such enforced intimacy does not produce and ultimately precludes permanent unions squares the policy of pressure with the basic rule of a tripartite system of policy: do nothing *vis-à-vis* a third party that might benefit the chief adversary.

Incompatibilities among rival non-aligned and neutralist countries and leaders themselves are a tactical asset for the West. They helped, for example, to restore Tunisia to moderate Bourgibism from a spell of extremism, seeking to coerce France into promptly evacuating the Bizerte base. Of larger significance are the incompatibilities that limit the degree of possible intimacy between neutralists and the Sino-Soviet bloc. Rival expansionisms are apt to produce even greater, or earlier, incompatibility between them than does the neutralists' will to independence. The ambitious lesser partner's concept of his independence tends to expand so as to comprise the disputed position and to exclude the stronger partner-antagonist from mere influence over it. The strain between the U.A.R. and the U.S.S.R. first came into the open over the Communist bloc's activities in coveted Iraq and in the Syrian province rather than in Egypt proper.

It is, of course, always possible that the discriminatory strategy may backfire and actually press the neutralist country into the Sino-Soviet bloc, as a result of the elite's pique or its Communist allies' triumph. The risk must not be overrated. Militant neutralism goes mostly with a fairly resistant one-party domestic system and remote geographic location: and neutralists can reverse themselves when they burn their fingers with the East, without completely burning their bridges to the West. For the same reasons, the West must press such regimes all the harder in order to make them move away from the bloc and closer to the center. A country's physical proximity to the bloc makes for greater immediate danger to national security; it is usually tempered by corresponding caution in the country's policy toward both

East and West, although regional disputes—such as Afghanistan's with Pakistan—may still occur and tax a discriminatory strategy to the utmost.

Such as they are, the risks can be further discounted by a gain. The gain is most likely to accrue when the circumstances surrounding the "loss" of a neutralist country increase desire for genuine non-alignment at large. To promote such circumstances may require the West to refuse help in salvaging a sinking elite. The refusal will pay off whenever subversion in a country remote from the Sino-Soviet bloc promises to be temporary and remain isolated, while the deterrent effect on other neutralists promises to be both widespread and lasting.

There is a more serious possible liability to be considered. The policy of discrimination on grounds of present behavior might interfere with the policy of assisting the development of potentially powerful countries, in the long-range security interest of the West itself. It is possible that, in such countries, the emotional satisfactions of a conspicuous foreign policy are soon offset by the reluctance to assume specific responsibilities prematurely. But if a conflict of objectives does occur, the long-term goal of building up such a country may have to be temporarily sacrificed for the immediate need of cutting its leadership down to size. Western aloofness may then produce compensating dividends, when it serves to highlight Communist encroachments and miscalculations while opposition to the developing country's costly foreign policy crystalizes within.

The two strategies' possible effect on multipolarization is a long-term aspect of their impact on the international system as a whole. Two more immediate issues arise in this connection. One bears on polarization between East and West; the other on the problem of international order in the non-Communist world.

The geopolitical pattern of polarization can be more or less symmetrical and neat. If a number of countries geographically close to the West's heartland should adhere more closely to the Sino-Soviet bloc politically, this would make for symmetry of the pattern, as long as the West retained its friends, allies, and positions geographically adjacent to the Sino-Soviet heartland. Should the West lose these positions and the Communist bloc fail to gain or long retain positions in the Western orbit, the pattern would be both symmetrical and neat: two compact blocs would face each other across adjacent non-aligned areas.

So far, the West has enjoyed asymmetry in its favor, progressively marred by setbacks in individual countries. The West's ability to uphold its wards and positions has been apparently on the decline in areas both remote from and adjacent to the Sino-Soviet bloc. At the time of the Guatemalan crisis, in 1954, local Communists had still to rationalize their failure to consolidate gains. They alleged the impossibility of taking over a country placed in the "iron fist" of Western imperialism, that is, in geographical proximity to the United States.[16] The doctrine may have been revised after the fist failed to bear down on Cuba; it was in any event being invalidated by revolutions in long-range military hardware and in short-term popular expectations. The two revolutions were complementary in opening up the American sphere to Soviet influence; after a century of disparity, initiated by Napoleon III's expulsion from Mexico, something like equality of access to areas of each other's immediate concern was apparently being re-established between the United States and the unfriendly European power of the moment. The emergence of equality highlighted a persisting disparity in the two superpowers' attitudes toward forceful action against less powerful states; and the practical handicaps flowing from the disparity for the United States have been further increased by superficial analogies between the Cubas and the Hungarys.

The combined impact of an inescapable equality and a

[16] R. M. Schneider, *Communism in Guatemala, 1944–1954* (1959), p. 80.

largely self-imposed disparity might precipitate a reordering in the existing geopolitical pattern. Even if the Sino-Soviet bloc does not attain an asymmetry completely favorable to itself, it might enforce a symmetrical and neat repolarization. Neither of the two compact blocs would then encircle the other by its outposts. Before this happened, Western positions and commitments in areas near the Soviet Union would have to be subverted, or be tacitly bartered for Soviet abstinence within the Western heartland and near the United States in particular. Such a bargain may well be the provisional objective of Communist forays in areas remote from the bloc; its ethical hazards would exceed those of intervention against small states' abusing their independence.

The discriminatory strategy might affect the pattern of polarization by pressing non-aligned countries into the Sino-Soviet bloc; the conciliatory strategy might influence the pattern only indirectly, but more profoundly, by conferring on non-aligned official and public opinion a virtual veto power over Western responses to Sino-Soviet probings and pressures. Such considerations might merely rationalize moderation induced by a growing regard for rising Soviet capabilities; while deeming itself self-restrained, the West would merely be self-deceived. The effects would not stay confined to the relationship of East and West; closely related are the two strategies' implications for an elementary order in the non-Communist part of the world itself.

International order requires that the major powers exert themselves within as well as on behalf of the non-Communist world. In the perspective of the conciliatory strategy, the responsibility is communal even before there is a community; in the perspective of the discriminatory strategy, it must be residually imperial even after there are no more Western empires—as long as the bigger ex-colonial countries do not choose to share in the task. To be policed are acts in excess of the lesser countries' rights and duties to uphold their essential internal and external independence; here belong threats to still weaker outside parties and inhibitions on the greater powers' security role. The objective is not rule by one or several powers; it is to evolve rules of mutually tolerable conduct within an embattled part of the world, and to prevent over-reactions to internal problems from generating disorder abroad.

The rules may continue to inhibit direct and forcible interference in internal affairs. This is apparently at variance with the fact that domestic factors tend to determine the international behavior of the most self-assertive neutralists. However, the inconsistency is less, the more consistent is the foreign policy of the great powers that aim at influencing the behavior of the lesser ones. Only consistency in demonstrating the limits of Western tolerance can substantiate these limits. Once they are established, the limits are perforce taken into account by local actors. Some actors will devise substitutes for equating anti-colonialism with anti-Westernism as a means for enhancing their local positions; some other actors will be compelled to reveal fully their commitment one way or the other. Apparently uncontrollable local power fields might then become more manageable; a concurrent polarization of forces within and between non-Communist countries need not be unfavorable to the West. Many of the local actors who aim to reduce Western presence think and act within the framework of a permissive or vacillating Western strategy. They would re-examine their attitudes if the inescapable choice were between assistance on terms satisfying vital Western interests or the transfer of Western friendship elsewhere.

Some such rationale has inspired the policy of the Fifth French Republic toward its colonial dependencies. The sanction of withholding all French assistance was meant to encourage continued association with France in larger community or special partnership. The sanction was implemented against Guinea, when she chose complete independence; the sanction was threatened in order to influence Algeria's decision between severance of ties and continued association. As applied to Guinea, the policy was discredited within its own terms. The alienation of the penalized country was not given time to pay off in deterrent effect on other French-African countries, soon given virtually complete independence in a reversal of policy. Apart from being consistent, moreover, the policy must also be concerted. It is a feasible strategy for the West as a whole rather than for any one, or any but the most powerful, Western country—notably if such a country's allies cannot be counted upon likewise to deny aid and forego influence.

The West cannot concert policy for a common order—or for joint action of any kind—without in some way touching upon the identity of the conflict to be regarded as the dominant one for the global system and the non-Communist system of states for some time to come. The choice is between the East-West conflict and the South-North issue of economic development and political independence for the non-industrial, mainly ex-colonial, countries. The conciliatory strategy implies belief that a choice between the two conflicts can be avoided, as long as the West avoids stressing preventive, and mainly military, approaches. The discriminatory strategy implies the belief in continuing contest over priority, despite adjustments in techniques of conflict; whenever choice is necessary, the East-West conflict and the immediate requirements of waging it must be treated as dominant.

In terms of the sweep and interplay of cultures and civilizations, the South-North issue may appear as ultimately transcending the more acute contemporary conflict in importance. The view is apparently confirmed by short-term impressions, when both the East and the West resort to indirect strategies and to economic weapons for fighting each other in the Southern Hemisphere; and it receives support from a statistical illusion, due to the sheer number of colonial and post-colonial crises in which the powers of the North (including the industrial Soviet Union) have on occasion been reduced to secondary roles.

It can be argued, on the other side, that changes in

method do not produce changes in identity, and that ups and downs in statistical incidence do not reverse the order of priority. A conflict is "dominant" when it can transform the international system in the process of being waged and, possibly, won by one party. It is not easy to see what the South-North contention means in terms of particular stakes or what a victory of the South as presently constituted would mean for the state system, unless it be multipolarity resulting from an enforced diffusion of Northern wealth and power. A partial diffusion and the transformation that may result are, however, being promoted only or mainly as a byproduct of the East-West struggle. If the stakes are indeterminate, so are the contestants. The major industrialized powers occasionally identify themselves with the South, and more insistently resist being identified with the "North" as the South sees it; but the South itself disposes so far neither of a major power of its own nor has it sufficient cohesion to override internal factionalism and produce an independent collective capability. And finally, commitments and loyalties won through parallel or supporting policies on the South-North issue are still less permanent and transferable to the other major issue than those won on the East-West issue.

In case of doubt, a conflict that can be defined more clearly in terms of actors and stakes, and can give rise to dependable ties, should be given primacy in resolving uncertainty over priority. This is not to say that the East-West conflict will remain dominant indefinitely. But it is not a matter of indifference whether it would be the West or the Soviet Union that would revise past policies and objectives more basically, should an ascendant South move to transform the South-North "issue" into a real conflict.

6
The Future of Alliances

THE FUTURE of alliances depends on changes in the international system, bearing on the number of major powers, the lines and forms of conflict, and the distribution of ultimate weapons among the powers. Speculations about the future are not predictions; but they help to guard against submission to events and fate.

Material Build-up and Multipolarity

In due course, the South may develop great powers of its own from among the non-aligned countries of today. The major powers of tomorrow, too, will have to come to terms with non-alignment of lesser countries when they assume greater responsibility for regional and global security in a more nearly multipolar international system. To anticipate such a state of affairs is a task for the powers of today.

Non-alignment helps greatly in attaining the status of a great power. It immediately increases the diplomatic influence of a state and secures outside assistance for increasing the big country's material power to match diplomatic influence. Consequently, non-aligned countries with great-power potential can afford to wait before they acquire in nuclear capability the final token of greatness. In this they differ from two other classes of countries. For aligned countries, nuclear capability may be a substitute for neutralism as a booster of diplomatic standing; and for neutralist countries without capacity for significant growth, some nuclear capability may soon become necessary to delay their decline relative to the better endowed former dependencies. If there be nuclear diffusion, a U.A.R. of the future may well precede India, which can wait and which stands to gain by waiting.

India has been the most frequently mentioned candidate for great-power status; others are Brazil and, if she does not disintegrate, Nigeria, or, if it aggregates, another regional superstate in Africa. The attempts to identify future great-power centers are exceptionally hazardous. Industrial potential is as important as sheer size; the former facilitates concentration of resources, the latter the dispersion of strategic facilities. The presently semi-industrialized big countries will take some time before they join the company of the industrial big powers. But at a later stage Brazil may surpass Britain in the West, and India may match or surpass Japan in the East.

National power which grows as a balanced whole of material and immaterial components is an "organic" one. Multiplication of the centers of great organic power must be distinguished from diffusion of diplomatic influence, based on the structure of the state system, and of nuclear capability, possibly superimposed on an otherwise undeveloped country. Should great organic power be dispersed, the global system would change in a double sense. One change would be in its structure, as the bipolar structure would yield to one genuinely multipolar. Another change would take place in the system of policy. It would not cease to be essentially tripartite; but the growing number and wider geographic and racial distribution of major actors would proportionately reduce the influence of the irresponsibles among the powerless ones.

As we know it, diplomacy originated in Europe and, as it spread out, fused with outlandish mores and with indigenous techniques of statecraft where such were present. Both within and outside Europe, diplomatic forms and procedures favored states worthy of the name, endowed with a central authority capable of upholding international commitments while restraining foreign alignments of factions. The real difference in standing and treatment was not between European and non-European principalities and powers, dear as the distinction is to the doctrinaire anti-imperialist. It was, rather, between eighteenth-century Poland and late nineteenth-century China, on the one hand, and the Low Countries and Siam, on the other. Poland and China were partitioned, because weaknesses in their domestic systems invited the destructive expression of balance-of-power politics. The more resistant internal order of the Low Countries and Siam had a part in making the balance of power work so as to produce a more positive result; both small countries secured their identity as neutralized buffer states between French and British power in Europe and Asia, respectively.

The color-blindness of European high diplomacy supplied its own irony. The signal event of anti-European and anti-colonial nationalism was Japan's victory over Russia; it was largely due to Nippon's altogether equal alliance with Britain (against an adverse coalition of European powers, France and Russia), concluded at the very peak of the colonial era. When more true great powers have risen in previously "colonial" areas, the West need not, therefore, substantially alter its traditions in order to adapt its diplomacy to the change. It can only welcome the relief from an inter-state politics, which has been papering over too many gaps between capability and influence.

Both the United States and the Soviet Union have been building up potential core-powers, each being more or less constrained to do it. The United States helped rebuild West Germany and Japan, and has been investing large resources in India, to offset Russia's part-creation, the "new" China. Demanding as it is in material effort, the diffusion of organic power calls for a parallel intellectual effort. Three main questions present themselves. One bears on domestic structures: which structures are likely to result in a foreign-policy behavior compatible with the interests of the United States or, for that matter, the Soviet Union? Little of what is known can be applied in relations between sovereign states; this matter has been dealt with elsewhere.[1] Another question, to be taken up shortly, bears upon the kind of international system in which self-interest of the new powers prompts behavior favorable to stability and security, regardless of domestic structures and passing attitudes toward issues such as those presently separating the West and the East. And the last question, now to be discussed, concerns the likely implications of global multipolarization at various stages of the longer run.

The object is to avoid—as nearly as possible in a system whose main merit is flexibility—the experience of Great Britain with Japan and of Russia with Prussia. Promoted as counterweights to other hostile powers, the protégés soon became antagonists. All risks cannot be avoided. Stalemated conflicts between truly great powers are most productive of terrible infants who seek to dominate the progenitors but who may also grow up to become their main support. When powerful agents are brought into a multipolar system from the outside to redress its balance, they may dwarf their sponsors almost immediately in producing a bipolar pattern. France and Spain did so when they were brought as allies into the Italian state-system; and so did America and Soviet Russia with regard to Europe. On the other hand, when the sponsoring powers themselves are strong, they will re-

[1] In my *New Statecraft: Foreign Aid in American Foreign Policy* (1960), Chap. 4.

main longer in control of the forces they helped activate in one form or another. It took centuries before France's and subsequently Russia's junior ally, Brandenburg-Prussia, became, as Germany, the arch-enemy of both. It took less for the English-speaking colonists to deprive Britain of the fruits of a joint struggle for immunity against France in North America; but the child of defection grew up to be the all-important associate and ally of Britain in two World Wars.

The risk of the future is a possible contradiction in the present, when a great power builds up potentially powerful states and seeks to maintain its alliances at the same time. For the West, the contradiction might be most striking when the nation developing the capacity for being a regional core-power has been its ally. Sooner or later, such an ally is likely to have the relationship revised to fit a growing role and status, or even throw off the alliance tie altogether. To be formally unaligned with either East or West has become almost a condition of regional leadership; and dealignment may help satisfy grievances against both allies and enemies, such as the territorial grievances which Japan has against the United States and the Soviet Union. But, formerly allied or not, an ascending power will incline to supersede one or both of the regionally present superpowers as the nucleus of a regional grouping. An India-centered grouping, designed to contain Communist expansion, might supersede SEATO, for instance. But if India became Soviet Russia's protégé against China, SEATO might only add an anti-India slant to its anti-China slant, as the latter had prevailed over the anti-Soviet orientation. Roughly the same alternative would arise in the Western Hemisphere, if past allies of the United States, Brazil or Argentina, became strong enough to supplant the inter-American system with a Latin-American grouping of all or only some states of the region.

Much depends on the lesser countries in the affected region. They may be both anxious and able to use remote states, with political and military access to the region, to ward off subservience to one regional power or conflict between two regional powers. Or, conceivably, they might respond to the attraction of local powers, regardless of alternatives. When developments are unpredictable, however, fall-back positions are essential. This is an important truth for a power like the United States, which cannot avoid being "present" in several regions.

The more important precaution is a material one. It consists of helping the more promising among the smaller states to develop concurrently with the build-up of the potentially great regional powers. The pertinent objective of the lesser states' development unfolds as the larger local powers adjust policies to their increasing strength. Only in retrospect does one know what has been the "real" objective from the beginning. However, small-state responses at both polar extremes—resistance to domination and responsiveness to regional leadership—require economic and political strength. Moreover, by helping less developed states diversify their economies, foreign assistance may facilitate those regional associations which have so far been impeded by economic competition or by the fear of economic dependence. In that sense, at least, the chief security-stability purposes of economic build-up and of politico-military alliance can coincide.

There is an altogether vital proviso, however. The opportunity for outside assistance and build-up may be limited to a relatively short period of grace. This is the period during which potential great powers are not yet strong enough to thwart the extra-regional nation's activities in the lesser countries. They can react to these activities by giving a hostile slant to their non-alignment; it would be premature and self-defeating for them to go all the way to counter-alignment. And they cannot yet coerce the lesser states to sever their ties. Nor are conditions in the hypothetical period of grace ripe for a strictly regional organization. The resources of the rising powers are still inadequate for promoting regional stability, and the powers are not yet prepared to assume responsibility for regional security. Their claim to leadership is still latent; to the extent that it is actually put forward, it is based merely on their status as politically "independent" and potentially powerful states courted by the truly great powers.

In the same "period of grace," the lesser states are relatively free to manage their conflicts as they choose. They may adopt a common front against a rising local power, accept its arbitrament, or seek extra-regional support. And they need not allow their primary local conflicts to involve them in a globally dominant conflict in order to make sure of such extra-regional support. In other words, in the period of transition from global bipolarity to multipolarity, a regional system is apt to be essentially multipolar, largely autonomous, and relatively free from fixed alignments. It is by the same token more open to the activities of outside powers, which may aim at reconciling long-term structural goals with immediate national needs.

Once the potential of a regionally major state or states is realized, however, the relationship between global and regional structures is likely to change into one which rules out outside involvement. Only in exceptional circumstances, when the global system is unipolar, tightly bipolar, or infinitely multipolar, will the structure of the regional systems tend toward being identical with the global one. That is to say, effective power in regions will be concentrated in the imperial global power, polarized between local allies of the two global power centers (with few or no countries being unaligned), or else it may be evenly diffused among the local specimens of the great many "major" actors in the global state system. When the global system is loosely bipolar—i.e., encompasses many unaligned states—the regional systems will tend to be multipolar, consisting of various combinations of aligned and unaligned states. Things are different when the global system is finitely multipolar, that is, when it consists of a relatively small number of major states, so dispersed globally that no more than two are indigenous to one region. The regional system will then tend toward unipolarity when one such major power controls all local states; or it will tend toward bipolarity when two of the major powers polarize the lesser states through adversary alignments in function of their greater fear of one of the two greater states and of rivalries among themselves.

South and Southeast Asia, for instance, could be polarized around China and India (or China and Japan, or Japan and India), or the area might be "unified" by conquering China or by an India offering protection against China on terms excluding local small-state quarrels. Should India's protection be sufficiently effective, it might both compel and warrant the withdrawal of the United States as a regionally present power and ally; the same is true of Soviet involvement when China develops self-sufficient means of regional coercion.

Material precautions, such as diffusion of assistance in the "period of grace" are crucial. Withdrawal will be still easier when the retreating extra-regional power has also institutional fall-back positions and, finally, when changes in the structure fulfill some of the functions of superseded alliances.

The institutional fall-back positions consist chiefly of less comprehensive alliance combinations and less demanding forms of commitment. In both Europe and Asia, less inclusive alliances preceded the bigger ones. In the Communist camp, bilateral treaties preceded the Warsaw Pact in Europe and may precede a Hanoi Pact in Asia; in the Western camp, the progression was from the Anglo-French Dunkirk Treaty through the Western European Brussels Pact to the Atlantic alliance; from the ANZUS Pact (of Australia, New Zealand, and the U.S.) to the South-East Asia Treaty Organization; and, less auspiciously, from bilateral liaisons, notably of Britain and Iraq, to the Baghdad (and now Central) Pact. The Western European Union, institutionalizing the Brussels treaty, proved repeatedly a convenient stand-by for fitting Britain into Europe as a politico-military counterpoise to Germany; the ANZUS Pact, possibly enlarged by Britain, might likewise come to serve again a restricted purpose; and even the Balkan Pact, joining Greece and Turkey with Yugoslavia, has been kept formally in effect for possible future contingencies. To revive a dormant or moribund alliance may facilitate retreat from an abortive larger scheme. It may also be less provocative to rising or resurgent powers than if altogether new constellations were to coalesce in their orbit.

The alternative, and possibly supplementary, institutional fall-back position is that of a reduced commitment. Such a reduced commitment might be the middle range of the "graduated commitment"—a pledge to benevolent neutrality when the friendly power is faced with comparable force. The top-range pledge to intervene against "two or more" powers or qualitatively superior force remains the crucial deterrent to expanding the conflict; as such, it has been stressed earlier in the discussion. The concern at this point is a somewhat different, if related, one: to limit the guarantor power's or powers' involvement before and during a conflict, as an objective desired mainly for political reasons by most or all of the governments involved.

To guarantee lesser states merely against superior power combinations would reduce the Western and specifically American commitment where it had been to unqualified mutual assistance. This might require a compensating build-up of local forces, so as to keep them equal to unaided (or not more extensively aided) local adversaries; and it would require the building of local facilities potentially available to the guarantor for use in an emergency. On the other hand, self-dependence against an equivalent opponent might offset the perverse tendency of foreign assistance to abate the recipient's own efforts. Domestic and regional opinion would have less cause for attacking a foreign alliance as involving a small state and the entire region in great-power struggles.

Events might eventually make it desirable for the greater powers to apply the formula even to close small-state allies —for example, to a country like South Korea in the case of the United States. In the immediate future, however, the commitment might serve mainly to give a blanket guarantee to genuinely non-aligned small states in danger of attack or internal subversion aided by an expansionist, Communist or non-Communist state. The guarantee might help deter the Communist powers from joining in coalition against another small state or from encouraging local small states to join with each other in quasi-multipolar regional situations; and it might help deter any, including a non-Communist, government from joining another government or a rebellious faction in military action against a guaranteed regime.

To the extent that the deterrence would work both ways between the United States and the Soviet Union, or other adversary great powers, the effect would be similar to that of the Locarno formula of the 1920's. The guarantor powers would not now pledge common assistance against any one of the local antagonists guilty of aggression; but the guarantor powers' deterring each other would still discourage the local adversaries from acting violently against one another—this time by depriving both of the prospect of large-scale outside support.

The modified Locarno-type guarantee might be stabilizing. A formal prerequisite, we have noted already, is that only a minimum of other, more demanding, kinds of commitment operate in the system.[2] The material prerequisite

[2] Even if there were no other incompatibility between mutual–assistance and anti-coalition commitments, a political one might arise in contingencies in which global bipolarity cut across regional multipolarity. For example, it would be embarrassing if Turkey, as the defensive ally of the United States against the Soviet Union, should join a Middle-Eastern state making war on another regional state and the United States were obligated to prevent any other (including a non-Communist) power from joining the aggressor against a Middle-Eastern state. The tenor of the commitment follows closely that proposed by the Russians to Germany in the 1870's and adopted by Britain and Japan in their alliance treaty, which isolated and helped defeat Russia in 1904. See above, Chap. 1 n. 7.

is that both guarantor powers are self-restrained when it comes to invisible assistance under the legal cover of "benevolent" neutrality, before and during the conflict alike. Were the powers not equally self-restrained, but only equally expert at rendering covert assistance, they would bring about an indirect, likewise invisible or unadmitted, conflict between themselves. And, as the third possibility, if one of the guarantor powers could not effectively match the other's techniques of covert assistance, it would have to consider expanding the scope and raising the level of confrontation—to one in which either the small-state belligerents or the great powers themselves would be equivalent. To save the guarantee from being thwarted in its object (of deterrence and protection), the disadvantaged power would itself have to thwart the guarantee's intent (of limitation and reduced involvement), or be guilty of substantial default.

The guarantee would aim at securing friendly regimes —allied and unaligned—against indirect as well as direct aggression, carried out or supported by non-Communist powers as well as Communist ones. To that somewhat uncertain extent, the commitment would go beyond prior Western, and specifically American, commitments, in so far as these have been confined to aggression and subversion by forces of "international Communism" under the various instruments, understandings, and doctrines. To extend commitments in one direction may be necessary, even in a policy aimed at reducing their sum. Friendly governments have reason to expect allied support when they side with the West in the cold war and undertake internally unstabilizing development, defense, and "liberalization" efforts in concert with major allies or at their behest. Under such a guarantee policy, only the Royal Iraqi government could have laid claim to Western assistance. Actual or attempted overthrow of allied regimes in Turkey, South Korea, and France by officers' groups took place without any outside support or direction. The toppled regimes were, therefore, outside a guarantee policy against inter- or trans-national coalitions.

The merits and feasibility of intervention in individual instances are debatable matters; differences in the available time span, character of crisis, fortitude of the embattled government, and location of the insurgent groups will necessarily condition the possible, as well as the actually adopted, intra-alliance measures. But, from the viewpoint of the alliance system as a whole, a repeated failure of the major Western powers to save or avenge violent, physical liquidation of allied regimes can firm up the West's alliances no more than can irresolution in contending with external aggression and subversion in less-than-ideal conditions and deferential if not preferential treatment of some neutralist regimes.

What forms should the partly expanded, partly reduced, commitment take? Ideally, the commitment's form should be congruent with its object—that is, with the acts of third parties to which it refers. Formal commitments used to aim only at equally formal, including belligerent, acts of other states. In an exposé of the advantages of reciprocal assurances by the three Eastern European emperors, Bismarck made a distinction which is still pertinent:

Such a treaty and such a guarantee can have . . . for their object only overt acts of state. A treaty can give no safeguard against uncontrollable diplomatic interferences and intrigues. The struggle of diplomatic rivalry cannot always be ruled out even between the best friends and allies.

More recently, following World War II, Western allies have formally obligated themselves to joint action also against covert acts of subversion directed from without; but the obligation has been to a formal activity only—preliminary consultations—whatever may have been the informal co-operative arrangements of the allies' security organs.[3]

---

[3] For Bismarck's formulation, see *Die Grosse Politik*, Vol. III, No. 521, p. 152. (My translation.) in the same dispatch, Bismarck answers, "With a treaty more than without one," the doubts of the Austrian foreign minister

In practice, expediency will be the determining factor. Thus a formal commitment by treaty is desirable only when it increases the likelihood of observance and has a deterrent effect by and of itself. The same applies to explicit communication of one's informal self-assumed commitment. On the other hand, whereas a formal treaty is often desired as the symbolic expression of support for a particular regime, it may be a liability in relations with the regime's opponents. When the response of the target-state is largely independent of form, tacit understandings are preferable in the face of domestic resistance to the connection; it is easier to show support of a regime even if there is no treaty than it is to dispel enmity which can be inflamed by the readily understandable fact of a treaty. In revolutionary conditions a treaty is a handy propaganda target as the instrument of neo-colonial dependence, source of material burdens and security risks for the lesser ally, and the object of violations by the major partner. For the major power, to be sure, tacit and informal guarantees may mean duty without gratification, notably if the absence of a treaty makes it more, rather than less, difficult to secure the necessary minimum of potentially usable facilities. A merely tacit commitment increases, however, the range of choices regarding its implementation; by the same token it diminishes the adverse repercussions which failure to intervene effectively has on a treaty network.

In an essentially bipolar or only quasi-multipolar system, such as that presently prevailing, a written or tacit graduated commitment would mainly be extended by great powers to lesser ones; it would be supplementary to measures practically feasible under the U.N. system. Were the commitment to be reciprocal, a small-state party would have to

---

about the possibility of trusting Russia. The commitment to "consultation" is to be found, e.g., in Article IV of the North Atlantic Treaty, as well as in Article III of the Mutual Defense Treaty between the United States and the Philippines (August 30, 1951).

pledge benevolent neutrality in, for example, a Sino-American or Soviet-American war and outright assistance if a small-state neighbor joined the Communist great powers. The object then is material equality between adversary sides and formal equality between the friendly parties.

In a global system that has become one of several major power centers, the commitment against "two or more" powers would again apply mainly to relations among the great powers themselves, as in the past. The United States, a Western European Union, the Soviet Union, China, and, say, India might then only take the place of Britain, France, Prussia-Germany, Russia, and Austria-Hungary. There would have to be no formal, explicit commitment for the non-belligerent powers to deter each other from intervening in a conflict between equal belligerents. A first "necessary" defense alliance has been known to release pressures for counter-alliance and polarization; and even a mere anti-coalition guarantee, that is formalized in advance of a conflict, may cause tensions in the system by inviting other powers to seek alternatives to the position of one-sidedly neutralized actors.

At the very least, for reciprocal guarantees against coalitions to work in a relatively flexible multipolar system, no two states should be allied in a mutual-assistance alliance against a third state. Then nothing hampers any great power from acting against any other if it joins in an attack by a third power against a fourth. In principle, mutual-assistance commitments for defense between any two powers would not be incompatible with reciprocal guarantees against coalitions among all the powers. Power A could still restrain its mutual-assistance ally B from attacking C in alliance with D, since the aggressive character of the act would disengage A not only from the defense commitment to B but also for support of C against a coalition. In actuality, however, the more intimate commitment would be suspect of outweighing the claims of the anti-coalition guarantee in commonly ambiguous circumstances concerning "aggression"; this would encourage other states to reinsure themselves likewise.

Nuclear Diffusion and Multilateral Deterrence

The no-alliance rule has been the fond hope of the ideological opponents of alliances. The rule may prevail as a matter of expediency when all or most great powers have nuclear capability. They need not have, for the purpose, anything like nuclear parity prior to the first use of nuclear weapons in a contingency. The consequence might be a new form of deterrence; not only mutual between two nuclear powers, but also multilateral for the system as a whole. Multilateral deterrence can obtain among a few nuclear powers with comparable capabilities; or it can constrain a greater number of states with highly unequal nuclear capabilities. The problem is one for the future, and weapons systems change; this lessens the merit of only a general discussion but allows of no other.

If several greater powers had a comparable nuclear capability, the conditions of stability would not be substantially different from those governing mutual deterrence in a two-power situation. But stability would then depend not only on each power's estimate of an adversary's capability to retaliate with a second strike for the aggressor's first; it would also depend on any two potential belligerents' appraisal of the behavior and position of third parties subsequent to the nuclear exchange. The immediately uninvolved state might prove to be the third laughing party, if it benefited from the mutual diminution of the belligerents after an undecisive first strike. Or, such a state might prove to be the third striking party, if it hit the side gaining a cumulative advantage after an effective first strike.

The basic impetus to intervention by the third, reserve powers would be self-interest. They would wish to preserve the multipolar structure of the state system rather than any particular member of the system, as the best available safeguard of stability in a centrally uncontrolled nuclear environment. The coincidence of self-interest with the world's general interest would tend to discourage bellicose powers from initiating a conflict, and belligerent powers from expanding the methods and objectives of warfare to the point of eliminating or seriously weakening an opponent.

The use of conventional weapons only would be at a premium. It would avoid degrees of reciprocal destruction which would substantially enhance the relative standing of uninvolved states; and, by retaining an unimpaired nuclear establishment, the belligerents would guarantee themselves against two adverse developments: they could veto attempts by other states to exploit their embarrassment during the conflict or after it; and, however suicidally, any one of the belligerents could veto any other power joining his adversary in the conventional struggle, on pain of employing nuclear weapons to equalize the disparity. Unused nuclear capability, kept in reserve, would perform the function which a reserve power's guarantee against adverse coalition performed in the past. The two kinds of "reserve power" might actually reinforce each other in restraining both belligerent sides from the pursuit of an overwhelming victory by one method or another. The components of the over-all restraint would be: the ability of both belligerents to resort to nuclear weapons; the desire of other states to spare any one belligerent the necessity to do so; and the ability of third states to wipe out a possible advantage from a rash employment of nuclear weapons by any one belligerent side.

There would result a kind of automatic "collective security," combining multilateral deterrence and reciprocal anticoalition guarantees of each by all others. The presumption would be in favor of intervention against any belligerent gaining decisive advantage through the use of nuclear weapons or of allied power in any form. The postulated system would realize some of the main preconditions of effective "collective security." For it to work, multiplicity of roughly equal powers must be linked together by self-interest in preserving the existing system and by the capacity (now achieved in the long-range vehicles of delivery) to bring national and collective power to bear anywhere. A measure of common concern in the security of each must be translated into impartial action in a crisis.

When organic and nuclear power is diffused, common concern and impartiality are no longer dependent on the sense of justice and political detachment of governments. They rest more securely on the fact that each is potentially both a *de facto* ally, or "second," *and* a secondary target of any other state, whether friend or enemy prior to a nuclear conflict.[4] For the purpose of preventing or moderating a nuclear duel, A is the second of both C and B, even though he may be formally allied to B and to B only.

A's authority stems from the fact that he is potentially a non-belligerent victor over both ally B and non-ally C in terms of relative residual capability following upon the duel. A's interest in precluding or moderating a nuclear exchange stems from the fact that he is no less a potential sufferer. Unless the multipolar structure is preserved, A faces in the longer run the possibility of an unequal confrontation with the successful belligerent, present ally or not, without having any longer the advantage of restraint being exerted by the existence of third laughing or striking parties. More immediately, A is the potential secondary

---

[4] The term "second," like "provocation," belongs to the universe of the duel of honor. The second is most literally, and was originally, the friend who fights a parallel duel with the second of his friend's adversary. Alternately, the second kept himself in readiness to step in if the friend's adversary played it false and brought in reinforcements to save life rather than vindicate honor. In that sense, the guarantor against "two or more" states acts as a second to his contracting partner. The second's role in "arms control" between duellists evolved into that of an intermediary for agreeing on rules and weapons and for attempting reconciliation.

target during the exchange between B and C. Both parties to a mutually damaging nuclear exchange are interested in lowering the balance of power and deterrence in the period immediately following the war. They can reliably do so only by diffusing destruction. The winning party is both more interested in the postwar balance and better able to divert some of its power of destruction to third states. Any danger, however, that the nuclear exchange between any two states will trigger precautionary strikes against uninvolved third states gives these states a powerful reason for concern and impartiality when discouraging resort to force and to higher levels of force.

Once the national power of several great states is practically infinite, no aggregation can meaningfully increase that power and decrease the effects of the adversary's countermeasures. In an imaginary multipolar system of great powers with nuclear capability and means of long-range delivery, alliances would therefore become unnecessary. In some ways they would also be impossible. Once deterrence broke down, the retaliatory and precautionary action would have to match the diffuse and multilateral character of the deterrence. A particular commitment to a particular state could only inhibit the necessary freedom of one's responses in an unfolding military crisis. The "pure" system of Hobbes would come true, both aggravated and stabilized by the capability of each to kill not only every actor but all other actors—and be killed in return.

For some time at least, however, the nuclear capabilities of third states are likely to lag considerably behind those of the two superpowers. As they are developed, the two-power nuclear situation would be succeeded by a two-tier situation —one of two highly unequal classes of nuclear powers—rather than by a multi-power situation strictly speaking. In analyzing and speculating, one may dwell on the futility of a small capability for the possessor and on diffusion's disastrous portent for the international system as a whole. Or, as will be done in the following pages, one may weight the intangibles of politics rather than the strictly technological and numerical factors and reach less ominous conclusions for international stability.

There are two main aspects of stability, and the significance of the distinction increases as a two-power nuclear situation gives way to a two-tier situation. One aspect of stability concerns military capabilities; stability requires that the composition and distribution of these capabilities do not impel any of the two contestants to strike first in order to reap advantage from action or preclude the consequences of inaction. The other aspect has to do with politico-military pressures; stability requires that no contestant be in a position to exploit his strategic capabilities for limited gains without actually striking. The two aspects of stability—one regarding strategic military capabilities, the other regarding political strategies—have so far affected the relations of the two superpowers directly. Progress toward mutually "invulnerable" deterrents has enabled the Soviet Union to step up pressures against the West; the Soviets have been shielded by the existing measure of stability on the nuclear plane and they could exploit the consequently revealed or released imbalances in non-nuclear capabilities as well as the asymmetries in the geopolitical configuration of the adversary systems.

The resulting political instability is fraught with the danger that political strains will outweigh the technological factors of stability and trigger the two superpowers' retaliatory capabilities sooner or later. The expansionist side is, however, likely to be less restrained by this danger in a two-power situation than the defensive side. It has to be concerned about the reactions of only one nuclear opponent, and the more pragmatic is the approach of the defensive power's leadership, the more secure is the expansionist in assuming that he can always backtrack in time if necessary.

The divergence in the conditions of nuclear-strategic

and political stability can widen into an inverse relationship: an increase in the first entails decrease in the latter. The defensive side can draw on three main expedients for dealing with the problem. One is to destabilize the strategic-nuclear balance by means of a military build-up or a qualitative technological breakthrough favoring the defensive side; another is to stalemate the full range of forces available to opponents on every level, down to that of internal subversion. As these expedients prove to be difficult to attain and more difficult to maintain, it may become necessary to fall back upon the third expedient: diffusion of unequal strategic-nuclear capabilities among greater and lesser states.

When such a diffusion takes place, a second tier of nuclear capabilities is added to the great-power tier. The interaction of the two tiers supplements then the interplay of the two or three main levels of capabilities controlled by the major powers—the strategic-nuclear, the mainly conventional, and the guerilla-type unconventional or subversive. In origin, the nuclear capability of lesser states can be "independent" or "derivative," depending on whether it was researched and developed at home or stems from a more advanced ally. In size and function, the capability can be "self-sufficient" or be merely "detonative" of the strategic capabilities making up the great-power tier.

A lesser state's nuclear capability is in different ways self-sufficient when it is "great" or altogether "small" in terms of the prevailing state of the arts. To rank as "great" in the abstract, the capability must be such as to compel the adversary to commit so much of his nuclear forces against the lesser state as to put himself at a serious disadvantage *vis-à-vis* his major opponent. The latter is then under no immediate compulsion to strike out pre-emptively; his abstinence may be insured by the threatening posture of the aggressor's nuclear ally, if any. The two uninvolved powers may even join in arbitrating a cessation of the conflict on terms consistent with the lesser state's political independence and the system's stability.

The more likely nuclear capability of a lesser state is less than "great" in the above sense, however. One kind is a small capability, sufficient only to punish the aggressor for the destruction of the small country and partly vindicate its nuclear suicide. The physical damage to the greater power may be quite minor and need not match the value of the conquest; the opposite is likely to be the case with the political damage.

The lesser state's ruling group may actually strike out first, in the face of otherwise irresistible pressure from without or within; but it is the greater power responsible for such pressure that will be made responsible also for its consequence. The first use of nuclear weapons in a nuclear environment will have an impact on international politics exceeding both that of the first atom bomb over Japan in a conventional environment and that of the diffusion of still unused nuclear weapons. The fact that nuclear forces of non-participants survive the exchange intact is likely to offset any tendency to stampede toward a manifestly ruthless expansionist. The further fact that the aggressor's major adversary remained passive during the unequal contest is likely only to harden his attitude; he will have to intensify his commitment to third states in order to avoid being isolated and overwhelmed in turn. Any pressure that may be directed against the expansionist great power by states anxious to avoid the dilemma and the fate of the resisting small state represents the intangible part of the small state's over-all, partly posthumous, capability to be taken into account by the expansionist power from the outset.

As an alternative to a substantial and a very small capability, a lesser state may conveniently possess one of medium size and quality. Such capability is not in principle self-sufficient. It need instead be just sufficient, and may be necessary, to trigger the strategic capabilities of the great powers in pre-emptive strikes against each other; it is then immaterial for the lesser state and for international stability which of the greater powers actually strikes first in order to avoid being caught off balance during or immediately following a nuclear exchange involving the smaller state.

Diffusion of nuclear capabilities of any kind would convert the international terrain into an uncharted mine-field; the very danger of untoward detonation would tend to deter the application of politico-military pressures anywhere. A greater state's strategic superiority over a lesser one would be of little use, if attempts to exploit the superiority would threaten to strain or trigger the intrinsically stable balance between the expansionist and another great power and have unpredictable repercussions in the state system as a whole. The inverse relationship between the military and political aspects of stability, favoring the expansionist in a two-power situation, would be reversed to his detriment in a two-tier situation of multilateral deterrence.

The relative simplicity of forces and relationships in a single-tier, two-power situation is the optimum condition of equilibrium, or stability, when both powers are rational and conservative. Complexity, and unpredictability of political and military responses, may be the only deterrent to offensive thrusts by an expansionist power which is ruthless but rationally calculates its risks and probabilities of meaningful gains. The expansionist side can safely exploit, for small stakes on a low level of stress, divisions that nuclear diffusion may cause among status quo states, but when the stakes are high, the actual degree of a defensive grouping's unity cannot be foreseen before the crisis reaches a climax. The defensive side has the easier task. It can more safely assume disunity among expansionist adversaries whenever their unity is not clearly and manifestly apparent throughout the crisis, as long as the defensive powers' firmness rules out easy, unexpected gains.

The politically stabilizing effect of nuclear diffusion is not such as to rule out increases in the lesser states' conventional capabilities and advantages to over-all international stability from such increases. As long as strategic nuclear capability was monopolized by the United States and the

they also constitute a reservoir of power. The existence of such a reservoir would work against the second possibility—pre-emptive, essentially defensive strikes by one small state against another. Instability in a two-power situation is epitomized by one power's propensity to strike pre-emptively against another that seems to be gathering strength for an assault. The motivating, and not unreasonable, fear is that failure to act in the present spells disaster in the future. Such fear need not lead to a "preventive" action when a threatened small state can fall back upon at least one of rival great powers for protection against a local enemy.

The mere existence of antagonism among two or more major powers would thus be a stabilizing factor in the relations of nuclearized small states. Any cooperation among the greater powers in controlling the nuisance potential of the smaller ones would be an extra bonus for stability. Were the great powers to intervene in a small-state conflict jointly or on opposing sides, they would most probably use only conventional instrumentalities. These would be all the more likely to suffice in dealing with the lesser states, even when using nuclear weapons against each other, if the small states' concern was with gains at each other's expense and not with survival; the conflict would probably be denuclearized while being enlarged in the number of participants.

Any evolution toward a two-tier pattern of multilateral deterrence could not but accelerate changes in the role of alliances; and alliance arrangements would in turn have some effect on politico-military stability. By and large, alliances would be at a discount; the surviving arrangements would implement some of the traditional alliance functions or go beyond mere alliance.

Arrangements designed to deter and confine limited, chiefly non-nuclear, wars would aim at detracting from the power usable by the opposition, rather than at adding to the power of the ally. Or allies may chiefly restrain each other from aggravating a crisis and, between crises, assist each other in acquiring comparatively non-provocative, conventional and nuclear, capabilities. As nuclear weapons spread, so will "involuntary" adjustments in functions, commitments, and levels of integration among allies.

As regards functions, the diffusion of any kind of nuclear weapons among allies may compel a parallel expansion of conventional capabilities of individual allies and the alliance. And the most advanced allies may have to distribute "invulnerable" nuclear capabilities to take the place of independently researched and developed capabilities, likely to be primitive, vulnerable, and consequently—at least in theory—provocative. In doing so, the great-power donor can argue that such diffusion increases stability and the donating ally's potential for restraining the recipient. Such rationalization will have merit, with one reservation. Over-all stability will be enhanced by the adversary's having to assume that interallied restraints are not foolproof; they are actually likely to decline during a major crisis, when the free use of any available capability is least impeded by fear of the supplying ally's later sanctions.

Another stabilizing factor—next to "involuntary" extension of function—might be a similar extension of commitments. The possibility that a lesser ally might use his nuclear capability independently (and, in the eyes of some, irresponsibly) might incline the major ally to reduce his commitment to make up for decrease in control over the *casus foederis,* the capabilities of the immediately involved partner, and his conduct. But, in a crisis, the major ally may actually have to extend his commitment to the independent ally, in order to reassert the waning control and restraint; reduce the necessity for the lesser ally to act "desperately"; and restore the deterrent uncertainty of the adversary regarding possible chain reaction. When pre-emption threatens anyway in ambiguous conditions, the only alternative to extending commitment may be an explicit default, possibly guaranteed by measures of unilateral disarmament.

For a democratic alliance leader, however, it is as hard publicly to declare such a default as privately to decide on a potentially self-destructive intervention. The more attractive course is evasion; and to extend one's operative commitment may be the only way to avoid both unpleasant extremes—default and destruction—in the end.

France spurned Germany's demand for default and partial disarmament of the frontier in 1914, instead extending her commitment to Russia; Britain's failure to commit herself to intervention has since ranked as the immediate "cause" of the war. The extension of Britain's commitment to Czechoslovakia, virtually to match France's, in May, 1938, preceded the default of September. The manifest consequences of Munich, however, have since confirmed the case for the presumed efficacy of the formula adopted in May.

Nuclear diffusion will produce new dilemmas for allied governments and decrease their freedom in determining alliance functions and commitments. This may compel greater over-all integration.

In the West, the existence of a British and French nuclear deterrent, and the possibility of a West German one, are likely to supplement economic co-operation and competition as impetus to Western European political unity. Such a unity may be the only effective precaution against fragmenting the alliance; and a central authority is probably the only workable agency for joint control and command over a community deterrent. A mere alignment of independent Western European and North American deterrents, reinforcing each other in an active or merely auxiliary capacity,[6] might do for some time. The framework of such a relationship, the North Atlantic Alliance, might maintain a joint conventional capability, as a means of holding together the two component nuclear powers and limiting the incidence

---

[6] See pp. 129–131 on the "auxiliary" relationship as it might be improvised within the framework of a joint NATO deterrent; an independent European deterrent would make such a relationship easier to implement.

of potentially disruptive deterrent dilemmas. The disparity between a unified conventional capability and decentralized nuclear forces would not, however, be likely to endure. The alternative to erosion—or sudden disruption—of the connection between a Western Europe and a United States, independent of each other in respect to the supreme weapon, would be their all-out integration in a politico-military Atlantic Community.

Even when largely imposed by circumstances, institutional community can still bind only nations with strong feelings of solidarity—and some suspicion regarding each other's behavior if they are not closely associated. There would continue to be less intimate allies and protected non-aligned countries with nuclear capabilities. This is apt to promote an apparently contrary trend: toward an enforced "alliance" among major adversaries for carrying out an essential function of genuine alliance—to detract from and to restrain usable power of other states. One alliance effect between major adversaries may result from their reciprocal deterrence; the deterrence is likely to restrain lesser powers by reducing their prospect for decisive great-power support in a local conflict. A more self-conscious bond between the great powers might consist in their common bondage to unruly allies. The greater powers' trust in each other may be very small, and their self-restraint only reluctant; but they might still need a tacit understanding not to exploit each other's embarrassments when they try to keep in check unruly friends and allies.

There was a time when Russia preferred that Austria-Hungary be allied with Germany rather than be "on the loose" in the Balkans. And Austria-Hungary herself might have preferred that Serbia be allied with Russia, if the alternative were an irredentist Serbia tied to no power more "rational" than herself. The Soviet Union may come to prefer that Germany be allied with the United States as part of a European or Atlantic community, thus enabling the Western powers to feel and act alike with regard to Communist China's alliance with the Soviet Union.

Alliances become an instrument for peace when they add something substantial to the checks which mutual or multilateral deterrence impose on antagonists. This is most likely to happen when inter-allied restraints are reciprocal and dampen acts of self-assertion or provocation on the part of members of both adversary combinations.

For some kindred nations the chief virtue of alliance may have become its insufficiency. As the new military technology develops and spreads, the limitations of mere interdependence become apparent and push toward community, if only on the rebound from a last flirtation with independence. Interallied guarantees of assistance have been undergoing a crisis of confidence; the fear of separate deals and defaults impels allies to seek self-dependence while discussing the means for extending the alliance's functions and implementing joint commitments. The efficacy of a vital function of alliances—inter-allied restraints—declines as the usual suspicions grow. They concern the self-regarding motives which prompt restraints and the self-protective measures which might follow upon a breakdown of restraints among allies. In the age of nuclear diffusion, the crisis of alliances culminates when "self-protective measures" might conceivably mean precautionary strikes by involved allies against potentially overbearing uninvolved ones. Henceforth, only members of the same community can be certain to stake their existence for the partner's; can have the right and power to restrain him; and can be sufficiently trustful to spare him in any contingency. The essence of such a community is the substitution of "we" for "who" in questions like, Who will decide? Who will do or die?

There are, however, no short-cuts in politics, and least of all in politics among nations. Sovereign states will not make a decision entailing their disappearance in order to forestall hypothetical consequences of theoretically posited trends and events. Only as self-perpetuating national responses reveal their inadequacy can an integrative response be forthcoming.

The disarray of the Atlantic alliance has been due to an attempt to substitute for one national formula—the absolute guarantee by an invulnerable United States—another national formula—the ultimate guarantee of each vulnerable state by itself. A phase of disarray was inevitable once the postwar period of American ascendancy failed to witness the retreat of the Soviet Union into its national confines. The chief merit of France's disruptive unilateralism under de Gaulle was its timing; it awakened the allies to the need for a creative response before the Soviet Union was capable of forcing such a retreat upon the United States.

The Rise and Decline of Nations

The future is uncertain and changes as it becomes the past. The tendencies to polarization vie with tendencies to multipolarity, and these contend with forces for hegemony. Some alliances may become more than what they are presently, others less, and still others, nothing.

The policy of straightforward mutual-assistance alliances was severely damaged, and perhaps foredoomed, once nuclear stand-off disposed of all hope that the alliance policy might facilitate a Western break-through in the global conflict. Thereafter, the main choices were reformulation, de-emphasis, or partial abandonment of alliances. The West never did have a monopoly on the policy of alliances on a regional basis; the Soviets used the traditional technique for implementing their "Monroe Doctrine" in Central-Eastern Europe quite early. But the West, and the United States in particular, was sufficiently favored by the distribution of resources and security fears to apply the policy of alliance on a global basis. When both capacities and fears took an adverse turn, the West and again specifically the United States came to face one of the most difficult tasks of diplomacy: how to soft-pedal awkward commitments without extinguishing the vital ones, and how to endorse non-alignment of others without being repudiated by one's allies.

The problem has been most acutely posed on the peripheries of the Sino-Soviet bloc. As the 1960's opened, the West seemed to be on the point of employing its diplomacy to effect a transition from the strategy of alliances and alignments in the peripheral regions to the next dominant strategy. Both West and East had used their diplomacy before for the same purpose—covering up retreat from other temporarily dominant strategies. The favored strategy of the next phase which, if any, might bring about a decision is competition in depth over economic and political growth on earth and, secondarily, penetration into the highest and remotest points in space. The newly emphasized strategies are essentially domestic. This is certainly true of the growth and development of national substance, as well as of space-launchings from national territory, more or less as part of the arms race. And it can be made true also for internal subversion and counter-subversion, when restraints and fictions are applied to a strategy that dominated without serious competition an earlier phase of the cold war.

In the circumstances, diplomacy has been occupied with two interrelated assignments: to insulate the domestic strategies from international implications, when desired; and to exploit limited gains and limit losses from this or that strategy internationally, as symbols of a supposed rise or decline, peaceableness or aggressiveness, of the two superpowers and their allies. Concurrently, negotiations and other techniques of diplomacy have been used to identify inessential items of temporarily de-emphasized or obsolete strategies, which might become subjects for trade in the next phase. In the area of security, a question arose as to whether some of the alliance commitments or, more generally, modes of implementing alliances, might become negotiable—perhaps for arms-control measures and politico-territorial adjustments under novel forms of international or inter-bloc guarantees.

As was the case in protracted conflicts before, diplomacy's concurrent task has been to employ the actors and absorb the attentive publics, while the drama of the day's dominant conflict unfolds toward a dénouement or merely into the next act, introducing new actors with new, or revised, roles.

Outer space has been emerging as one more level of international politics and strategy. This has further complicated the already complex relations of the domestic, regional, and global levels, each of them governed by more conventional politics than the immediately "higher" and vaster one. A reciprocal encirclement of the superpowers is difficult to accomplish on finite ground; it may be in prospect by means of orbital bomb-carrying satellites. In due time, facilities in outer space may supplement existing capacity for mutual surveillance, deterrence, and destruction. Military clashes may then be diverted away from the earth to outer space—to determine the ranking of powers in this world and dominion in other worlds.[7]

Temporary advantages in the race for reciprocal encirclement in outer space have served the Communist campaign to disrupt the loosening chain of horizontal "capitalistic encirclement" by Western bases. Beyond that, the Communist camp has sought to impart the impetus of rising morale and prestige to the vertical "socialist encirclement" of the West by a relatively more rapidly growing and expanding East. Increasingly, particular gains in political prestige and specific achievements of science have become the only halfway measurable indices of boundless, and largely unusable, power as well as a vital factor in highly vulnerable national morale.

The protagonists in the Communist camp have been vocal

[7] K. Knorr, "On the International Implications of Outer Space," *World Politics* (July, 1960), pp. 564–84; and *Developments in Military Technology and Their Impact on United States Strategy and Foreign Policy*, A Study Prepared at the Request of the Committee on Foreign Relations, United States Senate, by The Washington Center of Foreign Policy Research, The Johns Hopkins University, December 6, 1959, p. 76.

in presenting the more avowable among their successes as evidence for the "necessary" triumph over the crises-ridden capitalist West. There may be immediate, tactical advantages to be derived from such affirmations. To affirm trust in a benign necessity of outcome both obligates and enables one to refrain from potentially destructive modes of waging the contest while it lasts. The certainty of an approaching consummation may induce even revolutionary militants to tolerate exercises in orthodox diplomacy. And the apparent utopianism of a far-fetched end, by reassuring the adversary about the present, may encourage him to negotiate provisional agreements; immediately favorable to the revolution, such agreements are subject to revision and reversal as conditions change. Finally, the display of ideological certainty about the outcome may discourage "vain" resistance by the uncommitted, while screening failures of the actually very pragmatic means of attraction, erosion, and subversion.

Any affirmation about the future constitutes a fact in the present; as such, it may promote or impede the prediction's realization. The real necessity is not the Communist one, or any other pertaining to the shape of the future. A kind of necessity sways only the mode of inter-state conflict while it lasts; and it informs the open-ended tendency for any major conflict to be submerged in the relative rise and decline of old and new actors, without triumph for any faith or any one power or group of powers as they were constituted at the struggle's beginning.

The rise and decline of nations in the balance of organic power is a basic fact of international relations. Alliance policy promotes or hinders the process itself and sways its bearing on the fortunes of individual states, by adding to or detracting from the resources which are brought into action at a particular time. The relevant international system itself can be static or expanding along with the power factors available for distribution among states. And the system can be chiefly managed by conservative powers that are declining relative to comparably powerful states—thus Austria in the 1820's and France in the 1920's—or the main ordering influence can come from powers which, while internationally conservative, are still on the rise—thus Germany in the 1880's or the United States in the late 1940's and in the 1950's. When the rising power is also a revolutionary one, it is likely to aim at organizing an empire—at least as a preliminary step to a new global order.

The contemporary state system has been an expanding one—both in politically relevant physical space and in the factors and methods of competition. And the major powers contending for leadership in organizing the system have both been dynamic, rising states. The United States and the Soviet Union have shown a comparable capacity for growth at comparable stages of development. And, despite instances of a higher rate of temporary or initial growth elsewhere, the two superpowers seem capable of further outdistancing the upcoming allies or rivals in the longer run. It may well be that this evolutionary, organic factor will invalidate historical precedents more fundamentally than does the revolutionary character of modern weapons.

A rising power may be one of two things. It may be a meteor, projected into fleeting pre-eminence by a leader's genius, by a self-consuming national élan, or by a momentary international balance of forces. Or the power may grow out of a steadily expanding organic base. The rise of Prussia differed from the passing ascendancy of Sweden as markedly as the rise of the United States and the Soviet Union has differed from the rise of Japan. But meteoric and organic elements can overlap, as they did in Prussia's fitful advance to great-power status through triumphs and humiliations.

Too rapidly rising lesser allies may incommode established great powers. Both Prussia and Sweden were much too ebullient partners in France's progression toward supremacy. On the other hand, declining Spain became a drag on her major ally once the Family Pact failed to make up to France for what she had expended for Bourbon preponderance. In the next phase, it was Britain who was steadily gaining relative to France, being only temporarily set back by the second, only meteoric, French ascendancy under the greater of the Napoleons. Britain's rise showed, by contrast, the advantage of a nation which knows how to utilize partly new economic and political factors in an expanding world system, while other states contribute the protective stalemate most of the time.

Only gradually did British-style manipulation of system-wide mechanisms lapse before the sheer weight of mass. The broadening base of the two major European states to the east of Britain and France took longer to organize politically and economically; but once organized, each of the two states dwarfed the smaller and earlier organized units to the west. The trend's first beneficiary (and subsequent victim) was the Second and Third German Reich, once the self-consciously fostered military power of Prussia coalesced with the subterraneously gathering strength of Germany as a whole. Only together with Russia and the United States, growing from a still larger mass base, were the British able to share in the defeats of Germany; and the defeats were not least due to Germany's failure to find other than stagnant or declining allies in both World Wars. The sole and only apparent exception was Japan in World War II, attempting at least one-hundred years too late to telescope into decades Britain's slow rise to empire from a narrow insular base. The Soviet-American alliance of World War II combined two states with both massive and expanding organic power; and the Sino-Soviet alliance has introduced another "first," by uniting two such states with ties of both alliance and specific ideology.

The imminent prospect is the confrontation of the Sino-Soviet alliance with a like combination of two dynamic, ideologically related super-states—the United States and unified Western Europe. The potential for growth and military preparedness of these powers is so great that differences in the rates of growth become less important. They reflect variations in phases of industrial development, not sustained trends of relative rise or decline. But political behavior matters more as a carefully watched symptom than do economic indices, once the issue of superiority has been posed.

A spectacular transfer of supremacy, between France and Spain, initiated the modern state system in the wake of the Thirty Years' War. As it drew to its close, the protracted conflict was marked by greater than usual uncertainty about the actual relation of power between the major contestants. Under such conditions the directly uninvolved, third powers are especially apt to misjudge the intention, and underrate the capability, of the challenger to replace the dominant power. Their desire for vicarious revenge on the party with a longer history of dominance is as important as is their desire for incidental self-aggrandizement. As for the declining nation, if Spain's behavior prior to the Peace of the Pyrenees has anything to teach us, she is apt to stall and seek a mere truce, pending a favorable shift in the balance of power. The hope is that the chief opponent may break up internally and that other states may awaken to the realities of the situation and rally to the defense of the status quo. When the hopes fail to materialize, the declining power will attempt to pass off as a real concession the legitimization of the opponent's prior gains. The rising adversary's gains are all the more effective if they are individually small but continuous. They are then most likely to exert more than proportionate pressure on the morale of the declining power and still fail to alert the other states. Small but steady gains enable the rising power to appear strong but moderate, mainly concerned in fending off encirclement by the declining power. And they strengthen the rising power no less for the final challenge, designed to effect a symbolic transfer of hegemony.[8]

In 1659, the symbolic event was the Infanta's marriage to the future *grand monarque* on French terms. The event

[8] On the Franco-Spanish transition, see J. Valfrey, *Hugues de Lionne* (2 vols., 1877–81).

was so understood by the contemporaries and, as such, was resisted by Spain so long as she could; in due course, it served as a basis for the French claim to all Spanish possessions. The contemporary equivalent might be the reorganization of the United Nations on Soviet terms. It, too, would consecrate the equality of the upstart power; and it would combine the symbolic with the material advantage to be derived from a legal-political device for reducing the rival in due course to a subordinate position.

The lesser, third powers have a decisive role to play in the drama. As did Cromwell's England in the earlier contest, they can join the rising adversary of a dominant power in order to share in the spoils. Or they may help the henceforth conservative power uphold the balance. This is unlikely to happen when that power appears to be in decline. When the balance between the chief contestants is uncertain, the best, stabilizing, role for concurrently rising third states is to serve as reserve powers, making it more risky and less necessary for either of the contestants to resort to ultimate force. The Soviets profess to fear that the United States would strike out in despair to avoid surrender when patently losing the race. And the West cannot be certain that the most revolutionary of the Communist powers would not do something similar when it discovers that "historical necessity" is not enough for winning. The best long-term assurance against either occurrence is an international system in which no major contestant can decisively lose to the other or win over him, but both are forced to transform the system by building up other powers despite themselves and to some unavoidable degree against themselves.

More than ever, the role of alliances and alignments is only preventive as the balance of new power is growing out of the contemporary East-West conflict; defensive alliances forestall disasters and only incidentally do some good. The preventive role is not negligible, however; good alliance policies can help equilibrate contending forces and interests, as ever new structures take shape within and among nations.

Index

A

Adenauer, Konrad, 66, 179–180
Afghanistan, 22, 28, 208, 213, 249
Alexander I, 49
Algeria, 252
Alignment: attractions and, 13–14; balance-of-power principle and, 26–27; conflicts and, 14–26; gains and liabilities of, 29–30, 98, 103, 105, 108–111, 114–115, 175, 190, 205; interests and, 27–29, 81–82, 106, 139; reasons for, 30–39. *See also* Alliances; Dealignment; Realignment; Subalignment
Alliances: cohesion of, 66, 87, 175; constitutional character of, 69–70; domestic oppositions and, 103–104, 111; functions of, 116, 279–280, 291; future of, 272, 279, 283–284, 285–286; historical continuity and, 3–8, 10, 11; ideologies and, 10, 15, 61–66, 90, 170, 187, 191, 210; interallied restraints and, 34–36, 40, 78, 138–147, 176–185, 187, 280–281, 282–283; neutralist view of, 206–207, 208–210; polarization and, 15–17, 19, 41, 163–164; political cultures and, 10–11, 67–68; politico-economic development and, 104–106, 107, 165–167, 261, 289–290; types of, 30–33, 34, 75–78, 102, 109, 133–134, 174, 241, 267–268. *See also* Alignment; Graduated commitment; Guarantee
ANZUS Pact, 262–263
Arab League: the Baghdad Pact and, 209; offensive alliance as, 40
Argentina, 14, 259
Austria (before 1867): conflicts and alignments of, 15, 16, 34–35, 90–91, 191, 194; dealignments and, 43, 46, 53, 55; international role of, 288; realignments and, 57–60, 89. *See also* Austria-Hungary
Austria, neutralization of, 203, 230
Austria-Hungary, conflicts and alignments of, 17, 18, 32–33, 34, 35, 36, 37, 140–141, 142, 282
Axis (powers). *See* Germany; Italy; Japan

B

Baghdad Pact: impetus toward, 23, 119; neutralism and, 20, 209, 227, 228. *See also* Central Treaty Organization
Balance of power: alignments and, 25, 27, 234, 291; guarantee against coalitions and, 136; separate peace and, 54–55; within alliances, 113–114. *See also* Equilibrium; Stability

293

Bandung Conference (powers): "blocs" and, 222; Sino-Soviet alliance and, 188, 228; Warsaw Pact and, 228–229, 231
Bavaria, 15, 43
Belgium, neutrality of, 203, 206.
Bipolarity: kinds of, 161–162, 261; tripartism and, 164. *See also* International system; Polarization
Bismarck, Prince Otto von: alliance policies of, 35, 126, 266; alliance system of, 17, 32, 36, 103
Brandenburg, 15. *See also* Prussia
Brazil, 256, 259
Bulgaria, 14, 19, 126
Burma, 204, 208, 213, 217, 232
Buol-Schauenstein, Count Karl Ferdinand, 60

C

Cambodia, 88, 143, 213
Canada, 14, 245
Capabilities: distribution of within alliances, 88–90, 95, 112, 280; employment of, 90–93; kinds of, 162, 256; nuclear, 93–95, 256, 269, 274–275; relation to pressures of, 97, 99–100. *See also* Diffusion; Integration; Multipolarity; Pressures
Castro, Fidel, 233. *See also* Cuba
CENTO. *See* Central Treaty Organization
Central Treaty Organization: antecedents of, 262; integration in, 120; neutralism and, 211. *See also* Baghdad Pact
China, imperialism and, 183–184, 257. *See also* Communist China; Taiwan
Churchill, Sir Winston, alliance ideology and, 62, 66

Clarendon, George William Frederick Villiers, Earl of, 142
Clemenceau, Georges, 6
Collective security, nuclear diffusion and, 270–271
Colonialism, 208–210, 215, 216, 218, 219–220, 225, 238, 245-246, 253, 257
Communist China: alignment alternatives of, 197–198; conflicts and alignments of, 20, 22, 23, 262; Indochina and, 135, 137–138; nuclear weapons and, 131, 185, 186; politico-military strategies of, 101, 186; SEATO and, 88, 121; Taiwan and, 175, 184–185. *See also* Sino-Soviet alliance; Sino-Soviet bloc
Compensation: coercion and, 102–103, 112–113; interallied restraints and, 139, 179, 181–183; 190-192; neutralism and, 216; theory and practice of, 101–102, 105, 190–192
Compromise: compensation and, 102; theory and practice of, 81–83, 86
Conciliation, strategy toward neutralism as, 237–238, 239, 243–244, 246–249, 251–253. *See also* Containment
Conflicts: dominance of, 14–15, 164–165, 253–254, 261, 287, 290–291; initiation of, 140; limitation of, 33–34, 52, 129–131, 134–138, 141–142, 144, 265, 270, 279
Consultations: avoidance of, 85–86; negotiations and, 70–73, 83, 173; parties to, 73–75, 172–173; provisions for, 142; scope of, 75–80
Containment, strategy toward neutralism as, 237, 238–239, 243–244, 246–249, 251–253. *See also* Conciliation

Crimean War, limitation of, 142
Cuba, 14, 40, 126, 173, 250
Czechoslovakia: conflicts and alignments of, 19, 23; Soviet Union and, 143, 215, 236; Western powers and, 87, 143, 281

D

Dealignment: dilemmas of, 54-55; economics of, 48-49; ideologies and, 63; neutralism and, 204–205; partners in, 42–43; reasons for, 46–48; strategies and modalities of, 43–46, 48, 49–53, 58, 153–157, 188–190, 192–193
Denmark, 15, 19
Deterrence: active, 128; alliances and, 30, 36, 136; foreign bases and, 145; graduated, 242-243; multilateral, 164, 269–272, 278–279; mutual, 8, 127, 264–265; mutual assurance and, 127; neutralism and, 208, 211; notions of, 127, 152; passive, 128
Diffusion, nuclear weapons of: alliances and, 93–96, 128–129, 276–277; great powers among, 269–272; great and small powers among, 272–273, 274–276; military strategies and, 164, 269–272, 277–279. *See also* Multipolarity
Diplomacy: methods of, 70-71, 109–110, 149, 150–151, 153, 163–164, 240, 257; nuclear age in, 96, 141, 147–148, 152, 156–157, 284–286; styles of, 67–69, 150

E

Eden, Sir Anthony, on alliance solidarity, 82-83, 86

Egypt. *See* United Arab Republic
Equilibrium, contemporary aspects of, 8–9, 162, 169, 276, 291. *See also* Balance of power; Stability
Erosion, strategy as, 232, 234–236, 238–239, 242, 244, 287. *See also* Subversion

F

Fleury, Cardinal André-Hercule de, 38
Foreign aid: balance of rewards and, 240–241, 252; build-up of countries and, 249, 255–257, 259–260, 263
Foreign bases: ideal types of, 145, 263; interallied restraints and, 144–147; neutralism and, 211, 226–227
France: alignment alternatives of, 195–197; alliance concepts and traditions of, 4, 5, 6–7, 76, 90, 106–107, 114–115, 133; conflicts and alignments of, 14, 15, 16, 17, 18, 19, 21–22, 32–33, 34–35, 38, 40, 89, 110, 138, 142, 194, 258, 262–263; consultations and, 77, 79–80, 85; dealignments and, 43, 45, 46; diplomatic style of, 67–69; European integration and, 180, 199–201; German unification and, 176–179; Indochina and, 135, 137–138, 231; Little Entente and, 37, 87–88; NATO and, 112–114, 143–144, 146, 154, 180–181, 284; neutralism and, 8, 237, 246, 248, 252–253; realignments and, 56, 57–58, 89; regime of, 265; SEATO and, 125; supremacy of, 288–289, 290–291. *See also* Western alliance system

Frederick II, of Prussia: consultations and, 85–86; preventive action and, 99; on separate peace, 47, 63–64

G

Gaulle, Charles de: alliance ideology of, 64–67; alliance policy of, 171, 180, 284
Gentz, Frederick von, 62
Germany: the Axis and, 33, 85, 86, 91–92, 110; conflicts and alignments of, 6, 16, 17–18, 37, 87–88, 107, 138, 140–141; dealignments and, 44, 46, 48–49; expansion of, 183–184, 289. See also Germany, Eastern; Germany, Western; Prussia
Germany, Eastern: German unification and, 182–183; regime of, 190
Germany, Western: alignment alternatives of, 195–198; conflicts and alignments of, 23, 194; consultations and, 74–75; European integration and, 180, 199; national unification and, 175–177, 181, 190, 193; NATO and, 23, 88, 94, 104, 107, 113, 143–144, 154, 175–181; neutralism and, 215, 246; nuclear weapons and, 94, 178, 181, 281. See also Western alliance system
Ghana, 241, 247. See also Nkrumah
Gomulka, Wladislaw, 172
Graduated commitment: graduated deterrence and, 241-242; fall-back position as, 263–268. See also Guarantee
Great Britain: alignment alternatives of, 196–198; alliance concepts and traditions of, 4–5, 7, 31, 36, 76, 82–83, 90, 208–209; conflicts and alignments of, 16, 17, 18, 21, 38, 107, 142, 191, 194, 257–259, 262–263; consultations and, 77, 79–80, 85; dealignments and, 43, 46, 47, 51, 52, 55; diplomatic style of, 67–69; European integration and, 113, 198–201; growth of, 289; NATO and, 108, 122, 146, 176; neutralism and, 205–206, 215, 237; nuclear weapons and, 94, 131, 156, 179, 281; realignments and, 56–59, 89; SEATO and, 119, 143. See also Western alliance system
Greece, 19, 263
Guarantee: coalitions against, 32–33, 36, 136–137, 257, 268–269, 270; regimes of, 265–266; small states of, 8–9, 145–146, 264–265, 267–268. See also Alliances; Graduated commitment
Guatemala, 236, 250
Guinea, 216, 252–253. See also Sékou-Touré

H

Hapsburg powers. See Austria, Spain
Hungary, 19, 259

I

Ideologies: alliances of, 61–63; alliances about, 64–67, 206–207. See also Alliances
India: conflicts and policies of, 19, 20, 23, 28–29, 208, 213, 214–215, 218, 230–231; potential regional core-power as, 210, 225, 256, 259, 262. See also Nehru
Indochinese War, limitation of, 135–136, 137–138

Indonesia, 214
Integration: cohesion and, 116–117; foreign bases and, 144–145; independence and, 65–66, 72–73, 93–95, 105, 117, 124, 128, 137, 147, 150, 156–157, 283–284; interallied restraints and, 143–147, 176; interdependence and, 114, 123–124, 283; mobility and, 132–133; modes of, 117–119, 122–123, 173–175; negotiations and, 152–153, 156; solidarity and, 75–76, 102, 134, 148, 153, 282; Western alliance system in, 119–122; Western Europe in, 198–201, 281
Inter-American system, implementation of, 120–121, 259. See also Organization of American States
International order, non-Communist world of, 238–239, 251–253
International system: bipolarity and, 25, 168; definition of, 12; domestic systems and, 20–23, 165–166, 214, 258, 285; kinds of, 287–288, 289; multipolarity and, 25–26, 141–142, 168–169, 249, 254, 255, 256, 272; regional systems and, 19–20, 22–24, 259–262; regional vs. domestic systems and, 24–25; regional vs. global systems and, 25, 80, 261–262; reserves in, 140, 270, 279, 291; strategies in, 242–244; structure of, 12, 161–167. See also International order; Outer space
Iran, 221, 232, 236
Iraq, 20, 23, 103, 119, 236, 248, 265. See also Kassim
Israel, 20, 40
Italy: the Axis and, 91, 110; conflicts and alignments of, 19, 87–88; dealignments and, 43, 44, 50–51, 52, 55; NATO and, 122; realignments and, 56

J

Japan: the Axis and, 33, 43–44, 85, 86, 91–92, 110; conflicts and alignments of, 257, 259, 262; dealignments and, 48–49, 50–52; economic attractions on, 14; neutralism and, 212, 215, 245, 246, 247; rise of, 258, 259; SEATO and, 88; U.S. alliance and, 104, 146

K

Kassim, Abdul Karim, 235, 243–244. See also Iraq
Kaunitz-Rietberg, Prince Wenzel Anton von, 57–58
Korean War: limitation of, 135, 142, 173; truce negotiations and, 147

L

Laos: internal conflicts in, 21, 136; neutralization of, 230–231, 236; SEATO and, 122, 143
League of Nations: consultation forum as, 7; grand alliance as, 5–6
Lisola, Baron Franz Paul von, 62
Little Entente, cohesion of, 87–88, 97
Locarno Pact, 36, 67, 107, 264
Louis XIV: French supremacy and, 290–291; separate arrangements and, 43, 44, 155
Low Countries, 257

M

MacArthur, Douglas, 142
Mali, 247
Mao-Tse-tung, 171, 173. *See also* Communist China
Mazarin, Cardinal Jules, on separate peace, 48
Metternich, Prince Klemens von, 53, 59–60
Mexico, 14, 250
Mollet, Guy, 86
Morocco, 20, 22, 216–217, 241
Multipolarity: future potentialities of, 258–284; kinds of, 161–162, 256, 261–262. *See also* International system

N

Napoleon I, 45, 49, 59
Napoleon III, 142, 250
Nasser, Gamal Abdel, 209, 217, 234, 235, 243–244. *See also* United Arab Republic
NATO. *See* North Atlantic Treaty Organization
Negotiations: alliances and, 148–150, 285; compensations and, 102; compromise and, 82, 147–148; consultations and, 70–73, 83; methods of, 150–152, 153–157
Nehru, Jawaharlal: policies of, 234; view of alliances of, 209, 216. *See also* India
Neutralism: characteristics of, 203–207, 218, 234–235; domestic factors and, 214–216, 233–234, 244, 248, 252; economic needs and, 218; impartiality of, 226–227, 229; international stabilization and, 219, 221–231, 249–252; nuclear weapons and, 256; organization of, 222–224; rationale of, 207–213; regional expansion and, 217, 241, 264–265; strategies toward, 232–254. *See also* Neutrality; Non-alignment
Neutrality: benevolent variety of, 263–265; security strategies and, 7, 60, 203, 204; treaties of 31–32. *See also* Neutralism; Non-alignment
Nigeria, 217, 247, 256
Nkrumah, Kwame, 234, 235, 241. *See also* Ghana
Non-alignment: characteristics of, 203–207, 218, 221; international stabilization and, 219, 221-231; motives for, 207–208, 217, 218, 260. *See also* Neutralism; Neutrality
North Atlantic Treaty Organization: antecedents of, 262; bipolarity and, 161–162; conceptions of, 76, 78, 79–80, 82–83, 103, 108–109, 122, 180–181; deterrent for, 161–162; European integration and, 198, 281; integration in, 118, 122, 134, 281–282; neutralism and, 210, 227; practices of, 77, 83–84, 85; reasons for, 21, 23; strategies for, 94, 100, 112, 114–115, 117, 129, 132–133, 134, 284. *See also* Western alliance system
Nuclear weapons. *See* Capabilities; Diffusion; Diplomacy; Integration

O

OAS. *See* Organization of American States
Organization of American States, 80
Outer space, 286

INDEX 299

P

Pakistan, 20, 23, 28–29, 245, 249
Philippines, 88
Poland: conflicts and alignments of, 13, 14, 19, 23, 88, 178; international status and, 171–172; internal divisions of, 25, 257
Polarization: kinds of, 163, 268; neutralism and, 249-251, 252. *See also* Alliances; Bipolarity
Portugal, 245
Pressures: access to allies and, 13, 259–260; cohesion of alliances and, 97–99, 102–103, 104, 225, 227–229, 244–245; negotiations and, 148; relation to capabilities of, 97, 99–100. *See also* Capabilities
Prestige. *See* Status
Provocation: kinds of, 125–127; interallied controls and, 145–147; neutralist doctrines and, 208, 210; notion of, 124–125; "seconds" and, 271
Prussia: conflicts and alignments of, 16, 18, 19, 32–33, 34–35, 90–91, 112; dealignments and, 43, 47, 48, 53, 55; realignment and, 57–59; rise of, 25, 258–259, 288

R

Realignment: alliance ideology and, 63, 194–195; alternatives to, 113, 124; reasons for, 56–58, 138, 181–182; strategies and modalities of, 58–60, 192–194, 195–198, 200. *See also* Dealignment
Rumania, 87–88, 126
Russell, Lord John, 142
Russia: conflicts and alignments of, 14, 17, 18, 19, 32–33, 35–36, 40, 89, 112, 136, 138, 258–259, 282; dealignments and, 49–50; realignments and, 58; rise of, 25. *See also* Soviet Union

S

Saxony, 15
Schumacher, Kurt, 66–67
SEATO. *See* South-East Asia Treaty Organization
Security: cohesion of alliances and, 106–107, 110–111; efficacy of alliances and, 117; immunity and, 220–221; reason for alignment as, 30–34, 38, 39
Sékou-Touré, 217, 235. *See also* Guinea
Senegal, 241, 247
Separate peace. *See* Dealignment
Serbia, 19, 283
Siam, 257. *See also* Thailand
Sino-Soviet alliance: interallied restraints in, 40, 175, 184, 187; neutralism and, 210, 218; peculiarity of, 289; strains within, 185–186, 191, 192–193, 225; Western strategies toward, 188–190, 282–283. *See also* Sino-Soviet bloc
Sino-Soviet bloc: bipolarity and, 161–162, 169, 226; divided countries and, 40, 175, 182-185; "historical necessity" and, 286–287, 291; neutralism and, 227–228, 230–231, 232–236, 248–251; relationships within, 40, 92, 167, 169–175, 190; Western "provocation" of, 126–127, 286. *See also* Sino-Soviet alliance; Warsaw Pact
South Korea, 22, 190, 264, 265. *See also* Korean War
South Vietnam, 122, 143

Soviet Union: 14, 15, 22, 23, 31; alignment alternatives of, 196-198, 200; conflicts and alignments of, 6, 13, 20, 87–88, 92; dealignments and, 45, 47, 48, 50; growth of, 166–167, 288, 289; politico-military strategies of, 97–98, 101, 151, 154, 155, 157, 182, 222–223, 257–258, 262, 273, 282–283. *See also* Russia; Sino-Soviet alliance; Sino-Soviet bloc

Spain: the Axis and, 52; conflicts and alignments of, 15, 19, 258; dealignments and, 43, 52–53; realignments and, 56; rise and decline of, 25, 288, 290–291

Stability, domestic: cohesion of alliances and, 103, 106–107, 110–111, 265; efficacy of alliances and, 117; non-alignment and, 214–215, 217–218, 221; reason for alignment as, 34–38, 39, 98

Stability, international: buffer belts and, 202–203; conditions of, 128–129, 131, 162, 163, 166, 191, 269, 273–274, 276, 279, 280; equilibrium and, 8-9; interallied restraints and, 139–140; non-alignment and neutralism and, 210–211, 219, 221–231, 241; satellite belts and, 202–203. *See also* Deterrence; Diffusion

Status: cohesion of alliances and, 107–108, 110–112, 171–172; diplomatic styles and, 68, 71; efficacy of alliances and, 117, 178–179; global power and, 79; negotiations and, 155; non-alignment and neutralism and, 214, 224, 240, 255, 261; reason for alignment as, 27–39, 98

Subalignment, among allies, 112–114, 149, 173–174, 183

Subversion, strategy as, 232–234, 242, 244, 266–267, 285, 287. *See also* Erosion

Sweden: conflicts and alignments of, 15, 16, 19, 110; dealignments and, 43, 44–45, 48; realignments and, 57; rise of, 25, 288

Switzerland, 203

Syria, 236, 248

T

Taiwan: restraints on, 184, 185; unification of China and, 175, 182–183, 190

Thailand, 88, 119, 121–122, 213, 245. *See also* Siam

Tito (Josip Broz), 173, 229. *See also* Yugoslavia

Tripartism: political policy in, 163–164, 248, 256–257; economic policies in, 218; military strategy in, 164, 269–272; non-aligned countries and, 203, 204, 222, 224

Tunisia, 217, 248

Turkey: Baghdad Pact and, 119; Balkan Pact and, 263; conflicts and alignments of, 19, 20, 265; NATO and, 122

U

United Arab Republic, 19, 20, 40, 218, 248, 256. *See also* Nasser

United Nations Organization: consultation forum as, 7; grand alliance as, 5–6; non-commitment and, 222–224; particular commitments and, 267; regional alliances and, 6; reorganization of, 291

United Provinces (Dutch): conflicts and alignments of, 22, 23, 25, 108, 126; dealignments and, 43, 47, 52; rise of, 25

United States: alignment alternatives of, 195–198; alliance concepts and traditions of, 3–8, 69, 76, 82–83, 90, 284–285; the Axis and, 33, 43–44, 49, 83; the Baghdad Pact (CENTO) and, 119; consultations and, 77, 79–80; dealignments and, 50, 54; European integration and, 200–201, 281–282; growth of, 166–167, 259, 288, 289; Indochinese War and, 135, 136, 137–138; the Inter-American system and, 120–121, 250–251; NATO and, 31, 130–131, 176, 181; neutralism and, 205–206, 211–212, 222, 237–238, 241, 245, 253; Pakistan and, 28–29; politico-military strategies of, 9, 36, 93, 99–101, 128, 144, 182–185, 188, 189, 257–258, 262, 277, 291; restraints on, 142, 143, 146–147; SEATO and, 31, 88, 119; separate negotiations and, 156–157. *See also* Western alliance system

V

Vergennes, Charles Gravier, Count de, 35

W

Warsaw Pact: antecedents of, 262; neutralism and, 210; relationships within, 40, 169–170, 175. *See also* Sino-Soviet bloc

Western alliance system: colonialism and, 208–209, 212, 215, 216, 227; divided countries and, 40, 175–185, 187, 190; integration in, 119–122, 168–169, 175; mobility and, 132; multipolarity and, 259; neutralism and, 230–231, 237–254; nuclear diffusion and, 276–277, 284–285; provocation and, 127; relationships within, 40, 80, 92–93, 103, 167, 170–175, 266; strategies toward Sino-Soviet alliance of, 188–190, 226; Western European union and, 200–201

Western European Union: European nuclear force and, 178; evolving concept as, 198–201, 262–263, 289; West Germany's membership in, 143

Wilson, Woodrow, 6, 62

Y

Yugoslavia: the Balkan Pact and, 263; conflicts and alignments of, 19, 87–88; Soviet Union and, 15–16, 173. *See also* Serbia; Tito

AUGSBURG COLLEGE & SEMINARY
George Sverdrup Library
MINNEAPOLIS 4, MINNESOTA
WITHDRAWN